ORIGINS OF COMMERCIAL BANKING

ORIGINS OF COMMERCIAL BANKING

Prem Nagpal

CYBER TECH PUBLICATIONS
4264/3, Ansari Road, Daryaganj, New Delhi-110002 (India)
Ph.: 011-23244078, 011-43559448 Fax: 011-23280028
E-Mail: cyberpublicationsdelhi@yahoo.com
Website: www.cybertechpublications.com

ORIGINS OF COMMERCIAL BANKING

Prem Nagpal

First Edition 2010

Published by :

G.S. Rawat for **Cyber Tech Publications**
4264/3, Ansari Road, Daryaganj, New Delhi-110002 (India)
Ph.: 011-23244078, 011-43559448 Fax: 011-23280028
E-Mail: cyberpublicationsdelhi@yahoo.com
Website: www.cybertechpublications.com

Printed at: Asian Offset Printers, Delhi-53

Preface

Access to finance by the poor and vulnerable groups is a prerequisite for poverty reduction and social cohesion. This has to become an integral part of our efforts to promote inclusive growth. In fact, providing access to finance is a form of empowerment of the vulnerable groups. Financial inclusion denotes delivery of financial services at an affordable cost to the vast sections of the disadvantaged and low-income groups. The various financial services include credit, savings, insurance and payments and remittance facilities. The objective of financial inclusion is to extend the scope of activities of the organized financial system to include within its ambit people with low incomes. Through graduated credit, the attempt must be to lift the poor from one level to another so that they come out of poverty.

This study of the activities of commercial banks in financing urban real estate is one of a series completed under the Urban Real Estate Finance Project of the National Bureau's Financial Research Program. Other studies in the series deal with the effect of governmental intervention in the real estate market; the characteristics of real estate as they affect the financial requirements of that market; the mortgage lending activities of life insurance companies, savings and loan associations, and the Home Owners' Loan Corporation; the comparative markets and investment experience of various institutions lending on the security of urban property; and the relation of mortgage financing to economic fluctuations.

A special satisfaction is felt in the completion of this study, arising from its unusually broad-based support. Contributing to the work were a foundation, three groups representing private financial institutions, and two federal bank supervisory agencies.

Specifically, financial support was received for the study in grants from the Association of Reserve City Bankers, the Life Insurance Investment Research Committee, acting for the Life Insurance Association of America and the American Life Convention, and the Rockefeller Foundation; many of the data on which the' study rests were collected with the technical assistance of the American Bankers Association and the Board of Governors Of 'the Federal Reserve System; finally, the research itself, which was conducted under the responsibility of the National Bureau of Economic Research, was' done under a cooperative agreement between the National Bureau and the Federal Deposit Insurance Corporation. The task was a difficult one, even with the combined resources available from these several quarters, but it would have been impossible except through such a cooperative effort.

—Author

CONTENTS

CONTENTS

1

Introduction

A commercial bank is a type of financial intermediary and a type of bank. Commercial banking is also known as business banking. It is a bank that provides checking accounts, savings accounts, and money market accounts and that accepts time deposits. After the Great Depression, the U.S. Congress required that banks engage only in banking activities, whereas investment banks were limited to capital market activities. As the two no longer have to be under separate ownership under U.S. law, some use the term "commercial bank" to refer to a bank or a division of a bank primarily dealing with deposits and loans from corporations or large businesses. In some other jurisdictions, the strict separation of investment and commercial banking never applied. Commercial banking may also be seen as distinct from retail banking, which involves the provision of financial services direct to consumers. Many banks offer both commercial and retail banking services.

POSSIBLE MEANINGS

Commercial bank has two possible meanings:

- Commercial bank is the term used for a normal bank to distinguish it from an investment bank.

This is what people normally call a "bank". The term "commercial" was used to distinguish it from an investment bank. Since the two types of banks no longer have to be separate companies, some have used the term "commercial bank" to refer to banks that focus mainly on companies. In some English-speaking countries outside North America, the term "trading bank" was and is used to denote a commercial bank. During the great depression and after the stock market crash of 1929, the U.S. Congress passed the Glass-Steagall Act 1933-35 (Khambata 1996) requiring that commercial banks engage only in banking activities (accepting deposits and making loans, as well as other fee based services), whereas investment banks were limited to capital markets activities. This separation is no longer mandatory. It raises funds by collecting deposits from businesses and consumers via checkable deposits, savings deposits, and time (or term) deposits. It makes loans to businesses and consumers. It also buys corporate bonds and government bonds. Its primary liabilities are deposits and primary assets are loans and bonds.

- Commercial banking can also refer to a bank or a division of a bank that mostly deals with deposits and loans from corporations or large businesses, as opposed to normal individual members of the public (retail banking).

Origin of the Word

The name *bank* derives from the Italian word *banco* "desk/ bench", used during the Renaissance by Florentine bankers, who used to make their transactions above a desk covered by a green tablecloth. However, traces of banking activity can found even in ancient times. In fact, the word traces its origins back to the Ancient Roman Empire, where moneylenders would set up their stalls in the middle of enclosed courtyards called *macella* on a long bench called a *bancu*, from which the words *banco* and *bank* are derived. As a moneychanger, the merchant at the *bancu* did not so much invest money as merely convert the foreign currency into the only legal tender in Rome- that of the Imperial Mint.

The Role of Commercial Banks

Commercial banks engages in the following activities:

- processing of payments by way of telegraphic transfer, EFTPOS, internet banking, or other means

- issuing bank drafts and bank cheques
- accepting money on term deposit
- lending money by overdraft, installment loan, or other means
- providing documentary and standby letter of credit, guarantees, performance bonds, securities underwriting commitments and other forms of off balance sheet exposures
- safekeeping of documents and other items in safe deposit boxes
- sale, distribution or brokerage, with or without advice, of insurance, unit trusts and similar financial products as a "financial supermarket"
- traditionally, large commercial banks also underwrite bonds, and make markets in currency, interest rates, and credit-related securities, but today large commercial banks usually have an investment bank arm that is involved in the mentioned activities.

TYPES OF LOANS GRANTED BY COMMERCIAL BANKS

Secured Loan

A secured loan is a loan in which the borrower pledges some asset (e.g., a car or property) as collateral (i.e., security) for the loan.

Mortgage Loan

A mortgage loan is a very common type of debt instrument, used to purchase real estate. Under this arrangement, the money is used to purchase the property. Commercial banks, however, are given security - a lien on the title to the house - until the mortgage is paid off in full. If the borrower defaults on the loan, the bank would have the legal right to repossess the house and sell it, to recover sums owing to it. In the past, commercial banks have not been greatly interested in real estate loans and have placed only a relatively small percentage of their assets in mortgages. As their name implies, such financial institutions secured their earning primarily from commercial and consumer loans and left the major task of home financing to others. However, due to changes in banking laws and policies, commercial banks are increasingly active in home financing. Changes in banking laws now allow commercial banks to make home mortgage loans on a more liberal basis than ever before. In acquiring mortgages on real estate, these institutions follow two main practices. First, some of the banks maintain active and well-organized departments whose primary function is to compete actively for real estate loans. In areas lacking specialized real estate financial institutions, these banks become the source for residential and farm mortgage loans. Second, the banks acquire mortgages by simply purchasing them from mortgage bankers or dealers.

In addition, dealer service companies, which were originally used to obtain car loans for permanent lenders such as commercial banks, wanted to broaden their activity beyond their local area. In recent years, however, such companies have concentrated on acquiring mobile home loans in volume for both commercial banks and savings and loan associations. Service companies obtain these loans from retail dealers, usually on a nonrecourse basis. Almost all bank/service company agreements contain a credit insurance policy that protects the lender if the consumer defaults.

Unsecured Loan

Unsecured loans are monetary loans that are not secured against the borrowers assets (i.e., no collateral is involved). These may be available from financial institutions under many different guises or marketing packages:

- bank overdrafts
- corporate bonds
- credit card debt
- credit facilities or lines of credit
- personal loans

Commercial banks are in the business of providing banking services to individuals, small businesses and large organizations.

While the banking sector has been consolidating, it is worth noting that far more people are employed in the commercial banking sector than any other part of the financial services industry. Jobs in banking can be exciting and offer excellent opportunities to learn about business, interact with people and build up a clientele.

Today's commercial banks are more diverse than ever. You'll find a tremendous range of opportunities in commercial banking, starting at the branch level where you might start out as a teller to a wide variety of other services such as leasing, credit card banking, international finance and trade credit.

If you are well-prepared and enthusiastic about entering the field, you are likely to find a wide variety of opportunities open to you. Carefully read through the material below as you decide whether you've got what it takes to pursue a career in commercial banking.

Commercial banks are banks that are in classic business of accepting deposits and making loans. As against merchant banking where primary responsibility is to help people find money. Thus they help companies to raise capital through issue of equity or bonds etc

In few countries like US and Japan commercial banking is separate from investment banking by law. Few countries like UK we find that commercial banks carry out investment activities through a subsidiary. Only in countries like Germany where we find Universal Banks like Deutsche that is both a commercial and I-bank. The legislation that kept banks and investment banks separate—Glass Steagall—was struck down by Congress in 1999. So banks are now moving into highly visible spheres of activity, such as investment banking, mutual funds, and brokerage.

Commercial banks hold customers' money and supply loans, in exchange for check-writing fees and interest collected from loans. The work of commercial bankers is critical—retail consumers get their credit lines extended, their checking accounts upgraded, their mortgages, cars, and home improvement loans approved.

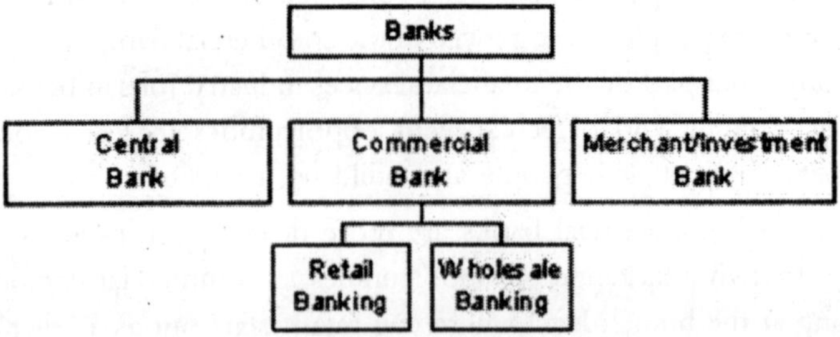

A commercial bank can either be a retail bank or a wholesale bank or both.

Retail Banking

- Retail banking involves high street branches, dealing with the general public, shops and very small businesses. Retail banking covers current accounts, cheque facilities, saving accounts, and loan facilities like overdraft, personal loans and mortgages.
- The use of cheque and cheque clearance are of prime importance. Here we are talking about high volume low margin business.

Wholesale Banking

Wholesale banking covers banks lending to larger entities like corporate, governments etc It also includes activities like money markets, foreign exchange and finance for trade

Small businesses are also highly dependent on the goodwill of commercial bankers. Even as dot coms, angel investors, and VCs monopolize the news, most small businesses continue to fund their growth with commercial loans. Such loans allow them to secure new inventory, cover payroll, remodel their stores, buy registers, and manage their overseas accounts receivables.

Commercial bankers perform core financial analysis to assess risk, creditworthiness, and the likelihood a business will succeed. They play a key part in deciding the best business initiatives, expanding existing businesses, developing new markets and clients, and creating new products for e-commerce, the Internet, international markets, and consumers. In addition, Commercial bankers have to combine business acumen with strong accounting and interpersonal skills. After all, commercial bankers are at the front lines of the banking business. Ideally, they know their clients' lives intimately and can recommend additional products and services. Commercial bankers are a key distribution point and referral source for the rest of a bank's financial services activities.

Many commercial banks are consolidating in order to branch out and provide other services such as mortgage, mutual funds, investment banking, and insurance. As other financial firms expand their services, commercial banks are diversifying to keep up, and often a merger with a peer company is the best way to do this. Since 1995, more than 200 large and small banks have merged. Consolidation usually results in layoffs and fewer job opportunities, but jobs in banks that are more diversified offer more opportunities for career development. And a growing number of non-banks are pioneering new ways of delivering financial services, providing more jobs in the finance industry.

If you like intense project work, with a good deal of financial analysis and customer contact—if you like helping new families and new businesses create brilliant futures—commercial banking might be for you. You'll just have to function in a larger organization, trying to build synergies with other product groups across different customer and product platforms.

Commercial Bank Term Loans

A basic commercial bank loan is called a term loan. In reality, bank term loans are often short-term, but because they are renewed over and over, they become longer term loans. Bankers prefer self-liquidating loans where the use of the loan money ensures an automatic repayment scheme. Most term loans are in amounts of $25,000 or more. Many have fixed interest rates and a set maturity date. Payment schedules vary. Term loans may be paid monthly, quarterly, or annually. Some may have a balloon payment at the end of the term of the loan.

TYPES OF TERM LOANS

The American Bankers Association generally recognizes two types of term loans. The first is the intermediate term loan which usually has a maturity of one to three years. It is often used to finance working capital needs. Working capital refers to the daily operating funds that small business owners need to run their businesses.

Intermediate term loans can also be used to finance assets such as machinery that have a life of around one to three years, such as computer equipment or other small machinery or equipment. Repayment of the intermediate term loan is usually tied to the life of the equipment or the time for which you need the working capital.

Intermediate term loan agreements often have restrictive covenants put in place by the bank. Restrictive covenants restrict management operations during the life of the loan. They ensure that management will repay the loan before paying bonuses, dividends, and other optional payments.

Long-term Bank Loans

Banks seldom provide long-term financing to small businesses. When they do, it is usually for the purchase of real estate or a large business facility. The bank will only lend 65% - 80% of the value of the asset the business is buying and the asset serves as collateral for the loan.

Other factors that small businesses have to deal with in bank loan agreements are interest rates, creditworthiness, affirmative and negative covenants, collateral, fees, and prepayment rights.

2

Origins of Commercial Banking in the United States, 1781-1830

Early U.S. commercial banks were for-profit business firms, usually structured as joint-stock companies. Many, but by no means all, obtained corporate charters from their respective state legislatures. Although politically controversial, commercial banks, the number and assets of which grew quickly after 1800, played a key role in early U.S. economic growth.

Commercial banks, savings banks, insurance companies and other financial intermediaries helped to fuel growth by channeling wealth from savers to entrepreneurs. Those entrepreneurs used the loans to increase the profitability of their businesses and hence the efficiency of the overall economy.

DESCRIPTION OF THE EARLY COMMERCIAL BANKING BUSINESS

As financial intermediaries, commercial banks pooled the wealth of a large number of savers and lent fractions of that pool to a diverse group of enterprising business firms. The best way to understand how early commercial banks functioned is to examine a typical bank balance sheet. Banks essentially borrowed wealth from their liability holders and re-lent that wealth to the issuers of their assets. Banks profited from the difference between the cost of their liabilities and the net return from their assets.

Assets of a Typical Commercial Bank

A typical U.S. commercial bank in the late eighteenth and early nineteenth centuries owned assets such as specie, the notes and deposits of *other* banks, commercial paper, public securities, mortgages, and real estate. Investment in real estate was minimal, usually simply to provide the bank with an office in which to conduct business. Commercial banks used specie, i.e. gold and silver (usually minted into coins but sometimes in the form of bars or bullion), and their claims on other banks (notes and/or deposits) to pay their creditors (liability holders). They also owned public securities like government bonds and corporate equities. Sometimes they owned a small sum of mortgages, long-term loans collateralized by real property. Most bank assets, however, were discount loans collateralized by commercial paper, i.e. bills of exchange and promissory notes "discounted" at the bank by borrowers.

Discount Loans Described

Most bank loans were "discount" loans, not "simple" loans. Unlike a simple loan, where the interest and principal fall due when the loan matures, a discount requires only the repayment of the principal on the due date. That is because the borrower receives only the discounted present value of the principal at the time of the loan, not the full principal sum. For example, with a simple loan of $100 at 6 percent interest, of exactly one year's duration, the borrower receives $100 today and must repay the lender $106 in one year. With a discount loan, the borrower repays $100 at the end of the year but receives only $94.34 today.

Commercial Bank Liabilities

Commercial banks acquired wealth to purchase assets by issuing several types of liabilities. Most early banks were joint-stock companies, so they issued equities ("stock") in an initial public offering (IPO). Those common shares were not redeemable. In other words, stockholders could not demand that the bank exchange their shares for cash. Stockholders who wished to recoup their investments could do so only by selling their shares to other investors in the secondary "stock" market. Because its common shares were irredeemable, a bank's "capital stock" was its most certain source of funds. Holders of other types of bank liabilities, including banknotes and checking deposits, could redeem their claims during the issuing bank's open hours of operation, which were typically four to six hours a day, Monday through Saturday. A holder of a deposit liability could "cash out" by physically withdrawing funds (in banknotes or specie) or by writing a check to a third party against his or her deposit balance. A holder of a banknote, an engraved promissory note payable to the bearer very similar to today's Federal Reserve notes, could physically visit the issuing bank to redeem the sum printed on the note in specie or other current funds, at the holder's option. Or, a banknote holder could simply use the notes as currency, to make retail purchases, repay debts, make loans, etc.

After selling its shares to investors, and perhaps attracting some deposits, early banks would begin to accept discount loan applications. Successful applicants would receive the loan as a credit in their checking accounts, in banknotes, in specie, or in some combination thereof. Those banknotes, deposits, and specie traveled from person to person to make purchases and remittances. Eventually, the notes and deposits returned to the bank of issue for payment.

Balance Sheet Management

Early banks had to manage their balance sheets carefully. They "failed" or "broke," i.e. became legally insolvent, if they could not meet the demands of liability holders with prompt specie payment. Bankers, therefore, had to keep ample amounts of gold and silver in their banks' vaults in order to remain in business. Because specie paid no interest, however, bankers had to be careful not to accumulate too much of the precious metals lest they sacrifice the bank's profitability to its safety. Interest-bearing public securities, like U.S. Six Percent bonds, often served as "secondary reserves" that generated income but that bankers could quickly sell to raise cash, if necessary. When bankers found that their reserves were declining too precipitously they slowed or stopped discounting until reserve levels returned to safe levels. Discount loans were not callable. Bankers therefore made discounts for short terms only, usually from a few days to six months. If the bank's condition allowed, borrowers could negotiate a new discount to repay one coming due, effectively extending the term of the loan. If the bank's condition precluded further extension of the loan, however, borrowers had to pay up or face a lawsuit. Bankers quickly learned to stagger loan due dates so that a steady stream of discounts was constantly coming up for renewal. In that way, bankers could, if necessary, quickly reduce the outstanding volume of discounts by denying renewals.

REDUCTION OF INFORMATION ASYMMETRY

Early bankers maintained profitability by keeping losses from defaults less than the gains from interest revenues. They kept defaults at an acceptably low level by reducing what financial theorists call "information asymmetry." The two major types of information asymmetry are adverse selection, which occurs *before* a contract is made, and moral hazard, which occurs *after* contract completion. The information is asymmetrical or unequal because loan applicants and borrowers naturally know more about their creditworthiness than lenders do. (More generally, sellers know more about their goods and services than buyers do.) Bankers, in other words, must create information about loan applicants and borrowers so that they can assess the risk of default and make a rational decision about whether to make or to continue a loan.

Adverse Selection

Adverse selection arises from the fact that risky borrowers are more eager for loans, especially at high interest rates, than safe borrowers. As Adam Smith put it, interest rates "so high as eight or ten per cent" attract only "prodigals and projectors, who alone would be willing to give this high interest." "Sober people," he continued, "who will give for the use of money no more than a part of what they are likely to make by the use of it, would not venture into the competition." Adverse selection is also known as the "lemons problem" because a classic example of it occurs in the unintermediated market for used cars. Potential buyers have difficulty discerning good cars, the "peaches," from breakdown-prone cars, the "lemons." Sellers naturally know whether their cars are peaches or lemons. So information about the car is asymmetrical — the seller knows the true value but the buyer does not. Potential buyers quite rationally offer the average market price for cars of a particular make, model, and mileage. An owner of a peach naturally scoffs at the average offer. A lemon owner, on the other hand, will jump at the opportunity to unload his heap for more than its real value. If we recall that borrowers are essentially sellers of securities called loans, the adverse selection problem in financial markets should be clear. Lenders that do not reduce information asymmetry will purchase only lemon-like loans because their offer of a loan at average interest will appear too dear to good borrowers but will look quite appealing to risky "prodigals and projectors."

Moral Hazard

Moral hazard arises from the fact that people are basically self-interested. If given the opportunity, they will renege on contracts by engaging in risky activities with, or even outright stealing, lenders' wealth. For instance, a borrower might decide to use a loan to try his luck at the blackjack table in Atlantic City rather than to purchase a computer or other efficiency-increasing tool for his business. Another borrower might have the means to repay the loan but default on it anyway so that she can use the resources to take a vacation to Aruba.

In order to reduce the risk of default due to information asymmetry, lenders must create information about borrowers. Early banks created information by screening discount applicants to reduce adverse selection and by monitoring loan recipients and requiring collateral to reduce moral hazard. Screening procedures included probing the applicant's credit history and current financial condition. Monitoring procedures included the evaluation of the flow of funds through the borrower's checking account and the negotiation of restrictive covenants specifying the uses to which a particular loan would be put. Banks could also require borrowers to post collateral, i.e. property they could seize in case of default. Real estate, slaves, co-signers, and financial securities were common forms of collateral.

A SHORT HISTORY OF EARLY AMERICAN COMMERCIAL BANKS

Colonial Experiments

Colonial America witnessed the formation of several dozen "banks," only a few of which were commercial banks. Most of the colonial banks were "land banks" that made mortgage loans. Additionally, many of them were government agencies and not businesses. All of the handful of colonial banks that could rightly be called commercial banks, i.e. that discounted short-term commercial paper, were small and short-lived. Some, like that of Alexander Cummings, were fraudulent. Others, like that of Philadelphia merchants Robert Morris and Thomas Willing, ran afoul of English laws and had to be abandoned.

The First U.S. Commercial Banks

The development of America's commercial banking sector, therefore, had to await the Revolution. No longer blocked by English law, Morris, Willing, and other prominent Philadelphia merchants moved to establish a joint-stock commercial bank.

The young republic's shaky war finances added urgency to the bankers' request to charter a bank, a request that Congress and several state legislatures soon accepted. By 1782, that new bank, the Bank of North America, had granted a significant volume of loans to both the public and private sectors. New Yorkers, led by Alexander Hamilton, and Bostonians, led by William Phillips, were not to be outdone and by early 1784 had created their own commercial banks. By the end of the eighteenth century, mercantile leaders in over a dozen other cities had also formed commercial banks. (See Table 1.)

Table 1: Names, Locations, Charter or Establishment Dates, and Authorized Capitals of the First U.S. Commercial Banks, 1781-1799

Name	Location (Year of Establishment)	Year of Charter (in U.S. dollars)	Authorized Capital
Bank of North America	Philadelphia, Pennsylvania	1781*/1782/1786**	$400,000 (increased to
		$2,000,000 in 1787)	
The Bank of New York	Manhattan, New York	(1784) 1791	$1,000,000
The Massachusetts Bank	Boston, Massachusetts	1784	$300,000
The Bank of Maryland	Baltimore, Maryland	1790	$300,000
The Bank of the United States	Philadelphia, Pennsylvania	1791*	$10,000,000
The Bank of Providence	Providence, Rhode Island	1791	$500,000
New Hampshire Bank	Portsmouth, New Hampshire	1792	$200,000
The Bank of Albany	Albany, New York	1792	$260,000
Hartford Bank	Hartford, Connecticut	1792	$100,000
Union Bank	New London, Connecticut	1792	$50,000-100,000
Union Bank	Boston, Massachusetts	1792	$400,000-800,000
New Haven Bank	New Haven, Connecticut	1792	$100,000 (increased to
		$400,000 in 1795)	
Bank of Alexandria	Alexandria, Virginia	1792	$150,000 (increased to
		$500,000 in 1795)	

Essex Bank	Salem, Massachusetts	(1792) 1799	$100,000-400,000
Bank of Richmond	Richmond, Virginia	(1792)	n/a
Bank of South Carolina	Charleston, South Carolina	(1792) 1801	$200,000
Bank of Columbia	Hudson, New York	1793	$160,000
Bank of Pennsylvania	Philadelphia, Pennsylvania	1793	$3,000,000
Bank of Columbia	Washington, D.C.	1793	$1,000,000
Nantucket Bank	Nantucket, Massachusetts	1795	$40,000-100,000
Merrimack Bank	Newburyport, Massachusetts	1795	$70,000-150,000
Middletown Bank	Middletown, Connecticut	1795	$100,000-400,000
Bank of Baltimore	Baltimore, Maryland	1795	$1,200,000
Bank of Rhode Island	Newport, Rhode Island	1795	$500,000
Bank of Delaware	Wilmington, Delaware	1796	$500,000
Norwich Bank	Norwich, Connecticut	1796	$75,000-200,000
Portland Bank	Portland, Maine	1799	$300,000
Manhattan Company	New York, New York	1799#	$2,000,000

Source: Fenstermaker (1964); Davis (1917)

* = National charter.

** = The Bank of North America gained a second charter in 1786 after its original Pennsylvania state charter was revoked. Pennsylvania, Massachusetts, and New York chartered the bank in 1782.

= This firm was chartered as a water utility company but began banking operations almost immediately.

Banking and Politics

The first U.S. commercial banks helped early national businessmen to overcome a "crisis of liquidity," a classic postwar liquidity crisis caused by a shortage of cash, and an increased emphasis on the notion that "time is money."

Many colonists had been content to allow debts to remain unsettled for years and even decades.

After experiencing the devastating inflation of the Revolution, however, many Americans came to see prompt payment of debts and strict performance of contracts as virtues. Banks helped to condition individuals and firms to the new, stricter business procedures.

Early U.S. commercial banks had political roots as well. Many Revolutionary elites saw banks, and other modern financial institutions, as a means of social control.

The power vacuum left after the withdrawal of British troops and leading Loyalist families had to be filled, and many members of the commercial elite wished to fill it and to justify their control with an ideology of meritocracy.

By providing loans to entrepreneurs based on the merits of their businesses, and not their genealogies, banks and other financial intermediaries helped to spread the notion that wealth and power should be allocated to the most able members of post-Revolutionary society, not to the oldest or best groomed families.

GROWTH OF THE COMMERCIAL BANKING SECTOR

After 1800, the number, authorized capital, and assets of commercial banks grew rapidly. (See Table 2.)

As early as 1820, the assets of U.S. commercial banks equaled about 50 percent of U.S. aggregate output, a figure that the commercial banking sectors of most of the world's nations had not achieved by 1990.

Table 2: Numbers, Authorized Capitals, and Estimated Assets of Incorporated U.S. Commercial Banks, 1800-1830

Year	No. Banks	Authorized Capital (in millions $U.S.)	Estimated Assets (in millions $U.S.)
1800	29	27.42	49.74
1801	33	29.17	52.66
1802	36	30.03	50.00
1803	54	34.90	58.69
1804	65	41.17	67.07
1805	72	48.87	82.39
1806	79	51.34	94.11
1807	84	53.43	90.47
1808	87	51.49	92.04
1809	93	55.19	100.23
1810	103	66.19	108.87
1811	118	76.29	142.65
1812	143	84.49	161.89
1813	147	87.00	187.23
1814	202	110.02	233.53
1815	212	115.23	197.16
1816	233	158.98	270.30
1817	263	172.84	316.47
1818	339	195.31	331.41
1819	342	195.98	349.66
1820	328	194.60	341.42
1821	274	181.23	345.93
1822	268	177.53	307.86
1823	275	173.67	283.10
1824	301	185.75	328.16
1825	331	191.08	347.65

1826	332	190.98	349.60
1827	334	192.51	379.03
1828	356	197.41	344.56
1829	370	201.06	349.72
1830	382	205.40	403.45

Sources: For total banks and authorized bank capital, see Fenstermaker (1965). I added the Bank of the United States and the Second Bank of the United States to his figures. I estimated assets by multiplying the total authorized capital by the average ratio of actual capital to assets from a large sample of balance sheet data.

Commercial banks caused considerable political controversy in the U.S. As the first large, usually corporate, for-profit business firms, banks took the brunt of reactionary "agrarian" rhetoric designed to thwart, or at least slow down, the post-Revolution modernization of the U.S. economy. Early bank critics, however, failed to see that their own reactionary policies caused or exacerbated the supposed evils of the banking system.

For instance, critics argued that the lending decisions of early banks were politically-motivated and skewed in favor of rich merchants. Such was indeed the case. Overly stringent laws, usually championed by the agrarian critics themselves, forced bankers into that lending pattern. Many early bank charters forbade banks to raise additional equity capital or to increase interest rates above a low ceiling or usury cap, usually 6 percent per year. When market interest rates were above the usury cap, as they almost always were, banks were naturally swamped with discount applications. Forbidden by law to increase interest rates or to raise additional equity capital, banks were forced to ration credit. They naturally lent to the safest borrowers, those most known to the bank and those with the highest wealth levels.

Early banks were extremely profitable and therefore aroused considerable envy. Critics claimed that bank dividends greater than six percent were prima facie evidence that banks routinely made discounts at illegally high rates. In fact, banks earned more than they charged on discounts because they lent out more, often substantially more, than their capital base. It was not unusual, for example, for a bank with $1,000,000 equity capital to have an average of $2,000,000 on loan. The six percent interest on that sum would generate $120,000 of gross revenue, minus say $20,000 for operating expenses, leaving $100,000 to be divided among stockholders, a dividend of ten percent. More highly leveraged banks, i.e. banks with higher asset to capital ratios, could earn even more.

Early banks also caused considerable political controversy when they attempted to gain a charter, a special act of legislation that granted corporate privileges such as limited stockholder liability, the ability to sue in courts of law in the name of the bank, etc. Because early banks were lucrative, politicians and opposing interest groups fought each other bitterly over charters. Rival commercial factions sought to establish the first bank in emerging commercial centers while rival political parties struggled to gain credit for establishing new banking facilities. Politicians soon discovered that they could extract overt bonuses, taxes, and even illegal bribes from bank charter applicants. Again, critics unfairly blamed banks for problems over which bankers had little control.

The Economic Importance of Early U.S. Commercial Banks

Despite the efforts of a few critics, most Americans rejected anti-bank rhetoric and supported the controlled growth of the commercial banking sector. They did so because they understood what some modern economists do not, namely, that commercial banks helped to increase per capita aggregate output. Unfortunately, the discussion of banks' role in economic growth has been much muddied by monetary issues. Banknotes circulated as cash, just as today's Federal Reserve notes do. Most scholars, therefore, have concentrated on early banks' role in the monetary system. In general, early banks caused the money supply to be procyclical. In other words, they made the money supply expand rapidly during business cycle "booms," thereby causing inflation, and they made the money supply contract sharply during recessions, thereby causing ruinous price deflation. The economic importance of early banks, therefore, lies not in their monetary role but in their capacity as financial intermediaries. At first glance, intermediation may seem a rather innocuous process — lenders are matched to borrowers. Upon further inspection, however, it is clear that intermediation is a crucial economic process. Economies devoid of financial intermediation, like those of colonial America, grow slowly because firms with profitable ideas find it difficult to locate financial backers. Without intermediaries, search costs, i.e. the costs of finding a counterparty, and information creation costs, i.e. the costs of reducing information asymmetry (adverse selection and moral hazard), are so high that few loans are made. Profitable ideas cannot be implemented and the economy stagnates. Intermediaries reduce both search and information costs. Rather than hunt blindly for counterparties, for instance, both savers and entrepreneurs needed only to find the local bank, a major reduction in search costs. Additionally, banks, as large, specialized lenders, were able to reduce information asymmetry more efficiently than smaller, less-specialized lenders, like private individuals.

By lowering the total cost of borrowing, commercial banks increased the volume of loans made and hence the number of profitable ideas that entrepreneurs brought to fruition. Commercial banks, for instance, allowed firms to implement new technologies, to increase labor specialization, and to take advantage of economies of scale and scope. As those firms grew more profitable, they created new wealth, driving economic growth.

HISTORICAL DEVELOPMENT

The restrictive policies of many states on branch banking led commercial banks to seek some method of circumventing the regulations in order to serve customers in their geographic area. One method of establishing a presence in more than one locality, even when state laws specifically prohibited actual branching, was through the system known as chain banking.

The Federal Reserve has defined chain banking as a system in which a network of separately chartered commercial banks is created, with the controlling stock interest in each bank held by a single group of individuals. Interlocking directorates among the banks are commonplace. Although chain banking networks were typically established in states that did not allow branching, they went unchallenged by those states in most cases, and many of them exist today as components of other organizations.

In the second half of the nineteenth century a new pattern of organization appeared in the from of the holding company, the operations of which became known as group banking.

In any type of business, a holding company may be formed as a corporate entity that exercises control over other companies through stock ownership. Although it was not legally defined as such by Congress until 1933, the bank holding company was one in which one or more commercial banks appeared as part of the overall organization. A holding company that controlled banks in several cities or towns was able to circumvent state restrictions and operate in a manner tantamount to actual branching. By 1920 a large-scale trend in this direction had been identified, and in many cases the holding company that had one or more banks in its structure had become a multimillion-dollar enterprise, often diversified into such fields as investments, real estate, securities, and restaurant chains. Many of the holding companies that controlled a bank during the depression achieved a higher survival rate than the independent banks. Until 1933 group banking did not come under federal or state supervision, simply because a holding company was not considered on the same basis as a bank . From today's perspective on bank regulation, it is of interest to note that the courts which were consulted on group banking generally held that banks should be run by their principle with a minimum of interference by agencies of government.

In 1927 the Federal Reserve identified a growing trend toward group banking, and by 1929 holding companies included 8 percent of all commercial banks, controlling 19 percent of total bank loans and investments. In some cases, a holding company was formed specifically to unify and strengthen a number of banks. Northwest Bancorporation and first Bank System, both headquartered in the Twin Cities, exemplify this type of voluntary association, formed during the Depression. The former now controls eighty-five banks in seven states with total assets of $11 billion; First Bank System controls ninety-one banks and trust companies in five states, with total assets of $10.3 billion. Many of the banks in both groups had enjoyed friendly correspondent relationships with one another. By being absorbed into holding companies, the smaller institutions gained capital, liquidity, and community loyalty resulting from stronger financial backing, and they were able to weather the economic storm of the early 1930s.

The tidal wave of bank failures during the Depression prompted Congress to begin a series of investigations, designed to determine whether the speculative nonblank operations of holding companies had contributed to the financial crisis. One result of these hearings was the inclusion in the 1933 Banking Act of the first federal attempt to regulate the operations of holding companies that controlled any commercial banks.

TRUST SERVICES

The fact that so many of the nation's oldest and largest financial institutions include the word "trust" as part of their legal names offers a clue to the history of fiduciary services in America. Many trust companies were organized in the early nineteenth century, often in connection with in surance companies, and operated under state charters to provide investment services. The equities of those who turned their assets over to these trusts resembled shares in an investment fund. By 1850, however, the trust companies had taken on a different character and were accepting demand and time deposits and making short-tern loans. This led to resentment among commercial bankers, who found that their competition was coming from entities that operated with minimal supervision and did not have to keep reserves as banks did. Trust companies also enjoyed tax advantages and were able to offer higher interest rates than banks.

To counter this competition, many state-chartered banks sought and obtained trust powers. At the same time, trusts were mushrooming out-side banking circles through the formation of various corporate "pools," designed to control the distribution of iron, steel, petroleum, and other goods. The Standard Oil Company trust (1879) served as a prototype. Monopolistic practices, engaged in by some of these trusts, led to federal legislation (the Clayton and Sherman Antitrust Acts) aimed against them.

Fiduciary functions, provided for individual and corporate customers, combined with commercial banking proved highly successful for statechartered banks. The growth of the trust area as an adjunct to other commercial bank functions received further impetus through the Federal Reserve Act passed in 1913. Section 11 (K) of that Act permitted national banks, for the first time, to apply to federal regulatory agencies for trust powers, but stipulated that such banks would also be subject to the restrictions that any state might impose.

Since 1913 the fiduciary functions of banks have increased tremendously in scope and importance, and over 4000 banks now offers some or all trust services-personal, corporate, or a combination of both. They act as administrators and executors of estates for individuals; provide safekeeping, custody, escrow, and managing agent services; act as registrars, transfer agents, dividend disbursing agents, and trustees under indenture for corporations; and manage pension, profit-sharing, and individual retirement accounts. They are considered to be America's most important single fiduciary group. At year-end 1978, the market value of the trust assets over which banks exercised investment discretion was over $279 billion; if the values of all other properties entrusted to them on a nondiscretionary basis were to be included, the figure would be very much higher.

Of the aforementioned $279 billion; the five largest banks in the trust field(Morgan Guaranty, Citibank, Bankers Trust, Mellon

National, and Harris Trust) alone held $82 billion and reported earnings of$305 million from trust operations in 1978, or an average 3.7 percent of their net operating income.

Competition in the fiduciary-services area is intense and, again, is often provided by organizations that are not subject to the restrictions applied to the commercial banks. Trust operations of the latter are constrained in many ways. Before they can offer any trust services, banks must obtain specific federal and/or state approval and meet capital requirements. At member banks, Federal Reserve Regulation F applies to trust performance and policies. Each bank's trust department is subject to federal and/or state annual examination and must also receive internal audits under the supervision of a Trust Committee of the directors. Any bank wishing to engage in trust operations must pledge specific securities as a means of protecting the assets under its control.

In addition, regulations of the Internal Revenue Service, Securities and Exchange Commission, and Federal Reserve (in the case of bank holding companies) apply to various aspects of trust services. The insurance companies, brokerage houses, law firms, and investment management and estate planning firms that compete with banks for trust business do not have to contend with this set of restrictions.

MULTINATIONAL BANKING

During his unsuccessful campaign for the United States presidency in 1940, Wendell Willkie espoused the concept of "One World" and published a book bearing that title. His basic thinking was that nations were actually interdependence, and that the actions of any major power inevitably affected all the others, regardless of the geographical distances separating them. Willkie's ideas surprised and alienated many Americans, whose attitudes were far more parochial and narrow. In 1940 America's gross national product had recovered from the depression, and the average individual's standard of living was far better than that of his or her counterparts in other countries. Hence the prevailing feeling was that the United States need not become involved with foreign nations and could very well exist alone, untroubled by the problems of others and indifferent to any marketing opportunities that other countries might offer. This feeling was articulated on the floor of Congress by banking and business leaders, who chose to operate outside the United States only on a limited basis.

Willkie's notion of the interdependence of all nations and his predictions of vastly expanded foreign trade for America supply a prelude to one of the major changes in our banking history. Traditional barriers and philosophical objections vanished as American banks began to move into every corner of the world. Foreign banks subsequently followed the same course of action and became a major force in our overall financial and economic picture. Were he still alive, Willkie might be gratified to see his wish and prophecy realized in the tremendous volume of transactions that are now processed each day under the generic heading of international banking.

The end of World War II was followed by the gradual rebuilding of the shattered economies of many countries, accompanied by a natural increase in demand for many products by the populations of those countries. Their own manufacturers' facilities had, in many cases, been destroyed during the war; therefore; they turned to America to supply the goods they needed. American corporations, identifying these new markets, began introducing their products into nations throughout the world. American chemical products were sold to German farmers; American food products began to appear on the shelves of British and French grocery stores; American cash registers and computers were sold to merchants and industrialists in many countries; and American exports assumed greater importance in our economy.

Many of those same American corporations found that they could obtain relatively inexpensive labor and raw materials outside the United States. Others needed imports of essential goods to manufacture their products. Foreign factories, distribution points, and import offices were opened to handle all phases of trade, and the names of America's industrial giants became as well known in Europe and the East as in the United States.

FOREIGN OPERATIONS OF U.S. BANKS

The expansion of American business abroad led commercial banks to perceive the wisdom of following the lead of their major corporate clients in identifying new markets and establishing overseas facilities. In steadily increasing numbers throughout the postwar years., they abandoned their isolationism and parochial attitudes and adopted a policy of following their customers. Wherever a corporation from the "Fortune 500" list was functioning, an American commercial bank sought the approval of the local government to open a branch or otherwise establish a presence. In 1947 only seven American banks had opened foreign branches; by 1970 sixty-one U.S. banks had foreign offices that held$50 billion in assets, and by the end of 1978 155 American banks had foreign-office assets of 4260 billion.

In the 20 years following the cessation of hostilities in World War II, short-term loans made by American banks to foreign borrowers increased almost 900 percent. A recent study of ten of the largest U.S. banks showed international contributions to their net earnings of 51 percent in 1977 and 46 percent in 1978.

The most important traditional components of foreign banking business continue, including loans, letters of credit, money transfers, collections of drafts and other instruments, foreign exchange, and trust receipt financing; in many cases, they have been supplemented by new services, but it is their sheer volume that is chiefly responsible for the growth in transactions and earnings. The world's economies have become increasingly interdependent. Any OPEC increase is felt throughout the global economy. Japan, Germany, and many smaller countries depend heavily on foreign trade, and the emergence of new nations and the expansion of currency trading have combined with this to create opportunities for banks to provide services to a far broader range of customers. American banks today participate in syndicates that extend large foreign credits. They penetrate the Iron Curtain by opening branches in countries that for years were sealed off from the Western world. They establish local facilities to provide installment loans and checking and savings accounts to consumers. They operate foreign subsidiaries engaged in various types of leasing. They have assumed a leading role as direct lenders to foreign governments. Their networks of "offshore" banking centers provide them with tax and operational-cost advantages and permit them to function under prevailing liberal regulations imposed by a local government.

TRANSFER SYSTEMS

Early in the twentieth century, American telephone companies in creased their marketing efforts, stressing all the advantages of telephone service for every type of user. Their campaigns were so successful that an entirely new technology had to be developed to handle the volume of telephone calls. The manual format, in which an operator personally placed every call, gave way to the dial telephone, and the letter, in turn, has undergone many further enhancements needed to support customer usage.

Similarly the nation's brokerage firms, as they became aware of the increased level of American family income in the postwar years, introduced a succession of advertising campaigns to attract new investors. The stockholder base of many corporations consequently grew, as did the volume of purchases and sales each day. The Brokerage firms found themselves swamped with a "back office" volume beyond their capacity as a result of the promotional campaigns they themselves had conducted. "Fails" (transactions in which purchased securities were not properly delivered) became so common that many firms had to be liquidated. In both cases an industry sold its services to the public, only to find that it could not cope with the transaction volume generated by its own efforts. Both situations may have influenced the thinking of bankers during the 1960s.

Banking has always been a paper-intensive field, with the check as its most widely used document. Normal annual growth in check volume in the years prior to World War II was handled with no great difficulty, and in the immediate postwar period this increase did not give rise to any real concern. The assumption was that the system would automatically be able to meet customer demands.

The growth of the postwar economy gradually brought about a change in thinking. Check usage increased at an unprecedented rate. Businesses expanded and required more checks to pay more suppliers. Checks replaced cash as the method of paying employees. Retail marketing efforts brought a new type of customers into the banks; the checking account was no longer a vehicle used only by the more affluent' The average consumer-more sophisticated, better educated, and with a higher level of income than his predecessors-came to recognize the advantages of checks as payment instruments.

As check usage steadily increased, fears were expressed that the banking system would prove unable to cope with the volume. The introduction of the magnetic ink character recognition system, with its accompanying automated technology for check processing, allayed these fears only for a short time. Predictions of imminent calamities in the system began to be heard. Bankers wondered if their industry might suffer the same fate as the brokerage firms and find itself submerged in a sea of paper, with consequent delays, errors, and increases in processing costs. A study, conducted in 1970 for the American Bankers Association, projected annual increases of 7 percent in check volume for the remainder of that decade. One individual, recognized as a data processing authority, claimed to have originated the phrase "checkless society" to indicate the direction in which he felt banks would have to move-that is they would have to find a substitute for checks as payment media. To some extant statistical evidence supported these fears and predictions. Check volume in 1948 had been 5 billion; by 1976 it had increased to 26 billion, and the most recent figures to an annual volume of 30 billion checks. Although several prominent bankers expressed confidence that the industry could cope with these increases, pressures for change continued and new approaches to the payment system were sought.

Costs were an important consideration. A study conducted in Atlanta in 1972 showed that checks cashed or deposited at the drawee bank (and therefore completely processed in-house) created per-item costs of $0.103; checks that had to be routed to other banks cost $0.137 each. More recently it has been estimated that the entire life cycle of a check costs the issuer $0.55, including postage and handing charges.

In retrospect it now appears that in many cases commercial bankers, equipment designers, consultants, and systems experts were caught up in a syndrome of overreaction in which each group vied with the others in projecting a totally new world of banking. A new society was envisioned on the assumption that all types of bank customers would enthusiastically adopt the latest technology. Checks would be eliminated, and visits to banks would be made unnecessary by the installation of computer terminals in customers" homes and offices, supermarkets, and other key locations.

These prophesies have been only partially fulfilled. There are, indeed, areas where EFTS services have been introduced with considerable success, offering benefits to both the bank and user. However, as a generalization, it appears that the early forecasts of universal adoption of EFTS were totally unrealistic. Instead of using the earlier phrase. "checkless society," today's bankers speak of a "less-check" system in which checks will be used, but in greatly diminished quantities. Evolution, rather than revolution, has taken place.

SOURCES OF BANK FUNDS

An apocryphal story claims that four officers, each representing a different commercial bank, met to discuss the planning processes their respective banks had initiated. "Our biggest concern," said the first banker, "is liquidity. We're prepared to pay far less attention to other considerations because we know many of our customers are really worried over recent bank failures and problems. They want absolute assurance that they can withdraw their funds from us at any time. We see our main job as emphasizing that availability for them. No matter what else we may neglect, we're going to guarantee liquidity at all times."

"That's all well and good," said the second, "but in our case we're much more conscious of the need for safety. Our customers have heard one scare story after another about all the bad loans that banks have made in the past few years and how much they've had to charge off. Liquidity can take second place in our thinking. We're focusing on risk and we're determined to let the world know how prudent and conservative we're become. We simply refuse to take the risks we took last year or the year before. Besides, how in the world can your bank build up liquidity to that extant? What do you plan on doing? Will you fill up every inch of space in every vault with currency?"

"You're both on the wrong track," said the third bank officer. "We're in business purely and simply to make monkey. Everything else must be secondary. Income is the key ingredient in our game plan. Stockholders, investment analysts, newspapers, and everyone else-they look at our bottom line. They all know our bank has had some substandard earnings the past few years, and it makes no sense for us to worry about anything else until we improve our image by increasing our net income. This year you'll see the difference. It's no secret: our emphasis is on a very ambitious profit plan, because that's the real name of the game today."

Like the three blind men in the fable who tried to describe an elephant, each of the three bank officers was partially correct, yet each was unable to see the complete picture. It was only the fourth officer who was able to put the entire problem into the proper perspective.

"All three of you have lost sight of one of the basics of today's bank management," he said. "Of course you're right when you say that no bank can neglect considerations of liquidity and safety, and of course you're correct when you say that income is tremendously important. But whenever you overemphasize any of those three elements at the expense of the other two, you're doing nothing but creating problems for yourselves. If you can't manage your bank's funds by balancing all three objectives, you've lost the battle."

AMERICAN BANKING

Because a commercial bank's customers a cross section of individuals, entities of government, businesses, and institutions, the manner in which the bank interfaces with them and provides services to them mirrors the environment. A bank's philosophy, and the extent to which its operations are restricted by laws, can be highly reflective of the outside world. Thus the mood and spirit of the earliest American colonists can be captured and highlighted if one examines the banks they created and the banking system, or lack of one,existing at the time.

When Sir Isaac Newton, in 1687, first promulgated the physical law that for every action there is an equal and opposite reaction, in no way could he have foreseen the applications of that same principle to many areas outside the purview of the sciences. Yet a moment' thought demonstrates that this can be done. An era of strict, prudish morality in society gives way to one of license and vice versa. Fashions go to one extreme, them revert to another. Overly sentimental literary style, romantic literary works, and soft music pass from the scene and are replaced by harsh realism, crude language, and dissonance; the latter, in turn, fade in popularity and a new reaction takes place. So it is with the historical development of the American banking system.

COLONIAL BANKING

The earliest colonists sought independence and personal liberty in all things. Many of them came from countries in which a high degree of government control, affecting many aspects of their daily lives, existed. In those countries, the banking scene was commonly dominated by a strong, central bank and a relative handful ofcommercial banks.To the colonists this concept was in direct conflict with the broad notion of individual freedom. They reacted by going to the opposite end of the spectrum and applied to banking the same liberties that permitted anyone to follow his or her leanings and open any other type of business. In direct contrast to the central government banks of England France, and Sweden, the colonists opted for minimal government supervision. Banks were opened through the granting of a charter by the colony (later, the state or commonwealth), but the requirements for approval of a charter do not appear to have been onerous. Thereafter, examinations of a bank' capital adequacy and prudent operations were infrequent and cursory. The notion of a strong, central unit in the federal government to regulate and examine banks was vigorously opposed, as was any plan for a "national" bank like those in European countries. As geographic areas in the expanding nation opened up for settlement, those individuals who wished to engage in the banking business were almost as free to do so as those who chose other entrepreneurial activities. The same basic concept of freedom that allowed a person to open a tavern, blacksmith's shop, or general store was applied to the formation and operation of a bank.

It required many years for the colonists to accept the fact that the very nature of banking requires a modus operandi different from those that prevail in all other industries. Opening and operating a bank cannot be treated on the basis that would be relevant elsewhere. The early settlers do not seem to have recognized the simple truth that a system that allows virtually anyone to open a bank and operate it with little or no regulation and supervision is also a system in which anyone can close a bank. The effect of this insecurity on the overall economy was disastrous. At a time when a sound banking system, in which the public could place its trust, could have contributed greatly to the nation's progress, it was sorely lacking.

The success stories of banks that had their origins in colonial times are few and far between. The original Bank of North America (Philadelphia, 1782) and the bank of New York and Bank of Massachusetts (both 1784) are notable exceptions in a general history of bank failures and widespread lack of public confidence. Many banks went out of existence because of outright mismanagement, despite what may have been the best of intentions on the part of their organizers; in other cases, the motivation for opening the bank may have lain in the hope of quick profits, followed by hasty departure from the area in order to repeat the process in some new community. Banks generally hoarded their limited supplies of gold and silver and disbursed loan proceeds by issuing their individual notes to customers. The concept of crediting loan proceeds to a customer's account had not yet taken hold. Each bank's notes presumably were to be used as a medium of exchange, but in actual practice were often rejected by merchants who naturally questioned whether the issuing bank was still in existence. In addition the party to whom these notes were tendered necessarily had to wonder if he would be able to redeem them in hard currency, such as gold or silver, by presenting them to the issuer.

Commercial banks offer a wide range of corporate financial services that address the specific needs of private enterprise. They provide deposit, loan and trading facilities but will not service investment activities in financial markets. Commercial banks can be described as a type of financial intermediary. In the US, the term is used to refer to any banking organization or division that deals with the deposits and loans of business organizations.

The term commercial bank is used to differentiate these banks from investment banks, which are primarily engaged in the financial markets. Commercial banks are also differentiated from retail banks that cater to individual clients only. In non English-speaking countries the term commercial bank is used interchangeably with the term trading bank. Commercial banks play a number of roles in the financial stability and cash flow of a countries private sector. They process payments through a variety of means including telegraphic transfer, internet banking and electronic funds transfers. Commercial banks issue bank checks and drafts, as well as accept money on term deposits.

Commercial banks also act as moneylenders, by way of installment loans and overdrafts. Loan options include secured loans, unsecured loans, and mortgage loans. A secured loan is one where the borrower provides a certain property or asset as collateral against the loan. The main condition of these loans is that if the loan remains unpaid, the bank has the right to use the property in any way they like to realize the outstanding amount. Unsecured loans have no collateral and therefore command higher interest rates. There are a variety of unsecured loans available today and these include credit cars, credit facilities such as a lines of credit, corporate bonds, and bank overdrafts. Mortgage loans that are provided by commercial banks are similar to secured loans but are used specifically to buy real estate property for commercial purposes. In most of these cases, the banks hold a lien on the title to the particular property purchased with the loan. If the borrower is unable to pay the loan back, the bank leverages this item against the loan to generate funds or recover the principal.

Commercial banks provide a number of import financial and trading documents such as letters of credit, performance bonds, standby letters of credit, security underwriting commitments and various other types of balance sheet guarantees. They also take responsibility for safeguarding such documents and other valuables by providing safe deposit boxes.

Currency exchange functions and the provision of unit trusts and commercial insurance are typically provided by the relevant departments in larger commercial banks.

COMMERCIAL BANKS IN INDIA

Commercial Banks in India are broadly categorized into Scheduled Commercial Banks and Unscheduled Commercial Banks. The Scheduled Commercial Banks have been listed under the Second Schedule of the Reserve Bank of India Act, 1934. The selection measure for listing a bank under the Second Schedule was provided in section 42 (60 of the Reserve Bank of India Act, 1934. Introduction of Banking:Banking operations started in India as early as 1870 with the establishment of the Bank of Hindustan, considered as the first bank in India. The second development in the banking sector happened with the incorporation of the Bank of Calcutta, the Bank of Bombay and the Bank of Bombay in accordance with the Presidency Bank's Act, 1876. All these banks joined hands to form the Imperial Bank of India. The reserve Bank of India was engaged in the performance of central banking activities before the establishment of the Reserve Bank of India. Activities of Commercial Banks:The modern Commercial Banks in India cater to the financial needs of different sectors. The main functions of the commercial banks comprise of transfer of funds, acceptance of deposits and then offering those deposits as loans for the establishment of industries, purchase of houses, equipments, capital investment purposes etc.

The banks are allowed to act as trustees. On account of the knowledge of the financial market of India the financial companies are attracted towards them to act as trustees to take the responsibility of the security for the financial instrument like a debenture. The Indian Government presently hires the commercial banks for various purposes like tax collection and refunds, payment of pensions etc. Modern Banking Techniques:The immense growth of the IT sector is reflected in the banking operation of the Commercial Banks in India. Presently, the IT companies are engaged in the creating software packages to facilitate, accelerate, and organize the banking operations. The Rangarajan Committee and the Reserve Bank of India has played a major role in the popularizing the concept of computer application in banking activities. The computerization process has reached its peak in the present scenario with the use of Total Branch Automation Packages. Products and Services offered by Commercial Banks in India:The Commercial Banks in India offer variety of products and services like Investment Advisory Services, Tax Advisory services, Cash Management services, debit cards, ATM cards, credit cards, personal loans, education loans, housing loans, car loans, Investment Advisory Services, and consumer durable loans.

3

Commercial Banking for the Rural Sector

INTRODUCTION

After the adoption of the New Economic Policy in 1991, the Indian economy is becoming more and more mature with the passage of time on account of structural changes undertaken in different sectors and areas. The GDP growth rate has been much higher than the neo-Hindu rate growth and it has averaged over eight per cent during the past three years. While there has been acceleration in the industrial sector, especially manufacturing and services sector, and the country is graduating from a low-income regime to a middle income regime, there has been deceleration in agricultural growth, which reflects as a broad-based slowdown in the productivity growth. Some of the poorest and most populous States have fallen behind. The commercialisation of agriculture, as also technology intensification has resulted in creation of substantial surplus labour in the agriculture sector. As a result, as per the results of the Economic Census 2005, employment growth in the non-farm sector is much lower and average employment itself has declined during the 1990s as comparted to the 1980s.

While growth is important, it is also imperative that growth becomes more inclusive because if certain regions, sectors or groups of people are denied economic opportunities for long periods, the spread and sustainability of growth itself is threatened. Hence, growth, to be inclusive, must take into account the betterment of every section of society. Hence, it is imperative to ensure that higher growth is also more inclusive. In the Draft Approach Paper to the Eleventh Five Year Plan, the Planning Commission has emphasised the need for faster and greater inclusive growth during the Eleventh Plan period. The banking sector, as the most important financial intermediary to mobilise the savings leading to increased investments, facilitating growth would, thus, play the most crucial role in attaining the stipulated economic objectives through expansion of the coverage of banking services by reaching the vast unbanked and underbanked population of the country.

HISTORICAL PERSPECTIVE

Adoption of a policy of social control over banks in 1967 and the nationalisation of 14 major scheduled commercial banks in 1969 have provedto be two major turning-points in the history of commercial banks in India. When the banks were nationalised in 1969, the primary focus was on social banking. government thought that it was necessary to 'control the heights of the economy and to meet progressively, and serve better, the needs of development of the economy in conformity with national policy and objectives'. The setting up of Regional Rural Banks in 1975 and nationalisation of another five banks in 1980 further revealed the concern of the government towards meeting the credit requirements of agriculturists.

Farmers in India have had to face a number of problems, one of them being great difficulty in getting credit because of the peculiar nature of agricultural credit. The element of uncertainty is greater in agriculture as compared to other sectors because even today a considerably high proportion of Indian agriculture is dependent on the vagaries of the monsoon. The agriculturalists (borrowers) want credit at relatively low rates of interest but the lender desires to charge a higher rate of interest to cover the risk of uncertainty. Therefore, one of the important objectives of the nationalisation of 14 major commercial banks in India, among others, was to make a provision of adequate credit for agriculture and the agricultural sector was included in the category of priority sectors. On the recommendations of a Committee of Bankers, the Lead Bank Scheme was introduced and throughout the seventies targets were set for commercial banks to open up branches in rural and semi-urban areas. In the years that followed, banks reached the targets and, in some cases, even surpassed them.

The total direct and indirect finance by the public sector banks to agriculture increased from Rs 162 crores in June 1969 to Rs 3881 crores in June 1981 (24 times) and the number of accounts increased from 1.7 lakhs of 96.99 lakhs. (Table 1). The number of branches in rural areas also increased from 1833 branches in 1969 to 17,656 branches in 1981 (over nine times) and that in semi-urban areas from 3342 branches to 8471 branches during the same period. This policy of target fixation continued in future years also. Consequently, the number of accounts, advances to the agricultural sector, as also the number of banks offices in rural and semi-urban areas increased.

In the meantime, the Working Group on Rural Banks (Chairman M. Narasimham) recommended in 1975 the setting up of Regional Rural Banks, as part of a multi-agency approach to rural credit. Accordingly, scheduled commercial banks' total advances (direct and indirect) further increased to Rs 16,750 crores in 1990-91 and the number of scheduled commercial banks' offices increased to 35,206 in rural areas and to 11,344 in semi-urban areas by 1991.

The Economic Reforms launched by the Indian Government in 1991 were designed to accelerate the overall growth and help India realise its full productive potential. Structural reforms were undertaken in industry, trade, foreign investment, fiscal front and various policy initiatives were undertaken in the area of agriculture. The basic objective behind all such reforms was to improve efficiency by encouraging competitiveness in the economy. These reforms were supported by reforms in the financial sector, including the banking system which has the prime responsibility for mobilising and allocating financial resources. Accordingly, reforms in the banking sector in the post-1991 era have been largely influenced by the recommendations of the Report of the Committee on Financial

System 1991 (Chairman M. Narasimham). The first phase of reforms focused mainly on enabling and strengthening measures. During the second phase of reforms, based on the recommendations of the Committee on Banking Sector Reforms 1998 (Chairman M. Narasimham), greater stress has been placed on structural measures and improvement in standards of disclosure and levels of transparency so as to align Indian standards with the best international practices.

While it is true that the policy environment during the nineties has been dominated by the liberalisation of the banking sector, greater concern with prudential norms for banks, risk management, etc. and most of the efforts have been concentrated in the urban and metropolitan centres, it is also true that priority sector lending, including agriculture, has also continued to grow. The total number of bank accounts in the agricultural sector with public sector banks have increased from 198 lakhs in 1995 to 253 lakhs in 2007 and the total outstanding advances for agriculture have increased from Rs 23,328 crores in March 1995 to Rs 2,05,091 crores in March 2007 (direct finance from Rs 20,562 crores to Rs 1,46,941 crores and indirect finance from Rs 20,766 crores to Rs 58,150 crores. The government has laid emphasis on agricultural credit in the post-1991 period also because agricultural credit, by promoting agricultural and related business, plays an important role in poverty alleviation and creation of employment. Keeping this in view, the Reserve Bank of India had advised the public sector banks to prepare Special Agricultural Credit Plans (SACP) in 1994-95. The SACP mechanism was also made applicable to the private sector banks in 2005-06. The disbursements by the public sector banks to agriculture under SACP have increased from Rs 25,654 crores in 2000-01 to Rs 1,22,215 crores in 2006-07.1 The private sector banks also made disbursements under SACP of Rs 31,1999 crores in 2005-06 and Rs 18,819 crores in 2006-07.

Keeping the importance of agricultural credit in mind the Tenth Five Year Plan envisaged a substantial increase in credit flow to agriculture from a level of Rs 2,29,956 crores achieved during the Ninth Five Plan to a level of Rs 7,36,570 crores during the Tenth Five Year Plan.

Under the government's policy, all domestic banks (including private banks) and foreign banks are required to provide 40 per cent and 32 per cent respectively, of their net banking credit to the priority sector. From Table 3, it would be clear that both public and private sector banks had achieved their overall target for priority sector lending in March 2006. However, the public sector banks fell short of the target of 40 per cent by 0.4 percentage points by March 2007 whereas the private sector banks had achieved their overall target. Foreign banks had also advanced 33.4 per cent loans to the priority sector, as against target of 32 per cent, as on last Friday of March 2007.

In recent years, two innovations, namely, micro- finance and Kisan Credit Card (KCC) Scheme, have emerged as the major policy tools to address the problems associated with the distributional aspects of rural credit. Today micro-finance, the Self-Help Group-Bank Linkage Programme (introduced in 1992), has emerged on the major micro-finance programme. At the end of March 2007, 29.24 lakh SHGs were linked to banks covering a total flow of credit of Rs 18,040 crores. Similarly, the Kisan Credit Card (KCC) Scheme was introduced in 1998-99 to provide adequate and timely credit support to the farmers in a flexible, hassle-free and cost-effective manner. Hence the KCC Scheme has become very popular and by the end of March 2007, 26.6 million KCCs have been issued by the public sector banks, with limits amounting to Rs 94,712 crores.

CRITICAL APPRAISAL

WHILE it is true that since 1991, the policy environment has been dominated by the liberalisation of the banking sector and greater concern for prudential norms for banks and risk management, most of these efforts have been concentrated in the urban and metropolitan centres and very little change has effectively come in the rural areas. Even today, majority of the rural branches are running in losses, the deposit mobilisation is not up to the desired level, there are problems in granting advances etc. In their anxiety to reach the target of 40 per cent to the priority sectors, banks have gone in for indiscriminate lending. There have been external pressures on the banking sector to lend to weaker sections. What is still worse, much of the priority sector lending has to be at a low concessional rate of interest. Despite these pressures, the total priority sector lending by public sector banks has come down from 43.6 per cent in March 2004 to 39.6 per cent in March 2007 and lending by the private sector banks from 47.3 per cent to 42.7 per cent during the same period (Table 3).

Another trend witnessed since 1991 is that scheduled banks are opening more and more branches in semi-urban, urban and metropolitan centres and the number of rural branches are going down. From Table 2 it would be clear that while the total bank offices have increased from 60,220 at the end of June 1991 to 71,781 offices in June 2007, the number of bank offices in the rural areas has gone down from 35,206 offices in 1991 to 30,633 offices in 2007.

Further, as the priority sector loans have been of small amounts, the public sector banks not been able to adequately monitor the distribution, follow-up and recovery of loans, resulting in squeezing of profitability and increase in non-performing assets. Non-Performing Assets (NPAs) of the end of March 2006 were 54.07 per cent for the public sector banks, as against 29.17 per cent for the private sector banks.

The official compulsions of keeping a high proportion of their deposits in liquid form and subsidisation of credit added fuel to fire. Over the years, there has been growth in staff, resulting in increased operating expenses—although in the recent past this ratio has gone down on account of compulsions of increased competition from private sector and foreign banks. Moreover, very few programmes focused on micro-enterprises or encouraged diversification away from agriculture. This led to a focus merely on geographical expansion of the rural areas, where the banks' branches offered credit in sizes which were too large to be made use of by the very poor. These practices led to a high default.

Suggestions

ENHANCING the growth rate in agriculture to 4.1 per cent, as envisaged in the Approach Paper to the Eleventh Five Year Plan, and improving its robustness would require substantial investment in irrigation and water management technologies, diversification and boosting productivity of different crops through improved seeds and plant-care practices. The move towards inclusive growth is a big challenge for the financial system of the country, including commercial banks. Banks would need to adopt an innovative, customer-friendly approach to increase their effective reach so that the share of organised finance increases. A participatory and partnership-based model for financial inclusion, coupled with community-linked financial initiatives is the need of the hour. In the near future customer-friendly products, delivery channels, relationship banking, dependency on IT systems and competitive pricing would be the driving forces. Banks will to move to a high-tech banking. The Internet would be the engine of the banking revolution in the decades to come and e-commerce would be its fuel. Therefore, the key to survival of banks in future will be the retention of customer loyalty by providing value-added services tailored to their needs.

First, traditionally banks have viewed rural areas as a segment purely in need of upliftment. This was based on the underlying philosophy of a social obligation. However, the future lies with those who see the poor as their customers, namely, financial inclusion. By 'financial inclusion' is meant the provision by the financial system, of financial products and services at an affordable price, to those who have been financially excluded. As banking services are in the nature of a public utility service, it is essential that banking and payment services are provided to the entire population without discrimination. The harsh reality is that the spread of banking facilities in India is uneven, with a substantial portion of the households, especially in the rural areas, still outside the coverage of the formal banking system. Almost 40 per cent of the adult population of the country is unable to access mainstream financial products.3 The Reserve Bank of India has recently adopted a decentralised approach in this regard with close involvement of

State Governments and banks and has used multiple channels to expand the outreach of banks. It is important to mention that the Union Bank has launched a new initiative called 'Village Knowledge Centres'. Here, technology is used to help the farmer improve his productivity. The Bank's staff at these village knowledge centres act as relationship managers, liaising between local authorities and farmers, facilitating the opening of accounts and ensuring that credit is provided to the needy. Such examples need to be followed by other banks.

Secondly, commercial banks should change their marketing concept. Under the new concept of marketing, the task of management should not so much be skill in making the customer do what suits the rest of the business, as to be skilful in conceiving and making business do what suits the interest of the customers.

Thirdly, stress should be laid on deposit mobilisation from the agricultural sector itself to finance its own credit requirements. Such a move will entail two steps—curtailment of unproductive expenditure and deposit of savings by the agriculturists in banks. It is common knowledge that villagers spend huge sums on unproductive social ceremonies, drinking, litigation, etc. Their outlook needs to be changed with the help of banking staff and utilising the services of the mass media. Villagers must be convinced that money spent on such social obligations is a waste and they themselves would gain in the long run if they would save and invest. The services of officers and staff of the community development projects may also be utilised for this purpose.

Fourthly, the more important aspect of the whole drive is the deposit of savings by the agriculturist in the banks. Vast sums of money are lying idle even today in rural areas. We think that, in spite of different agencies engaged in providing agricultural finance, the village moneylender continues to be a necessary evil. These moneylenders have great influence on the villagers. To mobilise the savings of the villagers, the services of these moneylenders—both professional and agricultural—can be utilised. The nationalised banks may appoint them as their agents. The banks should then ask them to encourage the villagers to deposit their money in the banks and approach the banks for loans through them. The banks may give them a sort of del credere commission, depending upon the quantum of business done by them, as is done in the case of agents of the Life Insurance Corporation, General Insurance Corporation, National Savings Organisation, etc. Such a step would help in mobilising savings. The appointment of moneylenders as agents has an added advantage. These moneylenders have been living in villages for a long time and are, therefore, accustomed to the rural way of life. They know the local language and can, therefore, mix well with the villagers. This is not the case with the qualified, educated and sophisticated bank staff. Many a time, superiority complex on the part of the bank employees drives away the villagers. As a corollary to this, it is also suggested that, as far as possible, the staff to be deputed in the rural branches, should be drawn from the villages or semi-urban areas themselves and better living conditions be assured for the bank employees.

Fifthly, there is need for a reorientation in the credit policy of banks. Priority sector lendings should be restricted only to the core sector. Banks should provide credit not merely on the basis of collateral security such as land and buildings but they should also advance loans to the agriculturists after assessing the 'absorptive capacity' and the increase in productivity that is feasible with the help of such loans. Crops should also be accepted on a loan of security. To assess the 'absorptive capacity' of the farmers commercial banks should maintain a staff of agricultural experts.

Sixthly, the commercial banks should also provide credit to the agriculturists on the basis of 'joint guarantee' given by the village panchayat or by a few well-known farmers of the village. The acceptance of such a basis will greatly help the farmers, particularly small farmers, in securing loans from commercial banks. This will also result in more purposeful advent of the commercial banks in the rural sector and will bring them into relationship with cooperative institutions. It will also ensure a fair understanding between them and encourage commercial banks to operate on the principle of collective service for a collective need.

Seventhly, one problem experienced by banks is that, many a time, villagers divert the loans from productive to unproductive uses. This needs to be stopped and it needs to be ensured that the credit is used for the purposes for which it is meant. Banks may think in terms of advancing credit to agriculturists in the form of agricultural inputs. While giving credit to farmers in the form of agricultural inputs, it should be ensured that inputs are supplied in adequate quantities and in time and complementary and supplementary facilities are also available.

Finally, it needs to be remembered that stray attempts would not solve the problem of agricultural credit. The credit system as a whole—government, commercial and cooperative—must be so knit together that it does not suffer either from a gap or an overlap. It is only then that the real fruits of credit facilities will be enjoyed by the country at large in the form of agricultural development which still the key to India's prosperity in future.

Table 2 : Distribution of Scheduled Commercial Banks' Offices (as on 30th June)

Year	Rural	Semi-urban	Urban	Metropolitan	Total
1969	1833	3342	1584	1503	8262
1975	6807	5598	3489	2836	18730
1981	17656	8471	5454	4126	35707
1986	29703	10585	7209	5790	53287
1991	35206	11344	8046	5624	60220
1996	32995	13561	9086	7384	63026
2001	32562	14597	10293	8467	65919
2002	32380	14747	10477	8586	66190
2003	32303	14859	10693	8680	66535
2004	32121	15091	11000	8976	67188
2005	30755	15174	11678	10942	68549
2006	30500	15644	12216	11441	69801
2007@	30633	16310	12925	11913	71781

@ provisional Source: 1. Report on Trend and Progress of Banking in India (different years) 2. RBI Handbook of Statistics on Indian Economy (different years)

Table 1 : Advances to the Priority Sector by Public Sector Banks

Sector	Number of Accounts (in lakhs)	Amount oustanding (Rs. crore)										
	June 1969	June 1981	March 1995	March 2005	March 2006	March 2007@	June 1969	June 1981	March 1995	March 2005	March 2006	March 2007@
Agriculture	1.7	96.99	198.42	201.71 (5.4)	237.98 (16.2)	253.00 (14.1)	162 (15.3)	3881 (15.3)	23328 (15.6)	109917	155220	205091
(i)Direct Finance	1.6	84.96	194.12	194.94 (1.3)	220.79 (12.3)	235.00 (12.4)	40 (11.6)	2955 (11.0)	20562 (11.2)	83038	112126	146941
(ii)Indirect Finance	0.1	12.03	4.30	6.77 (4.0)	17.19 (3.9)	18.00 (1.7)	122 (3.7)	926 (4.2)	2766 (4.4)	26879	43093	58150
Small-scale Industry	0.5	8.44	28.84	13.95 (8.5)	17.29 (14.0)	20.00 (15.5)	257 (9.5)	3351 (8.1)	25636 (8.0)	67800	82434	104703
Other Advances	0.4	30.56	107.84	98.08 (0.7)	103.13 (6.8)	102.00 (7.2)	22 (17.4)	1629 (16.1)	11838 (15.3)	125114	163756	201023
Total priority sector	2.6	135.99	335.10	313.74 (14.6)	358.40 (37.0)	391.00 (36.8)	441 (42.8)	8861 (40.3)	60802 (39.6)	307046	409748	521180
Net bank advances	-	-	-	-	-	-	3016	23950	165377	717419	1017656	1317705

@ provisional Source: 1. Report on Trend and Progress of Banking in India (different years) 2. Economic Survey (different years)

Table 3 : Priority Sector lending by Public and Private Sector Banks (By end March)]

Category(Accounts in Rs crores)..........................

Public Sector Banks (by end March)	Private Sector Banks (by end March)							
	2004	2005	2006	2007@	2004	2005	2006	2007@
Priority sector advances (a+b+c)	244456	307046	409748	521181	48920	69886	106586	143768
of which:	(43.6)	(42.8)	(40.3)	(39.6)	(47.3)	(43.6)	(42.8)	(42.7)
a) Agriculture	84435	109917	155220	205091	14730	21636	36712	52056
	(15.1)	(15.3)	(15.3)	(15.6)	(14.2)	(13.5)	(13.6)	(12.8)
b) Small Scale	58311	67800	82434	104703	7590	8592	10421	13063
Industries	(10.4)	(9.5)	(8.1)	(8.0)	(7.3)	(5.4)	(4.2)	(3.9)
c) Other	101710	125114	163756	201023	26600	38797	57777	76925
priority sectors	(18.1)	(17.4)	(16.1)	(15.3)	(25.7)	(24.2)	(23.2)	(22.9)

@ provisional Note: Figure in the brackets represent percentage to net bank credit for the respective groups

Source: RBI, Report on Trend and Progress of Banking in India (different years)

4

Role of Commercial Banks

This Chapter briefly traces the historical and contemporary imperatives to provide financial services to the rural poor in India and the institutional responses to the same.

EVOLUTION OF THE FINANCIAL LANDSCAPE

In post-independence India, in order to facilitate improvements in agricultural production and attain food self-sufficiency, the stance of policy was to ensure sufficient and timely credit at "reasonable" rates of interest to as large a segment of the rural population as possible (Rangarajan 1996). The strategy to achieve this was threefold: expansion of the institutional base, directed lending to disadvantaged borrowers, and credit provision at concessional rates of interest. The latter was justified in terms of the perceived mismatch between the longer term returns of farm investment in relation to cultivator households' short term consumption needs and requirements to service the loans. Fisher and Sriram (2006) identify three post-independence phases in rural credit provision. First, the 1950's up to the mid-1960's when cooperatives were the institutional vehicles of choice; second, the 1970's and 1980s when attention shifted to commercial banks and RRBs and third, the reform period in the early 1990's which saw the re-structuring of the banking system, the emergence of SHGs and a growing number of MFIs.

In terms of scale, spread, costs, risks, and the inter-temporal nature of credit markets, financial institutions and agents in India face formidable challenges in meeting the diverse financial service needs of the country's rural population.

The present rural financial infrastructure comprises a wide variety of formal, semi-formal and informal financial service providers, with distinctive cultures and characteristics. The number of organisations and agents is very substantial : 33,553 rural and semi-urban branches of commercial banks, 13,932 rural and semi-urban branches of Regional Rural Banks, 1.09 lakh primary cooperatives, 1,000 NGO-MFIs and around 20 MFIs registered as companies (Section 25) and nearly three million SHGs. Even more numerous are the myriad of informal agents constituting a great range of financial service providers across the country.

Different segments of the financial infrastructure have not developed uniformly or simultaneously, and their relative standing in terms of government policy and intervention has changed over time. Moreover, financial institutions have themselves influenced government policy (Jones 2006). In the following paragraphs, an attempt is made to trace the forces and compulsions that have led to the development of particular rural financial institutions in the country, to outline the changing fortunes and shares of these different systems, to show the present gap between rural financial needs and provisions, and to assess policy options to reduce this gap through institutional development, linkages and reform.

EVOLUTION OF COMMERCIAL BANKS

The foundation for building a broad base of agricultural credit structure was laid by the Report of the All-India Rural Credit Survey (AIRCS) of 1954. The provision of cultivator credit in 1951-52 was less than 1% for commercial banks. In the report it was observed that agricultural credit fell short of the right quantity, was not of the right type, did not fit the right purpose and often failed to go to the right people. With a view to give an impetus to commercial banks, particularly, in the sphere of investment credit, the nationalization of the Imperial Bank of India and its redesignation as the State Bank of India (SBI) was recommended.

Growth in Outreach 1951-91

From the position prevalent in 1951-52, commercial banks came a long way with a substantial spread of 32,224 branches in rural and semi-urban areas comprising 68% of their total outlets as on 31 March 1991. The outstanding deposits of such branches at Rs.67,855 crore as on the same date constituted around 35% of their total deposits, while loans outstanding at Rs. 43,797 crore comprised 36% of outstanding credit. The agricultural advances of the commercial banking system aggregated Rs. 16,687 crore and constituted 14% of total advances in March 1991. The rural and semi-urban branches of commercial banks covered 17.6 crore deposit accounts while the number of loan accounts serviced aggregated 3.7 crore.

Growth during 1991-92 to 2003-04

The period since 1991-92 has seen a fairly rapid expansion of credit to agriculture. Available data indicate that the flow of credit to agriculture by commercial banks and RRBs taken together increased to Rs. 60,022 crore in 2003-04. This implies a compounded annual growth rate of 22.2%. In fact, as compared with commercial banks (including RRBs), the flow of credit from the cooperative sector was much slower through this period. The compounded annual growth rate of credit for agriculture from cooperative institutions was only 13.7%. Further, the proportion of agriculture credit to total credit came down because of the rapid growth in nonagriculture credit.

The Government took some major initiatives during the period to boost agriculture production and productivity through enhanced credit flow and by way of building agricultural infrastructure, particularly irrigation and connectivity in rural areas.

Special Agricultural Credit Plan (SACP) was introduced by RBI for Public Sector Commercial Banks in 1994-95. Credit growth for agriculture and allied sectors under this caption reflected a CAGR of 36.45% during 2001-02 to 2005-06. SACP has since been extended to Private Sector Commercial Banks from 2005-06.

The SHG – Bank Linkage Programme was started as a pilot project by NABARD in 1992. It led to the evolution of a set of RBI approved guidelines to banks to enable SHGs to transact with banks. Initially there was slow progress in the programme up to 1999 as only 32,995 groups were credit linked during the period 1992 to 1999. Since then the programme has been growing rapidly and the cumulative number of SHGs financed increased from 4.61 lakhs on 31 March 2002 to 10.73 lakhs on 31 March 2004 and further to 29.25 lakh groups as on 31 March 2007.

Rural Infrastructure Development Fund (RIDF) was set-up in NABARD by GoI during 1995-96 with an initial corpus of Rs.2000 crore, to accelerate the completion of on-going projects of rural infrastructure. Banks which did not fulfill the priority sector credit requirement and agriculture credit mandate were required to contribute to this Fund. The fund has been strengthened every year with additional allocations in the Union Budget. A large number of irrigation and rural connectivity projects could get completed under RIDF.

RBI scaled down its contribution to the Rural Credit funds with NABARD to a token amount of Rs.1 crore per annum since 1993-94. However to enable NABARD to have reasonably strong leverage for accessing market funds, the share capital of NABARD was strengthened and increased to Rs.2000 crore (paid up) from Rs.100 crore at the time of its formation in 1982. Contributions to enhanced share capital have come from GoI and RBI. By prudent funds management, the institution has also built a strong base of reserves and has been using it in its business operations judiciously to keep lending rates to rural financial institutions at significantly lower than market costs.

Developments – Post 2003-04

Since 2003-04, there has been a substantial increase in the flow of credit to agriculture through commercial banks. Disbursements have increased from Rs. 52,441 crore in 2003-04 to Rs. 1,16,447 crore in 2005-06, reaching an annual growth of 43% each year. As envisaged in the GoI's strategy for "doubling of credit", 95 lakh new farmers have been brought under the institutional fold and 1,383 agri-clinics opened. Commercial banks have also played a major role in the promotion of the SHG – bank linkage movement with more than 11.88 lakh groups being linked to banks for provision of credit. Reforms in the commercial banking system include removal of procedural and transactional bottlenecks including elimination of Service Area Approach, reducing margins, redefining overdues to coincide with crop cycles, new debt restructuring policies, one time settlement and relief measures for farmers indebted to non-institutional sources.

The Task Ahead

Commercial banks are now slowly coming to appreciate the business potential in financial inclusion and also the need for better involvement. RRBs who are expected to function with the social heart of cooperatives and financial acumen of commercial banks have a significant role to play in financial inclusion, especially in the post-amalgamation scenario. The vast postal network, leveraging on their immense outreach, could also be an effective vehicle for purveying financial services.

While, there is evidence that commercial banks have been cognizant of their social responsibility in regard to small farmers, their focus on marginal and submarginal farmers, tenants, share croppers, oral lessees and non-cultivator households, viz., the very poor and disadvantaged sectors has been found wanting. In the circumstances, there is a need to evolve conscious strategies for providing easier access to affordable credit to the marginal, sub-marginal and other disadvantaged groups in the rural sector. Such strategies should combine using a variety of delivery channels, intermediaries and IT solutions apart from the traditional brick and mortar branch network.

The specific recommendations of the Committee for achieving targets under the NRFIP by leveraging the existing commercial bank branch network in rural areas are as follows :

Targets for rural / semi-urban branches

Currently, there are 33,478 commercial bank branches in rural and semi-urban centres in the country. Out of these, there are about 12,340 branches in the rural and semi urban areas of the Central, Eastern and North-Eastern Regions, where the majority of the financially excluded population live. It is understood that each branch of Grameen Bank in Bangladesh services at least 4,000-5,000 borrowers, with 6-7 field officers per branch. Given the existing staff strength, it should be possible for commercial banks (including RRBs) to provide access to credit to at least 250 hitherto excluded households per annum at each of their existing rural and semi-urban branches. For this, banks will have to strengthen their staff and use a variety of delivery mechanisms.

TARGETED BRANCH EXPANSION IN IDENTIFIED DISTRICTS

In several districts, the population per branch office is much higher than the national average, particularly in rural and semi urban areas. The list of such districts has already been circulated by RBI among banks. The DLCCs in these districts may identify centres for opening branches by commercial banks and RRBs. in the next three years.

For the North-Eastern Region, the financial sector plan has already identified such centres and branch expansion plan as laid out therein may be implemented. SLBC may monitor the branch expansion plan for each State.

Product Innovation

The excluded segments of the population require products which are customized, taking into consideration their varied needs. Their banking requirements being small, the issue of servicing and delivery in a cost-effective manner assumes significance. The need for savings by these groups require special attention, e.g. for meeting life cycle needs, creating assets, repaying high cost borrowings, meeting emergencies etc. The saving products offered at present do not effectively meet these needs. The services offered are also not suitable because of the spatial spread of the excluded people and also the small quantum of finance involved.

(a) Savings : Savings products to meet the specific requirements of the poor need to be evolved. One way of meeting this would be to utilize SHGs for tapping the small savings by providing incentives to the SHGs with suitable back-end technology support. The banks can develop medium and long term savings instruments by issue of pre-printed deposit receipts to the SHGs which in turn can be sold to the SHG members. Banks could be given the freedom to develop their own products, suiting local requirements and felt needs of the poor.

(b) Credit : With regard to credit products, the savings linked financing model can be adopted for these segments. The approach should be kept simple which should guarantee the beneficiaries a credit limit, subject to adherence to terms and conditions. The credit within the limit can be made available in 2-3 tranches, with the second and subsequent tranches disbursed based on repayment behaviour of the first tranche. This is to ensure that the vulnerable groups do not get into a debt trap; it also ensures good credit dispensation.

(c) Insurance : Banks can play a vital role in this regard – by distributing suitable micro-insurance products.

INCENTIVISING HUMAN RESOURCE – MEASURABLE PERFORMANCE INDICATORS

Lending to low income groups and increasing financial inclusion need motivated bank staff. Such motivation is a function of attitudes and beliefs as also a system of incentives / disincentives put in place by the bank's management for special efforts / failures to achieve desired levels of financial inclusion.

The Committee debated the issue of creating a separate cadre of rural bank employees. While the arguments in favour were supported by the large proportion of rural branches, quantum of deposits and credit, the arguments against were the high costs involved and compulsions regarding rotation of staff. It was, therefore, felt that existing staff posted to rural branches can be incentivised within a framework of performance parameters including covering of new households through deposit and loan accounts, increase in business in existing and new small loan / deposit accounts, increase in number of SHGs / Joint Liability Groups (JLG) formed and credit linked, efforts put in for promotion of asset management skills and developing linkages to promote credit absorption.

Funding

The Committee recognized that there is a cost involved in providing credit plus services and technology applications. Such costs may come down over a period of time with the resultant business expansion. Banks are expected to meet a part of the costs. However, in the initial stages some funding support thru' specially constituted Funds may be extended to them. This funding support, envisaged as a mechanism to reduce costs, may be provided to the banks on two counts - (i) promotional and developmental initiatives that will lead to better credit absorption capacity among the poor and vulnerable sections and (ii) application of technology for facilitating the mandated levels of inclusion.

Financial Inclusion Funds

The Committee proposes the constitution of two funds – the Financial Inclusion (Promotion & Development Fund), with NABARD, for meeting the cost of developmental and promotional interventions indicated below and the Financial Inclusion Technology Fund, with NABARD, to meet the costs of technology adoption. Each Fund will have an initial corpus of Rs. 500 crore, with a start-up funding of Rs. 250 crore each, to be contributed in equal proportion by GoI / RBI / NABARD and with annual accretions thereto. Banks will be eligible for support from the Funds on a matching contribution of 50% from the Fund in regard to districts other than tribal districts and 75% in case of branches located in tribal districts identified under the Tribal Sub Plan.

Financial Inclusion Promotion and Development Fund

The Financial Inclusion Promotion and Development Fund will focus on financing the following interventions :

Farmers' Service Centres (FSC) : With the creation of and support to FSCs a host of financial and farm advisory services are to be provided to the new / hitherto excluded customer segments. The Centres will network on the technology front with Agricultural Universities / KVKs, farmers clubs, the formal extension machinery of the State Governments, technical staff of banks, portals of national level commodity exchanges etc. Such FSCs can be financed by the banks on the pattern of agri clinics. In the initial stages, it may be necessary to provide them some support by way of viability gap funding.

Promoting Rural Entrepreneurship : Commercial banks may consider setting up institutions like farmer training centres and Rural Development and Self Employment Training Institutes (RUDSETI) for developing skills among farmers / rural entrepreneurs for effectively managing the assets financed.

Self-Help Groups : The process of financial inclusion can be greatly facilitated through the medium of linking SHGs with the formal sector. It has been observed elsewhere in the Report that the SHG movement is yet to catch up on a big scale in regions manifesting high levels of exclusion (Central, Eastern and North-Eastern Regions). The funding support for promotion, nurturing and credit linking of SHGs can be extended.

Developing HR – Addressing attitudinal issues thru' training : Various studies have confirmed that lending to the poor raises a number of issues ranging from sources and reliability of their incomes to lack of suitable bank projects for them to the elitist approach of the formal institutional credit delivery apparatus. These factors are the outcome of attitudes towards the poor, as generally not viable and profitable customers of the bank. Experience indicates that the poor, if guided properly, not only succeed as entrepreneurs, but are also good "repayers". However, changing this attitude or mindset is a challenge.

In a study conducted in Madhya Pradesh, it was found that attitudes of branch managers shape the branch lending behaviour. Two other important findings which emerged were that a majority of the branch managers held negative attitudes towards lending to the poor and about themselves, their work roles and situations and exhibited a general lack of motivation and confidence. Secondly, there was a positive correlation between the training received by the branch managers and their overall attitudes. Branch managers felt that in terms of frequency, and relevance to their work, training was inadequate, too theoretical, inappropriate for rural assignment, outdated and in some case a mere formality (Jones, Williams & Thorat).

Keeping in view the impact that training has on attitudes, a training module has been developed and tested for commercial banks and RRBs in the College of Agricultural Banking, Pune. The Committee recommends that banks use / adapt this programme for bringing about the right mindset amongst their branch staff posted to districts having a high share of population excluded from access to financial services.

Resource Centres

Resource Centres, apart from facilitating members of mature SHGs to graduate to micro-enterprises, also helps in ensuring long term sustainability of SHGs. The cost of setting up such centers can be met out of this Fund and / or the MFDEF. This is discussed in detail later in the report.

Federations

As indicated later in the report, funding support may also be extended from this Fund and / or MFDEF for voluntary establishment of federations.

Capacity building of BFs/BCs

Funding support, on priority basis, to be extended to specialized institutions which provide capacity building inputs to BFs/BCs, as discussed later in the Report.

Financial Inclusion Technology Fund

Technology Applications for Greater Financial Inclusion : Extending outreach on a scale envisaged under NRFIP would require the application of low-cost technology solutions, which have been discussed in greater detail elsewhere in the Report. This may also call for certain levels of funding support for rolling out such IT-based inclusive financial sector plan.

Guidelines for operationalising the Funds

NABARD, in consultation with RBI, may prepare detailed guidelines based on consulatations with commercial banks and technology service providers for operationalising both the Funds.

PROCEDURAL CHANGES

Simplifying Mortgage Requirements

The Talwar Committee had recommended acceptance of a simple declaratory charge as equitable mortgage. Enabling legislation has been passed in some States. This may be done by all the State Governments as it would simplify documentation processes considerably.

Exemption from Stamp Duty for Loans to Small and Marginal Farmers: Stamp duty adds to transaction costs incurred by farmers. Non-availability of stamps in required denominations results in borrowers paying higher than the prescribed stamp duty. The Committee recommends waiver of stamp duty requirements for loan documents of small / marginal farmers and tenant cultivators.

Saral Documentation for Agricultural Loans

NABARD, in cooperation with a core group of bankers, has prepared a one page document for agricultural loans up to Rs.1 lakh.

This document has been circulated among the scheduled commercial banks (including RRBs) with the approval of the Indian Banks' Association. The Committee recommends that this simplified document be adopted by all banks with a view to deepening credit outreach among the disadvantaged sections of the rural poor.

Nodal Branches (ADB Model)

Taking cognizance of the fact that the marginal and sub-marginal farmers require credit plus services in the form of extension services, in all districts identified as having the largest number of excluded people, the Committee recommends that one branch of the lead bank or the bank having the largest presence at the block / taluka level may be identified as the nodal branch to address the issue of exclusion. Lead banks or banks having the largest presence may strengthen these nodal branches with technical staff to provide agricultural / business development services in the farm and non-farm sectors respectively, comprising of technical inputs and extension services to the banks / farmers. These could either be provided by regular officers of the bank or local consultants / practitioners / agri-business clinics on a retainer basis. As the services of the nodal branch would be available to all other branches in the vicinity, an appropriate cost sharing arrangement may be worked out between various banks.

It is possible that in some districts the dominant presence is of the RRBs in which case sponsor banks may assist the RRBs in putting in place arrangements for technical staff for providing credit plus services for facilitating financial inclusion. NABARD may defray the cost of such technical staff, particularly, in the North-Eastern Region.

Business Facilitators/Business Correspondents (BF/BC)

With the objective of ensuring greater financial inclusion and increasing the outreach of the banking sector, the RBI has permitted banks to use the services of NGOs / SHGs, MFIs and other civil society organisations as intermediaries in providing financial and banking services through the use of BF and BC Models vide their Circular of 25 January 2006.

Business Facilitator Model

Under the BF Model, banks may use intermediaries such as NGOs, farmers' clubs, cooperatives, community based organisations, IT-enabled rural outlets of corporate entities, post offices, insurance agents, well functioning Panchayats, village knowledge centres, agri-clinics / agri-business centres, Krishi Vigyan Kendras and KVIC / KVIB units for providing facilitation services. It has been clarified that such services may include :

- Identification of borrowers and fitment of activities,
- Collection and preliminary processing of loan applications,
- Creation of awareness about savings and other products, education and advise on managing money and debt counseling,
- Processing and submission of application to banks,
- Promotion and nurturing of SHGs / JLGs,
- Post sanction monitoring,
- Monitoring and hand holding of SHGs / JLGs / credit groups / others, and
- Follow-up for recovery.

Business Correspondent Model

Under the BC Model, NGOs / MFIs set up under the Societies / Trust Act, Societies registered under Mutually Aided Cooperative Societies Acts or the Cooperative Societies Acts of States, Section 25 Companies, Registered NBFCs not accepting public deposits and post offices may act as BCs. Banks have been advised to conduct due diligence on such entities and ensure that they are well established, enjoy good reputation and have the confidence of local people.

In addition to the activities listed under the BF Model, the scope and activities to be undertaken by BCs will include

- Disbursal of small value credit,

- Recovery of principal / collection of interest,
- Collection of small value deposits,
- Sale of micro-insurance / mutual fund products / pension products / other third party products, and
- Receipt and delivery of small value remittances / other payment instruments.

The activities to be undertaken by the BCs would be within the normal course of the banks' business, but conducted through the entities indicated above at places other than the banks' premises.

Operating Norms

Banks have been permitted to pay reasonable commission / fees to the BFs / BCs, the rate and quantum of which is to be reviewed periodically. Such costs have to be borne entirely by the banks. Initially, it may affect operational margins, but over time, on account of the incremental business brought in, the arrangement is expected to become viable and self-sustaining. Further, banks have been advised that the agreement with the BCs should specifically prohibit them from charging any fee to the customers directly for services rendered by them on behalf of the bank. It has been clarified that the arrangements with the BCs shall specify :

- Suitable limits on cash holding by intermediaries as also limits on individual customer payments and receipts,
- The requirements that the transactions are accounted for and reflected in the banks' books by end of the day or next working day,
- All agreements / contracts with the customer shall specify that the bank is responsible to the customer for acts of omission and commission of the BF / BC.

It was explained to the Committee that notwithstanding the dispensation given to banks, the response of the banking system was somewhat low key and that the model is yet to be fully grounded.

Discussions with a cross section of bankers revealed that the muted response was in part due to :

- Disinclination on part of banks to absorb the costs involved on grounds of its impact on viability of operations,
- Lack of clarity regarding certain procedural complexities.

Taking the totality of circumstances into account, specially the need to facilitate greater financial inclusion, the Committee makes the following recommendations insofar as the BF/BC Model is concerned:

Business Facilitators

Originally, only individuals who were insurance agents could act as BFs while no individuals could be placed as BC. This was later on widened to include retired officials, viz., Government servants like postmasters, school teachers and headmasters, who were considered eligible by RBI to act as BF. These people have a standing in the local community and provide the needed comfort level to the banks. The banks may make use of this relaxation and use individuals as indicated above as BF.

Ex-servicemen in rural areas have the comforting support, not only of the institutionalized ex-servicemen's fraternity but also of their Regional Centres. These Centres act as guide and monitor both serving and retired armed forces personnel. During discussions with the Committee, it was indicated that ex-servicemen would volunteer to act as BCs in selected districts having a high concentration of ex-servicemen. The Committee is of the view that, initially, banks may appoint ex-servicemen and retired bank staff as their BFs.

Further, after identification and placement of BFs, the banks should ensure that the banking awareness created and potential identified by BFs get translated into business propositions by providing suitable banking services in the area. This could be attempted thru' mobile outlets, which could visit the various locations, as per a scheduled programme, so as to purvey banking services to the excluded.

To facilitate easy roll-out of this mobile banking model, banks should simplify and rationalize back-end processes and front-end procedures so that banking operations are made more customer-friendly.

Business Correspondents

With increasing competition, banks are getting to be quite wary of the reducing margins available to them on financial intermediation. Banks are, therefore, hesitant to opt for increasing their physical presence in upcountry/ remote locations entailing considerable capital/ operating costs. Under the present dispensation, small value clients (depositors) in remote locations get very little preference in accessing financial services. It is, therefore, imperative to have in place an arrangement which can cater to a large number of clients having irregular and low value transactions ensuring at the same time full protection of the interests of depositors. Such an arrangement is possible only by having a BC touchpoint in each of the 6 lakh plus villages serving as a customer interface at the front-end and backed by appropriate technology for its integration with the mainframe banking at the bank level. Keeping this in view, the following recommendations for the BC Model are made :

In addition to the institutions presently allowed by RBI to function as BCs, individuals like locally settled retired Government servants like postmasters, school teachers, ex-servicemen and ex-bank staff whose relationship with the banking system, through a pension account, has already been established, may be permitted to act as BCs.

Further, MF-NBFCs may be allowed to act as limited BCs of banks for only providing savings and remittance services.

The Committee recognizes the fact that technology has to be an integral part in sustaining outreach efforts thru' the BC model. Ultimately, banks should endeavour to have a BC touch point in each of the six lakh villages in the country. This is discussed in detail later in the Report.

With a view to encouraging the BCs to widen their client-base, a suitable incentive mechanism may be formulated by the banks, appropriately linked to the number of accounts opened / transactions put thru' by the BCs . This will go a long way in stabilizing the arrangement between the Banks and the BCs. Further, banks may consider identifying BCs even in areas where they have their own branches, so as to supplement their efforts in widening outreach and addressing access issues.

The Committee also observed that certain banks have already put in place intermediaries in the form of loan agents, who are akin to the BCs, (for undertaking loan disbursements and recovery) but in addition, also partake a certain element of risk / responsibility in case of loan defaults. In the initial stages, the BC model as envisaged by RBI could be implemented widely. In due course, when the BCs reach a higher level of turnover, they should bear commensurate financial responsibilities.

Banks may, at their discretion, appoint any individual/ institution of its choice as Business Correspondent, after exercising due diligence. This will facilitate greater acceptance of the BC Model by banks.

Funds may be provided to specialized institutions which provide capacity building inputs to BCs. Such funding support could be extended on priority basis to most excluded areas/ sectors of the society and met out of the Financial Inclusion Promotion & Development Fund.

SLBC convener banks may initiate discussion with their respective State Governments regarding routing government payments through BCs using the smart card or other relevant technology on a pilot basis.

SLBCs may undertake a study to identify organisations having the capacity to serve as customer service points and BC. In States like Andhra Pradesh and Kerala the VOs and Kudumbashree structures already exist and these can be used as customer service points.

Training modules for BFs/BCs may be prepared in vernacular and in culture sensitive pictorial forms.

ROLE OF COMMERCIAL BANKS IN MICROFINANCE

Deepening the outreach of the microfinance programme is an effective way in reaching out to the excluded segments. Commercial Banks have played a very important role in the SHG-Bank Linkage Programme. As at the end of March 2007, as many as 50 Commercial Banks are involved in the programme, having linked 15.95 lakh SHGs, forming more than 54% of the total SHGs credit-linked in the country. This programme should be strengthened and carried further, playing a key role in financial inclusion.

Financing Poor Farmers

Joint Liability Groups (JLGs) of the poor such as landless, share croppers and tenant farmers is another innovative mechanism towards ensuring greater financial inclusion. This mechanism has already been operationalised in a few regions under a Pilot Project of NABARD. Commercial Banks can actively promote such groups for effectively purveying credit and other facilities to such clients. RBI may encourage banks to adopt the JLG model for lending to SF/MF, tenant cultivators, share croppers and oral lessees.

Making Marginal Farm Holdings Viable and Enabling their Financial Inclusion

The Committee examined the credit absorption capacity among marginal farm holdings and is of the view that :

- Farm aggregation models including contract farming fully protecting the interests of farmers could be an option for enhanced viability. Credit-marketing linkage can also be effected through appropriate agreements.
- Access to irrigation will make a substantial difference on viability of small farms. A massive programme for financing minor irrigation structures (wherever ground water levels are safe and surface water potential is available) may be undertaken specifically targeting marginal farm households.
- Supplementary activities like dairy, small poultry, sheep-

rearing, etc. have to be specifically targeted for marginal farmers, tenants and non-cultivator households.

In this context, the Committee notes that against an estimated production of 91 million tons of milk in 2004-05, the demand for milk in 2021-22 would increase to 172 million tons as per estimates of the Planning Commission. To meet the demand, milk production should continue to grow at 4% per annum for the next 15 years. The growth of milk production could be augmented through a two pronged approach focusing on improving production in major milk producing areas and expanding infrastructure for procurement, processing, marketing and quality assurance. A National Dairy Plan (NDP) has been prepared to target production enhancement in 323 potential districts. Under the NDP the following has been envisaged:

- Financing dairy animals and dairy infrastructure to individuals, SHGs, cooperative societies, corporates, NGOs, etc after ensuring input and marketing linkages.
- Establishment and encouragement of viable institutional structures through grants for institutional development, incentivising reforms by cooperatives.
- Reform of existing dairy cooperatives.
- Study of low potential districts to assist State Governments for developing dairy activities and evolving suitable plans.
- Development of road and power infrastructure and watershed development in the identified areas under the NDP through RIDF loans to state governments.
- The NDP would be implemented through a consortium of NABARD, the National Dairy Development Board (NDDB) and the National Cooperative Development Corporation (NCDC). The funds required for breeding, nutrition and milk handling are estimated to be Rs. 18,500 crore over the next three five-year plan periods. The assistance from the GoI would be Rs. 225 crore for the first year (2007-08).
- It is recommended that similar initiatives may be considered for other sectors also like poultry, horticulture, etc.

- Technical counseling and farm advisory services have to be extended to such farms which are provided finance for undertaking the above activities.

TOWARDS BRANCHLESS BANKING - A NEW OPERATING MODEL

Developed by Corporation Bank

A project implemented by Corporation bank at select locations across four Southern States has used modern ICT applications at remote rural locations. The project uses biometric card based authentication devices, which are used by the bank's Business Correspondents at the villages. The Bank is providing basic banking services to the rural people through these low cost devices, without the concomitant costs associated with setting up of an Extension Counter/ATM or a Branch and thus aiming to bring down significantly the transaction costs in rural banking. This model reportedly brings in a win-win situation for both the Bank and its rural customer. The services are made available close to their homes, obviating the need to spend time and money on transport to reach the branch. The roll out and maintenance costs of this model are only a fraction of running a conventional branch. The Bank developed the new operating model to cover a large number of un-banked villages.

The various steps taken by the Bank in this regard were:

- A village survey was conducted to assess the present level of household income generation and the potential of credit requirements in future;
- The household survey report served as an enabling tool to arrive at a total economic view of the families surveyed, potential for savings and the extent of credit that can be delivered;
- While conducting the survey, the Bank observed that many of the villages were reluctant to visit the bank branches for various reasons like long distance to be travelled, time lost,

difficulty in following procedures and reluctance to visit branches for small value transactions.

- The Bank adopted a branchless banking model in select locations in four Southern States using a small Point of Transaction (POT) device developed by two local vendors using a bouquet of locally available ICT applications.
- The adoption of new technology facilitated basic identification of the customer based on the survey details, eliminated procedural hassles like filling up challans, cheques, etc. for depositing/withdrawing money, provided automated voice guidance to the users in local language, etc. The device adopted was sturdy with a battery back-up to supplement long hours of power outage and could be connected to a car battery. The device was installed at the premises of the Business Correspondent at the village and the customers at village could visit the Business Correspondent at their convenience to carry out cash deposit or cash withdrawal. To facilitate transactions at the Business Correspondent's level, biometric cards containing the photograph and the basic KYC details of the customer were provided to identified villagers.
- The Bank has recently introduced on a pilot basis a loan product which would facilitate loan withdrawals and repayments involving small sums at the Business Correspondent level.
- The Bank is also planning to introduce remittance products for the card holders and factor in Government payouts such as pension, NREGP payments, etc. through the card holder's account.
- The Bank plans to commence a project to disburse group loans through the Business Correspondent to SHGs.
- The Bank intends to provide ancillary services like Utility Payments, Mobile bill payments, etc., through this account.

5

Commercial Bank: Operations and Functions

The activities described in the preceding chapter as discount, deposit, and note issue are traditionally called the fundamental functions of commercial banks. "Function" here means the course of action which peculiarly pertains to or is appropriate to the institution. The operations of discount, deposit, and issue have been shown to be reducible to a guaranty of private credit or to a substitution of bank credit for private credit. These operations are not, of course, ends in themselves, but activities toward accomplishing ends. Some recent writers on banking call these immediate activities banking "operations" and their ends, banking "functions." Although in the further analysis of causation these so-called "functions" will be but "operations" to even more remote ends, it may be well to consider the activities so distinguished as functions.

In the other volumes of this book many other banking operations than discount, deposit, and issue will be described. Some of them have become traditionally associated with banks and are peculiarly appropriate to them. Banks could not continue in business unless they performed a wide variety of operations which competition has forced them to assume. These operations are usually incidental to discount, deposit, and issue, and are performed for borrowers or depositors and in consideration of their accounts. Other activities may be undertaken by a bank because it has an organization that can assume and execute the additional duties more economically than specialized organizations could do. Some of these activities may produce no small part of the bank's earnings and therefore seem quite essential; others are purely adventitious and occasion a large net expense, but are undertaken for the indirect benefits that accrue from general publicity.

The activities described in the preceding chapter as discount, deposit, and note issue are traditionally called the fundamental functions of commercial banks. "Function" here means the course of action which peculiarly pertains to or is appropriate to the institution. The operations of discount, deposit, and issue have been shown to be reducible to a guaranty of private credit or to a substitution of bank credit for private credit. These operations are not, of course, ends in themselves, but activities toward accomplishing ends. Some recent writers on banking call these immediate activities banking "operations" and their ends, banking "functions." Although in the further analysis of causation these so-called "functions" will be but "operations" to even more remote ends, it may be well to consider the activities so distinguished as functions.

In the other volumes of this book many other banking operations than discount, deposit, and issue will be described. Some of them have become traditionally associated with banks and are peculiarly appropriate to them. Banks could not continue in business unless they performed a wide variety of operations which competition has forced them to assume.

These operations are usually incidental to discount, deposit, and issue, and are performed for borrowers or depositors and in consideration of their accounts. Other activities may be undertaken by a bank because it has an organization that can assume and execute the additional duties more economically than specialized organizations could do. Some of these activities may produce no small part of the bank's earnings and therefore seem quite essential; others are purely adventitious and occasion a large net expense, but are undertaken for the indirect benefits that accrue from general publicity.

BANKS AS CREDIT MARKETS

Banking operations facilitate the production and distribution of goods. They do this by organizing the market for credit, by negotiating between lender and borrower, by rendering an ever larger volume of our collective wealth into "bankable" form and promoting, not only its transferability but also its actual transfer to the most effective uses. The lender repairs to the bank to deposit (lend, invest) his surplus, the borrower goes there to find accommodation; the bank is the organized credit mart. As a basis of credit the banker increasingly accepts stocks, bonds, mortgages, bills of lading, warehouse receipts, and other property rights in wealth that is not itself available as a basis of credit; possession of such titles can in this way be made the means of procuring bank funds, purchasing power, and finally control over other wealth useful in production and distribution. The banker determines largely the personnel of the business world; he is a shrewd judge of ability to produce and distribute efficiently; he seeks as customers those who by their financial record and originality, aggressiveness and opportunity, promise well, and he discourages the opposite sort of applicant. The American tradition holds that commercial banks should finance only short-term, self-liquidated transactions and should leave the provision of permanent capital to specialized investment institutions. The theory is that, since the liabilities of the bank are demand liabilities, the assets must largely consist of cash, and that short-term, self-liquidating paper is the most convertible and manageable earning asset. This traditional theory bears the approval of state and federal law, and the banking system conforms nominally to the theory; but an examination of the business (banking and investment) situation reveals the following facts:

1. No small part of commercial loans are provisions of permanent investment capital.
2. Industrial loans which finance the purchase of raw materials and labor to make a marketable product are quite as good bank assets as commercial loans to finance the marketing processes.

3. The so-called self-liquidating loans are largely liquid only with respect to individual banks and not to the banking system as a whole.
4. Liquidity is mainly a matter of high organization of the market for credits and of the markets for the various forms of collateral.

Extensions of Investment Credit

To the degree that banks invest in stocks and bonds of corporations, they contribute fixed capital to enterprises. The purchase of securities is the practical equivalent of loaning funds; loans to purchase securities which are then pledged to secure the loans are practically vicarious purchases of the securities. That there is a marked tendency for commercial loans to become continuous and permanent is due to the fact that production tends to become more and more capitalistic and continuous operation more and more necessary for efficiency, while improved facilities in distributing products lengthen the period of consumption and reduce the seasonal feature of business. Probably a fifth of commercial bank loans are now for investment purposes.

The one-time practice of banks of insisting that their borrowers "clean up" their loan account at least once a year has nearly ceased, except in lines of business having one or two definite seasons, and loans are indefinitely renewed time after time, or if borrowers are required to "clean up" they may borrow at one bank to "clean up " at another. Large borrowers sell their notes widely over the country through note-brokers; to pay a lot of notes maturing and due to holders in one section of the country, another lot will be issued and sold either to these same holders or to purchasers in other sections; thus the banking system as a whole supplies permanent working capital. The individual bank, however, may decline to renew a loan or to purchase the renewal paper, and thus not itself provide permanent capital.

When the whole banking system is considered, it is clear that commercial paper is only to a small extent self-liquidating. The banks renew loans freely, as just noted; their regular customers depend upon this accommodation, and large contraction or refusal to renew loans is quite impossible, especially in time of panic. When a borrower becomes strong enough to borrow through sale of his paper widely over the country and any holder refuses to purchase the renewal paper, he can borrow from other banks. The holder bank may also at any time sell the paper to another bank. Thus rediscount gives liquidity, but rediscount is simply a shifting of assets as between banks and as between forms of assets. One of the specific purposes in developing the federal reserve banks was that of providing central banks where paper holdings of needy banks might be converted into cash funds by this process of shifting assets. The capacity of the federal reserve banks to liquefy by rediscounting comes through their ability to tap unused reserves and to create federal reserve notes, which in the tills of the banks constitute not only a paying medium but also an actual reserve, although not termed "reserve" by the law.

Loan Ratios as Business Barometers

The sum of a bank's investments in securities and of its loans and discounts represents its contributions of capital to business. A part of these funds was originally deposited as cash in the bank; the rest have been created by the bank. Bank notes and deposit liabilities have been created and exchanged by the bank for various credit items of borrowers, while the borrowers possessing these bank notes, deposits, or actual government money, have been enabled to procure materials, labor, tools, plant, transportation, and the like. The funds put into investments and some indeterminate proportion of the loans (and discounts) represent contributions of permanent capital. The proportion of the loans which constitutes permanent advances of capital ranges in all probability from 20 to 50 per cent. The tendency is to increase. The ratio of cash reserve to investments, plus, say, 30 per cent of loans, is therefore a measure of the degree to which a bank contributes permanent capital to business. The ratio of cash reserve to, say, 70 per cent of loans, measures the temporary advances. Users of business barometers watch closely the less complex ratios of: (1) cash reserve to loans, (2) investments to aggregate assets, (3) loans to aggregate assets, and (4) the sum of loans and investments to aggregate assets. The history of the first, third, and fourth ratios is shown in the accompanying charts (Figures 2 and 3), and by subtracting the third from the fourth the second can be obtained. During the war the increase of bank cash reserves in this country did not keep abreast of the expansion of loans, the result being that the ratio of cash reserves to loans decreased precipitately. The loan account developed into an unprecedented state of extension; the banks met the urgent demands for funds to finance the war and war industries; an excessive proportion of the loans was collateraled by United States securities, and did not necessarily represent contributions of working capital to industries. The percentage increase of securities, largely United States war securities, purchased by the banks rose faster than the percentage increase of either loans or aggregate assets. As the purchase of securities is from the bank's point of view in many respects equivalent to a loan to the seller, these large purchases during the war had the effect of increasing the multiple to which banks create a loan fund on the basis of cash reserve. It might be said also that the contributions of permanent capital by banks were in effect increased both absolutely and relatively. Some liquidity was given to the war loans by

Figure : Graphic Chart Showing Ratio of Cash Reserves to Loans of New York Clearing House Banks. Brookmire curves used in this chart.

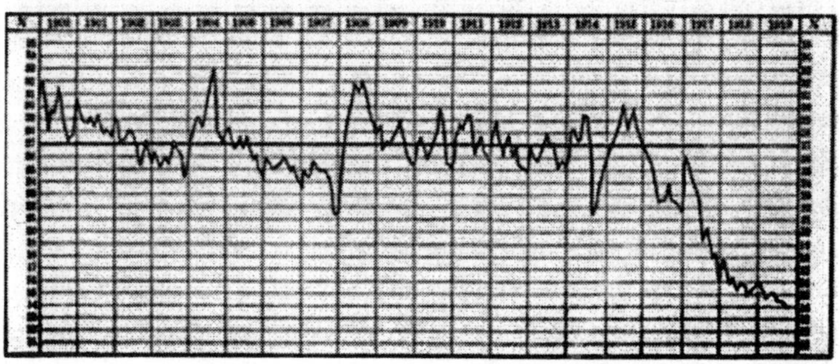

Figure . (a) Graphic Chart Showing Ratio of Loans to Aggregate Assets of All Banks Reporting to Comptroller

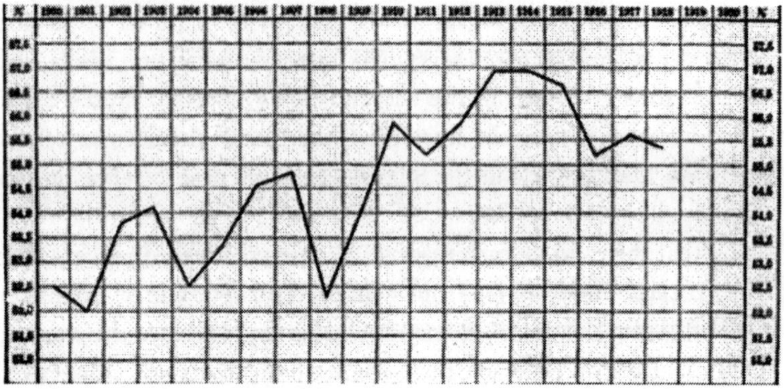

Figure. (b) Graphic Chart Showing Ratio of Loans and Investments to Aggregate Assets of All Banks

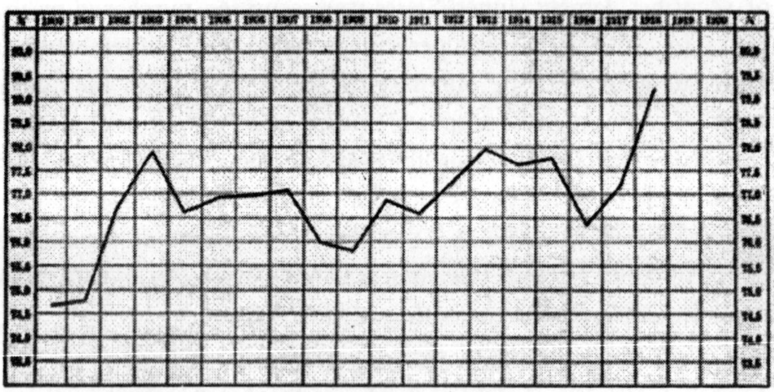

Reporting to Comptroller making paper backed by war securities eligible for discount with the federal reserve banks.

To put some fraction of a bank's funds into permanent investments is altogether safe and fitting, for in emergency they can be readily converted into cash through the stock exchange. Extensive dependence of all the banks on the securities market for such conversion, however, becomes positively dangerous. In order to accomplish a sale in a tight money market, not only must securities be sacrificed at great losses but the buyers go to other banks to withdraw funds to do the buying, thus making the market still tighter and tending to precipitate a panic. Accordingly the business world takes note of the ratios of loans and investments to total resources.

The banking situation of the country becomes more critical as the proportion of loans to aggregate resources increases, because such a change means an absorption of the loan fund; and it becomes even more critical as the ratio of investments to aggregate resources increases, for the additional reason that a larger proportion of banking funds is being tied up in long-term securities which are difficult to liquefy. Babson summarizes the barometrics of these ratios as follows:

1 i. During a period of business depression: (A) An Increase In The Ratio Signifies Renewed Activity. (B) A Decrease Signifies A Further Recession In Business. (C) No Change Signifies Continued Dullness.

2. During a period of improvement following a period of business depression: (A) An Increase In The Ratio Signifies Increased Activity. (B) A Decrease Signifies A Temporary Recession. (C) No Change Calls For Special Watchfulness.

3. During a period of prosperity: (a) An increase in the ratio signifies that fundamental conditions are becoming unsound. (B) A Decrease Tends To Prolong The Period Of Prosperity. (C) No Change Signifies Nothing Of Importance. 1 Babson, R. W., Business Barometrics, 1918, P. 272.

4. During a period of decline following a period of prosperity: (A) An Increase In The Ratio Signifies Further Trouble. (B) A Decrease Is The Natural Movement. (C) No Change Calls For Special Watchfulness.

EFFECT OF OTHER OPERATIONS ON THE BANK STATEMENT

So far as developed in the preceding sections, the operations of White, the bank, might result in a capital statement such as the following:

Assets

Loans and Discounts.......... $304,395

Cash:

Gold And Silver

Dollars.......... $22,104

Government Paper

Money.......... 3,033

Subsidiary Silver... 273

Minor Coins....... ______15 25,425

Investments.................. 68,945 $398,765

Liabilities

Capital...................... $100,000

Surplus..................... 50,000

Undivided Profits........... 10,323

Deposits................... 218,442

Bank Notes Outstanding....... 20,000 $398,765

It is now proposed to explain certain other simple but typical operations, and indicate their effects upon the bank's statement.

The accounts entitled "Due from Banks" and "Due to Banks " arise because the bank finds it expedient to open accounts with other banks, and to deposit certain of its funds with them. These depository banks are called "correspondents." Such accounts serve among others the following purposes:

1. They enable the bank to sell drafts against this distant metropolitan correspondent and charge exchange for the service.
2. The banks may arrange mutually to act as collecting agent one for the other, and possibly charge for the service.
3. In time of stress the local bank can count on accommodation from the metropolitan correspondent.
4. The correspondent may furnish special services for the local bank, such as credit advice, investment of funds, safe-keeping

of securities, and the like. The local bank may in turn carry accounts of banks for which it acts as correspondent.

Whenever a statement of the bank is made, therefore, among the assets will appear Due from Banks, and among the liabilities Due to Banks.

If a draft is sold by the local bank, the Due from Banks is reduced by the face amount of the draft. Undivided Profits is increased by the charge for exchange, and, if the face of the draft and the exchange charge are paid in cash, Cash will be increased by these amounts. If, however, the buyer of the draft pays by check on the selling bank, Deposits is reduced, and if by check on other banks, Due from Banks is increased.

When items are received for collection and credit, the local bank credits the remitter's (or depositor's) account with the face amount of the items - that is, credits Deposits and carries items among the assets as Collection Items in process of collection; when collected, either Cash or Due from Banks is increased. Checks on local clearing house banks are usually separated from checks on out-of-town banks and are reported as Clearing House Items.

The purchase of a site, a building, furniture, and fixtures, reduces the bank's Cash or its balances Due from Banks. Such payments by the bank are usually made by cashier's checks or drafts; while these checks are outstanding they appear among the liabilities, and when they are presented for payment, Cash will be reduced.

Stationery, wages, salaries, rent, taxes, and so forth are expense items that will likewise be paid by cashier's checks. Temporarily they will appear as Expense among the assets and Cashier's Checks among the liabilities; the ultimate disposition will be the reduction of Cash by payment of the checks and the reduction of the Undivided Profits.

Customers may deposit cash funds and take certificates of deposit, which will thereafter appear among the liabilities.

These certificates state that the customer deposited a certain amount on a given date, which will be repaid to him with interest at a stated rate provided payment is not demanded within a stipulated time.

If a depositor overdraws his account, the drawee bank may-exercise its discretion at paying the amount. If allowed the drawer's account (his Deposits) is wiped out, and the bank has a presumptive claim against the drawer for the deficit, which it lists among its assets as Overdrafts. Cash is reduced by the face amount. If this check had been presented through a correspondent bank the Due from Banks would be reduced by the face amount.

In the case of the issue of bank notes by a national bank, the issuing bank must first buy or borrow United States bonds to pledge with the United States Treasury as security; this reduces Cash and increases Investments, or else puts among the liabilities Bonds Borrowed and adds to Investments. The National Bank Law requires that a redemption fund of 5 per cent of the notes issued also be kept in gold at Washington; this reduces Cash but adds a new item, Redémption Fund, to the assets. The bank notes come to the paying teller, and he puts them into the Cash of the bank, and an equivalent liability, Bank Notes Outstanding, appears in the statement. Whenever any of the notes are presented to the bank for redemption, Cash in the statement is unaffected, for one form of cash is simply substituted for another; but when presented at Washington for redemption, the Redemption Fund is reduced and Bank Notes Outstanding is also reduced.

If Undivided Profits becomes large, the directors may decide to increase Surplus and declare dividends. Then Undivided Profits will be reduced at once by the amount put into surplus and dividends; the dividends will be carried temporarily as Dividends Declared but Unpaid; when paid, this item will disappear and Cash be reduced.

If the book values of certain assets are found too high, because they were originally overvalued or have meanwhile depreciated or have proved uncollectible, and it is necessary to scale down the valuations, the asset, Investments, or Loans and Discounts, or Real Estate, Buildings, Fixtures, or whatever asset it may be, is reduced, and Undivided Profits is reduced a like amount. The local bank may be pressed for funds, and be forced to borrow from its correspondent on the basis of its promissory note secured by discount paper from its note pouch. Its Cash and Due from Banks will be increased and Bills Payable will then appear among its liabilities.

The bank may issue letters of credit by which it agrees to accept certain drafts or bills of exchange drawn upon it. Later when these are presented for acceptance, the bank will incur specific liability for Acceptances. These liabilities are equalized by the introduction of the corresponding assets, Customers' Liability Under Letters of Credit, and Customers' Liability for Acceptances Executed.

TYPICAL BANK STATEMENT

The combined effect of these and other transactions is to render the statement into that of a typical commercial bank.

There is, however, no uniformity of style or titles in the published statements, whether of the same or different classes of banks. Uniform accounting is somewhat promoted by government supervision of banks and the requirement of periodic reports. Nevertheless in the publication of their financial statements wide variation occurs because bankers have different conceptions of what constitutes a good report, because the statements are adapted to different clienteles, and because the bankers have different motives to serve. These purposes are attained by combining items under varying heads. The following is a typical statement of a small bank.

Assets

Loans and Discounts......... $ 458,426

Cash....................... 44.975

Investments................ 95.000

Real Estate And Bank Building 21,000

Furniture And Fixtures....... 5.000

Expense.................... 1,252

Bonds Loaned............... 10,000

Collection Items............ 35.000

Clearing House Items........ 78,000

Redemption Fund........... 2,300

Overdrafts................. 4.621

Due From Banks............ 165,000

Customers' Liability Under

Letters Of Credit.......... 95,000

Customers' Liability For Acceptances Executed........ 80,000

Other Assets.............. 7.396 $1,102,970

Liabilities

Capital.................. $ 100,000

Surplus.................... 75,000

Undivided Profits........... 16,312

Dividends Declared But Unpaid.................... 4,000

Bonds Borrowed........... 20,000

Deposits.................. 487,345

Cashier's Checks........... 45,000

Bank Notes Outstanding..... 40,000

Certificates Of Deposit....... 55,000

Acceptances................ 80,000

Due To Banks.............. 48,000

Letters Of Credit........... 95,000

Bills Payable............... 20,000

Reserved For Taxes, Insurance 6,000

Other Liabilities............ 11,323 $1,102,970

CLEARINGS AND COLLECTIONS

In the process of executing the functions of loan, discount, deposit, and note issue, and of the incidental business of the bank, there come into its possession numerous forms of credit items which must be presented to the respective debtors for payment. Preliminary, however, to a discussion of the various operations performed by a bank with this end in view, involving as it would an explanation of clearing house procedure and out-of-town collection methods, consideration should be given to the factors that determine when a credit instrument will be presented for payment.

There are various factors which determine when a credit instrument will be presented for payment. These include the question whether the item has a fixed maturity, whether it bears interest, whether it can be used as a medium of exchange or as bank reserve, and whether the law requires presentment within a certain time.

Of the four common forms of bank liabilities to creditors, the first two - Bank Notes and Deposits - are generally payable on demand and do not bear interest, whereas the other two formsBills Payable and Acceptances - are payable at a time fixed by the date of acceptance and the terms of the papers and may or may not bear interest.

As a check cannot be readily used by the payee in making payments or for reserves and does not bear interest, the holder has funds which are useless, and at the same time he incurs a certain risk that the check will not be honored. In addition the statutory or common law may require him to present the item for payment within a certain time. Bank notes, on the other hand, attain to general acceptability because the holder may make payments with them and one bank may use the notes of other banks as reserves. If the law were to prohibit such uses, bank notes would be collected at once upon receipt, just as checks are; otherwise the holder would lose the use of the funds represented and the debtor would have them meanwhile without having to pay interest. Acceptances and bills payable having a definite maturity must be presented for payment at the time of maturity. If interest ceases at maturity it is financially profitable to present the item at that time and the law may also require such presentation so as to protect the indorsers of the instrument.

METHODS OF PRESENTMENT

The method of presentment of an item for payment is determined by its cost and by legal requirements. The costs include the clerical work, messenger service, loss of interest on idle funds, risks of carrying the items or moneys in the street or in the mails, and so forth. Items on institutions in the holder's city are collected either by messenger or through the clearing house. A clearing house is now established in every city of considerable size and the items collected by messenger include merely those on institutions not members of the clearing house, documentary items, special advice items, and large sight items. At the bank the city collection clerk dispatches messengers over prescribed routes with these collection items.

THE CLEARING HOUSE

The clearing house is an association which provides a common meeting place and facilities for collection messengers to exchange their reciprocal claims on each other and settle the net balances only. Suppose, for example, that in a city with five clearing banks, the claims on a certain day are as follows:

	Claims By Bank A	Bank B	Bank C	Bank D	Bank E	Total
Against Bank A.....		$1,285,434	$1,492,398	$ 923,619	$ 99,645	$3,801,096
Bank B.....	$ 663,957		482,337	537,948	113,151	1,797,393
BankC.....	559.S27	651,735		292,119	454,638	1,958,019
Bank D___	724,788	912,954	327,972		54,468	2,020,182
Bank E....	IS3.663	196,761	187,764	1,390,188		1,928,376
Total: Due to....	$ 2,101,93s	$3,046,884	$2,490,471	S3,143,874	$ 721,902	$11,505,066
Due from ...	3,801,096	1.797,393	1,958,019	2,020,182	1.928,376	11,505,066
	$ - 1,699,161	$1,249,491	$ 532,452	$1,123,692	$ - 1,206,474	

Then the equation of debit and credit balances is: (1,249,491 + 532,452 + 1,123,692) = (1,699,161 + 1,206,474) = 2,905,635

The banks A and E are net debtors to banks B, C, and D, and the payment of $2,905,635 balances settles their combined clearings of $11,505,066.

The economies of this clearing plan are evident. The items can be more expeditiously handled if put into one messenger's box and carried a short distance to the clearing house than if put into many boxes and carried to the respective drawee banks. Only the net balances of the day's exchanges need be paid in money and carried in the street, thus reducing risk and expense, and this expense may be further reduced by depositing funds with the clearing house for clearing house certificates which may be used to settle balances. Each bank needs to carry a much smaller amount of till money, for the sums due to and due from the bank are offset synchronously and the bank does not have to provide in advance cash enough to pay the whole of the sums due to other banks. Finally a great economy of time results, inasmuch as system and uniform rules are devised for the prompt exchange of items and settlement of balances. The effect of the whole process is to offset indebtedness and conserve the use of money.

OUT-OF-TOWN COLLECTIONS

To collect out-of-town items, one system is to effect arrangements whereby the correspondent acts as agent, collecting items on banks in its city through the clearing house and on banks in its vicinity through subcollecting agents. Since checks are payable at the drawee bank's window, the drawee bank remits for the proceeds after deducting exchange charges presumably to cover the expense of maintaining a balance with the sending bank against which drafts may be drawn to make remittances. The law holds a bank to the exercise of due care in choosing collection agents and to reasonable promptness in sending and remitting for items. Sending an item directly to the drawee bank, however, unless the principal bank expressly permits it, is held to be negligence, and therefore the collecting bank sends the item to sub-agents in the same city as the drawee bank. The terms of agreement between the depositor and the collecting bank as to collection charges, the time when items are credited to the account, and the reciprocity of collection services, are various. This system results in indirect routing of items to save collection charges, and therefore in too large an amount of funds being afloat in the mails. To cut down the expense of this system of out-of-town collections, co-operative "country" clearing houses have been established in some of the chief cities as adjuncts to the city clearing house. A member sends to the country clearing house such of its out-of-town items as it desires and is permitted to send. All items on one drawee bank, or on the banks of one city, are put into one envelope and mailed to that bank or the agent of the clearing house in that city. The bank or agent makes out one lump remittance to the clearing house, which settles with its members. This system of co-operative collections may go further and require all drawee banks to remit at par for all items sent to them, and then assess the expense of the country clearing house upon the depositing banks at so much per item or per dollar collected.

SERVICES OF COMMERCIAL BANKS

(a) Accepting deposits

The most important activity of a commercial bank is to mobilize deposits from the public. People who have surplus income and savings find it convenient to deposit the amounts with banks. Depending upon the nature of deposits, funds deposited with bank also earn interest. Thus, deposits with the bank grow along with the interest earned. If the rate of interest is higher, public are motivated to deposit more funds with the bank. There is also safety of funds deposited with the bank.

(b) Grant of loans and advances

The second important function of a commercial bank is to grant loans and advances. Such loans and advances are given to members of the public and to the business community at a higher rate of interest than allowed by banks on various deposit accounts. The rate of interest charged on loans and advances varies depending upon the purpose, period and the mode of repayment. The difference between the rate of interest allowed on deposits and the rate charged on the Loans is the main source of a bank's income.

(i) Loans: A loan is granted for a specific time period. Generally, commercial banks grant short-term loans. But term loans, that is, loan for more than a year, may also be granted. The borrower may withdraw the entire amount in lumpsum or in instalments. However, interest is charged on the full amount of loan. Loans are generally granted against the security of certain assets. A loan may be repaid either in lumpsum or in instalments.

(ii) Advances: An advance is a credit facility provided by the bank to its customers. It differs from loan in the sense that loans may be granted for longer period, but advances are normally granted for a short period of time. Further the purpose of granting advances is to meet the day to day requirements of business. The rate of interest charged on advances varies from bank to bank. Interest is charged only on the amount withdrawn and not on the sanctioned amount.

MODES OF SHORT-TERM FINANCIAL ASSISTANCE

Banks grant short-term financial assistance by way of cash credit, overdraft and bill discounting.

(a) Cash Credit: Cash credit is an arrangement whereby the bank allows the borrower to draw amounts upto a specified limit. The amount is credited to the account of the customer. The customer can withdraw this amount as and when he requires. Interest is charged on the amount actually withdrawn. Cash Credit is granted as per agreed terms and conditions with the customers.

(b) Overdraft: Overdraft is also a credit facility granted by bank. A customer who has a current account with the bank is allowed to withdraw more than the amount of credit balance in his account. It is a temporary arrangement. Overdraft facility with a specified limit is allowed either on the security of assets, or on personal security, or both.

(c) Discounting of Bills: Banks provide short-term finance by discounting bills, that is, making payment of the amount before the due date of the bills after deducting a certain rate of discount. The party gets the funds without waiting for the date of maturity of the bills. In case any bill is dishonoured on the due date, the bank can recover the amount from the customer.

Secondary functions: Besides the primary functions of accepting deposits and lending money, banks perform a number of other functions which are called secondary functions. These are as follows -

(a) Issuing letters of credit, travellers cheques, circular notes etc.

(b) Undertaking safe custody of valuables, important documents, and securities by providing safe deposit vaults or lockers;

(c) Providing customers with facilities of foreign exchange.

(d) Transferring money from one place to another; and from one branch to another branch of the bank.

(e) Standing guarantee on behalf of its customers, for making payments for purchase of goods, machinery, vehicles etc.

(f) Collecting and supplying business information;

(g) Issuing demand drafts and pay orders; and,

(h) Providing reports on the credit worthiness of customers.

Different modes of Acceptance of Deposits

Banks receive money from the public by way of deposits. The following types of deposits are usually received by banks:

(i) Current deposit

(ii) Saving deposit

(iii) Fixed deposit

(iv) Recurring deposit

(v) Miscellaneous deposits

(i) Current Deposit

Also called 'demand deposit', current deposit can be withdrawn by the depositor at any time by cheques. Businessmen generally open current accounts with banks. Current accounts do not carry any interest as the amount deposited in these accounts is repayable on demand without any restriction. The Reserve bank of India prohibits payment of interest on current accounts or on deposits upto 14 Days or less except where prior sanction has been obtained. Banks usually charge a small amount known as incidental charges on current deposit accounts depending on the number of transaction.

Savings Deposit/Savings Bank Accounts

Savings deposit account is meant for individuals who wish to deposit small amounts out of their current income. It helps in safe guarding their future and also earning interest on the savings. A saving account can be opened with or without cheque book facility. There are restrictions on the withdrawls from this account. Savings account holders are also allowed to deposit cheques, drafts, dividend warrants, etc. drawn in their favour for collection by the bank. To open a savings account, it is necessary for the depositor to be introduced by a person having a current or savings account with the same bank.

Fixed Deposit

The term 'Fixed deposit' means deposit repayable after the expiry of a specified period. Since it is repayable only after a fixed period of time, which is to be determined at the time of opening of the account, it is also known as time deposit. Fixed deposits are most useful for a commercial bank. Since they are repayable only after a fixed period, the bank may invest these funds more profitably by lending at higher rates of interest and for relatively longer periods. The rate of interest on fixed deposits depends upon the period of deposits. The longer the period, the higher is the rate of interest offered. The rate of interest to be allowed on fixed deposits is governed by rules laid down by the Reserve Bank of India.

Recurring Deposits

Recurring Deposits are gaining wide popularity these days. Under this type of deposit, the depositor is required to deposit a fixed amount of money every month for a specific period of time. Each instalment may vary from Rs.5/- to Rs.500/- or more per month and the period of account may vary from 12 months to 10 years. After the completion of the specified period, the customer gets back all his deposits alongwith the cumulative interest accrued on the deposits.

Miscellaneous Deposits

Banks have introduced several deposit schemes to attract deposits from different types of people, like Home Construction deposit scheme, Sickness Benefit deposit scheme, Children Gift plan, Old age pension scheme, Mini deposit scheme, etc.

DIFFERENT METHODS OF GRANTING LOANS BY BANK

The basic function of a commercial bank is to make loans and advances out of the money which is received from the public by way of deposits. The loans are particularly granted to businessmen and members of the public against personal security, gold and silver and other movable and immovable assets. Commercial bank generally lend money in the following form:

(i) Cash Credit : A cash credit is an arrangement whereby the bank agrees to lend money to the borrower upto a certain limit. The bank puts this amount of money to the credit of the borrower. The borrower draws the money as and when he needs. Interest is charged only on the amount actually drawn and not on the amount placed to the credit of borrower's account. Cash credit is generally granted on a bond of credit or certain other securities. This a very popular method of lending in our country.

(ii) Loans : A specified amount sanctioned by a bank to the customer is called a 'loan'. It is granted for a fixed period, say six months, or a year. The specified amount is put on the credit of the borrower's account. He can withdraw this amount in lump sum or can draw cheques against this sum for any amount. Interest is charged on the full amount even if the borrower does not utilise it. The rate of interest is lower on loans in comparison to cash credit. A loan is generally granted against the security of property or personal security. The loan may be repaid in lump sum or in instalments. Every bank has its own procedure of granting loans. Hence a bank is at liberty to grant loan depending on its own resources.

The loan can be granted as:

(a) Demand loan: Demand loan is repayable on demand. In other words it is repayable at short notice. The entire amount of demand loan is disbursed at one time and the borrower has to pay interest on it. The borrower can repay the loan either in lumpsum (one time) or as agreed with the bank. Loans are normally granted by the bank against tangible securities including securities like N.S.C., Kisan Vikas Patra, Life Insurance policies and U.T.I. certificates.

(b) Term loans: Medium and long term loans are called 'Term loans'. Term loans are granted for more than one year and repayment of such loans is spread over a longer period. The repayment is generally made in suitable instalments of fixed amount. These loans are repayable over a period of 5 years and maximum upto 15 years.

Term loan is required for the purpose of setting up of new business activity, renovation, modernisation, expansion/extension of existing units, purchase of plant and machinery, vehicles, land for setting up a factory, construction of factory building or purchase of other immovable assets. These loans are generally secured against the mortgage of land, plant and machinery, building and other securities. The normal rate of interest charged for such loans is generally quite high.

(iii) Bank Overdraft: Overdraft facility is more or less similar to cash credit facility. Overdraft facility is the result of an agreement with the bank by which a current account holder is allowed to withdraw a specified amount over and above the credit balance in his/her account. It is a short term facility. This facility is made available to current account holders who operate their account through cheques. The customer is permitted to withdraw the amount as and when he/she needs it and to repay it through deposits in his account as and when it is convenient to him/her. Overdraft facility is generally granted by bank on the basis of a written request by the customer. Some times, banks also insist on either a promissory note from the borrower or personal security to ensure safety of funds. Interest is charged on actual amount withdrawn by the customer. The interest rate on overdraft is higher than that of the rate on loan.

(iv) Discounting of Bills: Apart from granting cash credit, loans and overdraft, banks also grant financial assistance to customers by discounting bills of exchange. Banks purchase the bills at face value minus interest at current rate of interest for the period of the bill. This is known as 'discounting of bills'. Bills of exchange are negotiable instruments and enable the debtors to discharge their obligations towards their creditors. Such bills of exchange arise out of commercial transactions both in internal trade and external trade. By discounting these bills before they are due for a nominal amount, the banks help the business community. Of course, the banks recover the full amount of these bills from the persons liable to make payment.

Agency and General Utility Services Provided by Modern Commercial Banks

You have already learnt that the primary activities of commercial banks include acceptance of deposits from the public and lending money to businessmen and other members of society. Besides these two main activities, commercial banks also render a number of ancillary services. These services supplement the main activities of the banks. They are essentially non-banking in nature and broadly fall under two categories:

(i) Agency Services: Agency services are those services which are rendered by commercial banks as agents of their customers. They include :

(a) Collection and payment of cheques and bills on behalf of the customers;

(b) Collection of dividends, interest and rent, etc. on behalf of customers, if so instructed by them;

(c) Purchase and sale of shares and securities on behalf of customers;

(d) Payment of rent, interest, insurance premium, subscriptions etc. on behalf of customers, if so instructed;

(e) Acting as a trustee or executor;

(f) Acting as agents or correspondents on behalf of customers for other banks and financial institutions at home and abroad.

(ii) General utility services: General utility services are those services which are rendered by commercial banks not only to the customers but also to the general public. These are available to the public on payment of a fee or charge.

They include :

- Issuing letters of credit and travellers' cheques;
- Underwriting of shares, debentures, etc.;
- Safe-keeping of valuables in safe deposit locker;
- Underwriting loans floated by government and public bodies.
- Supplying trade information and statistical data useful to customers;
- Acting as a referee regarding the financial status of customers;
- Undertaking foreign exchange business.

6

Public Relations as Perceived and Practiced by Commercial Banks

The increasing competition in the business world has forced firms to become innovative as well as effective in their promotion activities. PR is a promotion tool that has gained increasing importance in recent times, since it is perceived as both cost effective and highly credible. PR is a set of communications techniques which are designed to create and maintain favourable relations between an organization and its publics.

This study aims to provide a better understanding of how banks utilize PR in communicating with their publics. The role of corporate reputation and trust development is also examined within this study. To this end, case studies were conducted of two large Swedish banks, SEB and Handelsbanken. The cases explain the roles, objectives, functions and tools of PR at the banks.

Findings show that banks do not define their communication activities as PR, but still utilize it to a high degree.

While objectives are different in the banks, one common priority is the building and maintaining of relationships with the publics. Banks utilize many different tools to reach PR objectives; many of these are used at the local branch level. Similarly, banks consider corporate reputation and trust as vital for the organization's capability to sell financial services, and therefore manage this with high priority.

INTRODUCTION

In this initial chapter the thesis will be presented with a background in promotion and public relations. This will lead to the problem discussion, which will be the base for stating an overall purpose and research questions.

Background

In recent time, increasing competition in the business world has forced firms to become more aware of price and costs, which has resulted in a shift in the promotion mix to a greater use of promotion tools that are cost effective in reaching the customer (Boyd et.al. 1998). The increasing media clutter and altering competition has also forced companies to take new stands when planning promotion activities, to be able to reach and keep the customer. To do this, a company needs to get and maintain a high amount of credibility in front of its customers. At the same time, modern marketing has been accused to be spending increasing amounts of resources in their promotion activities, which has resulted in products and services with higher prices for the customer. One promotion tool that has gained importance in recent times is public relations, with its feature to lower promotion costs and to increase promotion credibility. It is also perceived as both cost effective and highly credible (Williams, 1988; Kitchen & Papasolomou, 1997).

The communication between a company and its customer, also known as promotion, is a mix of tools that can be utilized in the marketing communication. Public relation activities are an important part of this mix (Kotler & Armstrong, 1994). Promotion is used by organizations to communicate with customers regarding their product offerings, and also to ensure that customers are aware of the available products (Rowley, 1998). Promotion is defined by Kotler (1999) as communication activities used to inform, persuade, or remind the target market about the availability and benefits of a product. Promotion covers all communication tools that can deliver a message to a target audience. According to Rossiter & Percy (1987), promotion aims to stimulate a purchase. It is seen as a direct form of persuasion based on external incentives rather than inherent product benefits. Boyd et.al. (1998), describe the promotion strategy as a controlled and integrated programme of communication methods and materials designed to present the organization and its products to customers, and to contribute to long-run profit. The promotion programmes are developed through the use of four broad components; advertising, sales promotion, personal selling and public relations.

Advertising is any paid form of non-personal presentation and promotions of ideas, goods or services. It is an effective tool when building awareness since many people is reached with the message. Examples of possible tools are print ads, radio, television, billboard, posters, catalogues and signs. (Boyd et al, 1998; Kotler, 1999).

Sales promotion is used to create incentives to stimulate purchase or sale of a product, usually in the short term. The method can be used to stimulate for a trial of your product. Examples of tools are coupons, product samples, contests and demonstrations. (ibid.).

Personal selling is the process of helping and persuading the prospects to make the purchase of goods or services. The communication is often done orally and involves personal interaction that can build up to a long-term relationship. Tools used are presentations, meetings and samples. (Boyd et.al. 1998; Kotler & Armstrong 1994).

Public relations is non-paid stimulation of demand for a product or service. It is a communication between the organization and the public to maintain good relations. Usual public relation tools are web sites, publications, speeches, publicity in newspapers, radio and television. (Boyd et.al. 1998; Hutton, 1999).

An appropriate promotion mix is created from the above mentioned tools and channels, depending on what is to be achieved. Company objectives can include; increased sales, improvement of market shares, improvement of brand recognition, informing, educating and to create competitive advantage. Depending on the objectives, different combinations of the tools can be utilized. (Rowley, 1998).

PUBLIC RELATIONS

Public relations, also known as PR, is defined as a set of communications techniques which are designed to create and maintain favourable relations between an organization and its publics (Jefkins, 1978). Beavers-Moss (2001) argues that PR is a form of communication that well supports and adapts to a company's various advertising components. As much as it works to strengthen these components, there is also one obvious difference between advertising and PR. Advertising controls the overall message of the organization and builds visibility, while public relations reaches in and provides the advertising message with credibility and trust (ibid.). While marketing builds brand, PR amplifies brand awareness. The trouble is that while PR and marketing are two sides of the same coin, in many companies the disciplines fail to cooperate. There is often also a failure to distinguish where marketing ends and PR starts. If people in the community are asked to mention five competitors in the same business and they do not mention yours, probably the competitors use PR more effectively (Lynn, 1999).

PR is arguably the broadest of the marketing communication disciplines, involving a wide range of activities and specializations used to deliver corporate and brand messages. PR has developed from efforts focused on selling products to a corporate advisory role. As a result, PR activities can be classified as long-term, brand building options. (Barnes & Schultz, 1999). Over the last decade communication with audiences considered important to an organization has developed into a central focus of corporate strategy (Dolphin, 2004). Companies want to build good relations with their shareholders, with suppliers, distribution channels and customers. External operators such as trade and professional associations, and local chambers of commerce are other organizations that companies might wish to influence. Also journalists and representatives from various publishers are groups with which the organization must maintain good relations (Holloway & Robinson, 1995). According to Wells et.al. (2003) public relations is a management function practiced by a wide range of organizations: companies, governments, non-profit organizations, the educational system, labour unions, politicians, organized sports, and the media. Their goal is to achieve positive relationships with various publics in order to effectively manage the organization's image and reputation. Its publics may be externals like customers, news media, investment communities, the general public, and governments, or internals like shareholders and employees (ibid.).

CHARACTERISTICS AND TOOLS OF PUBLIC RELATIONS

PR can be divided into a proactive and a reactive category. Proactive PR is concerning the company's marketing objectives. It is offensive, opportunity seeking, and a method to communicate brand merits typically used in combination with other promotion tools. Reactive PR is used in response to outside influences. It is undertaken as a result of external pressures and challenges brought by for example competitive actions, shift in consumer attitudes or changes in government policies. With reactive PR a company typically deals with changes that have negative consequences, for example trying to repair a damaged reputation or regain lost sales. (Shimp, 2000).

Kotler et.al. (2005) state that although public relations still captures only a small portion of the overall marketing budgets of most firms, public relations is an increasingly important brand building tool. Research has found that advertising does not build brands, but public relation does (ibid.). The practitioner of PR has many tools, which can be divided into two categories: controlled media and uncontrolled media. Controlled media include various activities such as, speeches, corporate advertising, in-house publications, and visual presentations that create product and company publicity. The sponsoring organizations pay for the media and in return, get total control over how and when the message is delivered. Uncontrolled media include press releases, press conferences, and media tours. These are the primary channels to deliver public relation messages to various Medias. Organizations control the original form and content of the release and content on media tours. However it is the media which decide what to present and how to do it. What the audience finally sees is not necessary what is stated by the organization. The most recent electronic media is categorized as semi-controlled. Corporate websites are controlled by the company, but other web sites like chat rooms and forums set up by critics are not controlled. Special events and sponsorships are initiated by the companies, but participation by the press and other important publics is not under control of the sponsoring company. Another important semi-controlled media is word of mouth, where the initial message often can be designed by the organization (Wells et.al. 2003, Kotler et.al. 2005).

As with other promotion tools and marketing activities, objective have to be set, messages and media vehicles have to be selected, and implementation of the PR plan with a follow up evaluation of the activities have to be done (Kotler et.al. 2005). To gain a competitive advantage, an ability to monitor and evaluate the activities becomes critical for most PR practitioners (Phillips 2001). Tracking of the outputs; how many news releases lead to stories in media, and outcome; attitude or behaviour change, is necessary to prove the effectiveness of the PR program to be able to learn and fine-tune future campaigns (Wells et.al. 2003).

Problem Discussion

Lages & Simkin (2003) present PR as an emerging science discipline and argue that PR research is in need of developing concrete measurement tools which will allow empirical evaluation and clearly identify its driving forces. The on-going conceptualisation is also moving PR more to a management discipline instead of its earlier label as a communication activity. According to Broom et.al. (1997) PR is still clearly lacking in definition and conceptualization. Without clearly explained concepts, researchers have a tough work to conduct empirical observations and construct meaningful theory. Presumably for this reason, the majority of past research in the area of PR is descriptive leaving a gap in explaining the actual activities observed in the business world. Broom et.al. (1989) argue that journals in PR are not responsive to the interest of practicing professionals and that publications provide little help to students, teachers, practitioners and managers to understand and utilize research in PR. There is relatively little cross-situational, theory building research to be found. More recent research has shown some improvement but the problem in the area of PR seems to remain.

PR in Service Firms

When marketing services that are both intangible and hard to differentiate, establishing trusting relationships is one key objective. According to Merenda (2004), nothing will establish trust more than credibility. This is done by enhancing demand for the organizations services. The ultimate way to market a service is to promote it by advertising, and then support the arguments by PR to build credibility (Beavers-Moss, 2001). Building credibility and trustworthiness are main issues in PR.

The existing research in the area of PR as a trust enhancer is based on data from different industries. Studies can be seen in service organizations in various markets. But there is still shortage of research in many specific industries. For example Saparito et.al. (2004) have investigated customer orientation and manager interface in trust building between banks and its customers. They recommend future researchers to look into other banking activities important for developing trust, such as PR. This research recommendation explains the significance of conducting research in the specific industry of banking, and further states the importance of this thesis direction.

PR in Banks

Earlier research shows that PR is one of the most important parts when considering the promotion mix in the banking industry. The nature of the business with a need of high levels of trust, explains the importance of public opinion to be successful. The bank's most effective tool to monitor and manage this opinion is through extensive use of PR activities. Recent research also shows that the banking industry has been caught in a negative trend regarding reputation, which could have been avoided through PR activities.

In the banking industry services provided are to a high degree similar, which makes it hard to make a comparison between banks and their offerings. Therefore in banking, credibility and value is mainly gained from the organization's reputation. It is also argued that reputation is the most valuable asset of a bank (Beavers-Moss, 2001). As stated by Dolphin (2004), corporate reputation is a fast developing area clearly gaining in importance for management and scholars.

Due to the obvious importance of PR activities in the banking industry, and because existing research does not fully describe the PR aspects continuously handled by banks to build upon their reputation, our aim in this study is to shed more light over the PR activities handled by banks. Some PR activities in banking have been studied internationally in different countries, but preliminary investigations showed that no one has researched the various aspects of PR in Swedish banks. The purpose and research questions are presented below.

Purpose: In view of the above problem discussion the purpose of this study is:

To gain a better understanding of how banks utilize PR in communicating with their publics.

Research questions: To be able to answer the purpose of the study we shall address the following research questions;

1. How can roles and objectives of PR in banks' promotion mix be described?
2. How can PR's functions and tools utilized by banks be described?
3. How can corporate reputation and trust as viewed by banks be described?

To explain the connection between the three research questions, and to be able to understand the entire picture of this study, the following can be stated; the first research question is approaching the area of PR in an overall strategic meaning. The second research question is handling the functions and tools that can be utilized to reach the roles and objectives within the banks. The third research question is concerning reputation and trust, which can be a result of the functions and tools utilized to reach the roles and objectives.

Demarcations

Since PR is such a vast area, it is not possible to cover all of its aspects in this study. The concept of PR as discussed in this study includes the elements possible to observe in the banking industry, and will follow the definition that; PR is a set of communications techniques designed to create and maintain favourable relations between an organization and its publics. The study is also limited to a corporate perspective with a focus on Swedish banks.

In this chapter literature relevant in the area of PR is reviewed and presented. The theories connected to the research area will be reviewed and presented in a conceptual framework, which will clarify the main topic to be studied and aid data collection. The existing literature in the area of PR is vast and numerous. To be able to answer the research questions and reach our purpose, we have been selective in the search of relevant theory and models. Some of the selected theories approach PR in general terms, while other theories handle more specific aspects within the area of PR. By selecting theories that fit into the focus of this thesis, we are able to create a conceptual framework, which is necessary to conduct this research.

ROLE AND OBJECTIVES OF PR

PR: Definitions

The research area of PR is vast and wide with numbers of definitions regarding the term PR and what it actually involves. People working with PR tend to view their activities as having a strategic impact, while many marketers views PR as only a tactical ingredient of the promotion mix. This confusion has hindered the development of the PR profession and added to the blurring of what exactly includes in the area of PR. (Lages & Simkin, 2003) A review of modern PR history gives a number of definitions, metaphors, and approaches to the field (Hutton, 1999). In the first two decades of this century the dominant theme in PR was "using communications to build and hold goodwill". The term has evolved and a review of recent PR definitions in literature and academic journals suggests a number of common themes, but there is still no true convergence. The most common components in the definition of PR appear to be "management", "organization", and "publics".

An example of a widely quoted definition is: "Public relations is the management function which evaluates public attitudes, identifies the policies and procedures of an organization with the public interest, and executes a program of action to earn public understanding and acceptance" (Hutton, 1999).

Lages and Simkin (2003) propose that PR scholars conceptualize PR as a management discipline, which is a change form the traditional view of PR as mainly a communication activity. Other authors referred by Lages and Simkin (2003) agree with Hutton (1999) and defines PR as the "management of communication between an organization and its publics"; and emphasize: "this definition equates public relations and communication management". PR is also defined as "the management function that identifies, establishes and maintains mutually beneficial relationships between an organization and the various publics on whom its success or failure depends". Further, Lages and Simkin (2003) define PR as "relationship management", which implies that the focus of public relations is the management of an organization's relationships with its publics through the four step management process of analysis, planning, implementation and evaluation. In this context PR is used to communicate strategically (ibid.).

Frank Jefkins (1978) define PR as: "Public relations consist of all forms of planned communication, outwards and inwards, between an organization and its publics for the purpose of achieving specific objectives concerning mutual understanding".

This definition points out that PR should be planned and organized similarly as production, sales and advertising programmes. The principal objective, mutual understanding means that the PR practitioner seeks to understand other people and their attitudes, as well as to create an understanding of his organization and its people, policies, products, or services. Such interaction is the essence of communication. By the term objective, the author means that the system of management by objectives is implemented to deliberately planned and sustained PR. Also a separate PR strategy can and should be planned, budgeted and executed alongside marketing. Ideally this should be part of a complete management system, using PR to achieve company objectives (ibid.).

PR: Objectives and Strategies

Dolphin & Fan (2000) discuss if PR is seen as a strategic function by corporate management. Their research indicates that a communication strategy is essential for any organization. It needs to be managed and formulated by the information director in close cooperation with the executive team. When shaping PR strategy, considerations must be given to the nature of the organization; to its vision, mission and to its key audiences.

The role of the information director is to act as a bridge between his organization and its audiences, and in this way create or sustain the corporate image or reputation. Obviously, PR has a key role to play in the strategic planning of an organization, and should therefore be closely linked to the organizations board room through an information director (ibid.).

Nakra (2000) agrees with this view, and states that PR activities must be involved early in the process when developing strategies for building and maintaining the corporate image and reputation. Reserving a seat at the corporate boardroom tables for PR executives, and involving them in strategy development, would be a logical first step. Jefkins (2000) describes the ideal organization structure with the PR department as independent, directly responsible in front of the CEO.

However if the PR executive is positioned in the marketing, advertising or sales promotion department instead, the use of PR can get strictly limited. According to Lages & Simkin (2003), the positioning of PR as a management discipline implies, that the PR activities are broader than communication techniques and broader than specialized PR programs, such as media relations. There are also arguments that PR is not efficient when practitioners master the technical skills without the understanding of when and why to use PR to make communication more competent for organizations (ibid.).

Wells & Spinks (1999) describe community relations as some of the most important activities of an organization. Establishment of ongoing, reliable and respected external communication processes should be a priority. Since public opinion is dynamic, the PR response also should be actively managed. This should also involve customer relations, since thousands of satisfied customers never will make an argument, but one unsatisfied customer probably will. Worcester (1997) also explains the attributes of the bank image in the eyes of the public as highly dynamic and never static. Even if it looks static, it is hardly ever so. Most organizations realize the necessity for effective communication with many audiences, such as its customers, clients and employees. However, many organizations fail to notice the importance of good communication with the community (Wells & Spink, 1999). Lynn (1999) argues that PR activities can clearly increase economic value for banks because it creates trademark and brand awareness in the community.

Hon (1998) points out that there is tremendous variability in organizations explanation of PR's goals and objectives, perhaps reflecting the diversity of organizations represented. Each organization divides its responsibilities differently, and not surprisingly, priorities tend to reflect the mission of the organization. Some practitioners mention communication goals that increase sales and revenue, and also bring in new business. Others talk more about PR's role in enhancing the image of the organization and disseminating positive messages. Hon (1998) discusses further that most of the companies in her research said that their PR department does have written, quantifiable goals and objectives, although several acknowledged that this systemization happened somewhat recently. Other statements were that PR goals and objectives have to be "strategic", meaning that public relations goals and objectives must be tied directly to organizational goals and objectives. The findings by Hutton et.al (2001) is in line with Hon (1998) and identifies widely disparate views of the purposes of PR, and also confirms that the diversity of PR strategy continues to be a major issue. Different objectives and philosophies may be appropriate for different companies, industries or business environments (Hutton et.al. 2001).

According to Wells et.al. (2003) PR objectives are designed to make changes in the public's knowledge, attitudes, and behaviours related to a company, brand, or organization. Usually these objectives focus on creating credibility, delivering information, and building positive images. Typical PR objectives include:

- Creating a corporate brand
- Shaping or redefining a corporate reputation
- Positioning or repositioning a company or brand
- Disseminating news about a brand, company, or organization
- Providing product or brand information
- Changing stakeholders attitudes, opinions, or behaviours about a brand or company
- Creating buzz - word of mouth
- Involving people with the brand (ibid.)

Defining Publics

Worcester (1997) emphasizes the importance of identifying the organizations important publics. Every bank should undertake careful evaluation of the audiences it must deal with in order of priority. In many financial institutions for example the customers often hold this position. Knowing accurately who to target first means that expenditure decisions can be based on relevance. Beavers-Moss (2001) states that after identifying the various publics of a bank, relationships should be established according to every group's needs and wants. Organizations are recommended by Wells & Spinks (1999) to establish ongoing communications with the public community in whole. Schultz & Barnes (1999) suggest instead that the relationship with specific publics should be emphasized. After deciding if the organizations publics are going to be defined wide or narrow, companies can utilize traditional segmentation bases such as Geographic's, demographics and psychographics. Other tools can also be used such as covert power segmentation, which involves identifying persons within a community who exert influence on a variety of issues or decisions. Reputation segmentation deals with identifying people who are influential within social networks.

Proactive PR versus reactive PR

PR can be characterized either as proactive or reactive. Proactive PR is dictated by a company's objectives. It is oriented offensively rather than defensively, and opportunity seeking rather than problem solving. The major role of proactive PR is to promote the organizations products and services. Integrated with other promotional activities, proactive PR give a product or service additional exposure, newsworthiness, and credibility. The last factor, credibility, largely accounts for the effectiveness of proactive PR. By comparison, reactive PR describes the conduct of public relations in response to outside influences. It is undertaken as a result of external pressures and challenges brought by competitive actions, shifts in consumer attitudes, changes in government policy, or other external influences. Reactive PR typically deals with change that has negative consequences for the organization, and attempts to repair a company's reputation, prevent market erosion, or regain lost sales. (Shimp, 2000).

HUTTON'S FRAMEWORK FOR DEFINING PUBLIC RELATIONS

Hutton (1999) has developed a three dimensional cube to provide a framework by which to analyze PR roles. There are three dimensions that explain the substantive differences among the various orientations or definitions of PR; interest, initiative and image.

Interest

The "interest" dimension can be described as the "balance of intended effects". It describes to what degree PR functions are focused on client interest versus public interest. In other words, is the focus mainly on the organizations direct customers or is the focus on the public in general?

Initiative

The "initiative" dimension explains to what extent the PR function is reactive versus proactive. This can be measured by PR activities designed to predict and help to shape up emerging organizational issues.

Image

The "image" dimension describes to what extent the organization is focused on perception versus reality, or image versus substance. This dimension represents the general focus of an organization's philosophy, thoughts and actions. When PR activities are analyzed in the context of this framework, there appear to be six relatively distinct orientations of PR practice: persuasion, advocacy, public information, cause-related public relations, image-reputation management, and relationship management.

Persuasion

Persuasion includes the philosophies of PR that are proactive and oriented toward persuading audiences to think or act in the way that benefit the organization. PR programs or campaigns that focus on promotion or to create consent fall in this category, distinguished from each other primarily by their strategic choice of tactics rather than their basic purpose. For example a promotion campaign that utilizes media publicity might be using an agenda-setting style of persuasion by attempting to place the client-organization's product on consumers' mental agendas, with the goal of increasing awareness and sales of the product. (ibid.)

Advocacy

This category is similar to persuasion in its intention, persuading audiences to think or act in ways that benefit the organization, but different in its level of initiative and in the fact that it arises out of controversy or active opposition. The function is to serve the role of defending the organisation in the court of public opinion, rather than a court of law. The presence of controversy or active opposition usually dictates the type of strategy and tactics used, and the reactive nature of advocacy public relations means that a PR counsel or function may not exist until triggered by a crisis or other catalyst. In addition to that, the focus of advocacy is often on persuading relevant audiences to think or act in certain ways. (ibid.)

Public Information

Public information refers to the style of PR in which an organization serves primarily as an educator and information provider. Examples include industry trade associations and other member service organizations, along with some government agencies that perform similar functions. (ibid.).

Cause related Public Relations

Cause related PR is similar to persuasion in its intention, to persuade the audience to think or act in specific ways. It is similar in its level of initiative, usually proactive. It is similar to advocacy, in the way that it may be reactive and nonexistent until triggered by a public event. In other ways it is the complement of advocacy, as long as it tends to serve a broader public interest rather than any special-interest group or individual. Cause related PR is often distinguished by its need to highlight strong but unorganized publics and media, trough lobbying and publicity. Examples of groups or organizations that practice cause related PR include for example the Red Cross organization and Amnesty International. The corresponding metaphor for cause-related PR is generally crusader. (ibid.)

Image/reputation Management

This role focuses on the image or reputation of the organization, as measured by its popularity or value as a supplier, buyer, partner, employer, lender, citizen or investment. Image/reputation management looks primarily to publicity, spin control and the creation and manipulation of symbols as its primary tactics. It has grown in importance recently, and has deep roots in the practices of early PR pioneers. A distinction might be made between image and reputation management to the extent that reputation could be considered less superficial than image, with a correspondingly greater emphasis on reputable behaviour as the foundation of a good reputation. (ibid.)

Relationship Management

Relationship management refers to the practice of PR as an exercise in identifying mutual interests, values and benefit between a client-organization and its publics. While acting primarily on the client's behalf, such an approach to PR seeks to operate in behalf of the client in a responsible manner, in line with the public interest, in belief that public support and consent are vital to achieving the organizations long-term objectives. The emphasis is on mutual trust, compromise, cooperation, and whenever possible, a win-win situation between the organization and the customer. (ibid.).

HUTTON'S HIERARCHY OF PUBLIC RELATIONS

Hutton (1999) has suggested a hierarchy framework for primary roles, functions and tactics/tools of PR. The benefit of such hierarchy is that it encourages scholars and practitioners to distinguish between the umbrella definition of PR and the primary purpose and objectives of PR in a given context. It also encourages a distinction between PR's roles, and the functions of PR, which are not end goals in themselves but means by which a given object is achieved.

FUNCTIONS AND TOOLS IN PR

Types of PR

In PR there are specific types of relations which all refer to relationships with various stakeholders.

Media Relations

Focuses on developing a relationship with media and find out who might be interested in the organizations story. The term "public relations" is by most people associated with publicity, which indicates the importance of this media function. The organization initiates publicity and provides appropriate information to media. A successful relationship between a PR person and the editor is built on a PR person's reputation for honesty, accuracy and professionalism. If this reputation is tarnished or lost, the PR person cannot function effectively as a liaison between a company and the media. (Wells et.al. 2003)

Employee Relations

Employee relation programmes communicate information to employees. The function of employee relations belongs both to PR and human resource management. These kinds of programmes are often called internal marketing. (ibid.).

Financial Relations

Financial relations includes all communication efforts aimed at the financial community, such as press releases sent to business publications, meetings with investors and analysts, and annual reports which the government require of public held companies. (ibid.)

Corporate Relations

Corporate relation programmes focuses on organization's image and reputation. The goal is to persuade the public to perceive the company in a positive light. According to Wells et.al. (2003) the public relation expert Fraser Seitel has stated that "it takes a great deal of time to build a favourable image for a corporation but only one slip to create a negative public impression." The goal of reputation management in a corporate relations program is to strengthen the trust that stakeholders have in an organization. Since corporate reputation is a perception, it is earned through deeds, not created by advertising. (ibid.)

Public Affairs

Focuses on corporate communication with governments and with the public on issues related to government and regulations. Issue management is another term for this function. In addition to government relations, public affair programs also monitor public opinion about issues central to the organization's interest and develop programs for communicating to, and with the public about these issues. (ibid.)

PR Tools

Wells et al (2003) describes three categories that divide the tools of PR, depending on the amount of control the company has in its communication. Since the tools which can be utilized in PR, are well known tactics in organizations, they are not described in further terms.

Controlled PR

When a company can control the use and placement of their PR tools they are utilizing controlled channels. Examples of tools in this category are:

- Publications: Brochures, flyers, newsmagazines
- Annual reports
- Displays, exhibits
- Product placements
- Speakers
- Photographs
- Staged events (open houses, anniversary celebration)
- **Uncontrolled** PR

When companies relies the use and placement of their PR to media, they are using uncontrolled channels. Examples of tools in this category are:

- Publicity (radio, TV and print media)
- News releases (print, audio, video, e-mail)
- Press conferences and media advisory (media kits, fact sheets, background information)
- By-lined articles
- Talk and interview shows
- Semi-controlled PR

When some aspects of the PR activities are controlled and initiated by the company, but other aspects remain uncontrolled, they are utilizing semi-controlled channels. Examples of tools in this category are:

- Special events and sponsorship
- Interpersonal communication
- Electronic communication (web sites, chat rooms)
- Word of mouth

When utilizing above mentioned tools, PR teams needs to work closely with the marketing department. PR tends to complement advertising activities. While advertising is pushing a banks desired message to its markets, PR is there to sprinkle the message with credibility. Banks often realize the importance of PR activities, but may differ in the way they are utilized in the marketing mix. (Beavers-Moss, 2001).

The PR Toolkit

Phillips (2001) provides a framework developed to set up and evaluate PR activities. The author proposes a five-step approach to research and evaluation. The steps are:

1. Audit research about the organization, products and services, and an audit of communications with audiences. Research can help identifying these as well as track the progress of

the campaign and its outcome. Looking into existing research saves time and money. Involving senior management at this stage demonstrates the strategic role that PR can play.

2. Objectives. These must reflect the strategic business goals of an organization. PR should be co-ordinated with advertising, direct marketing, and sponsorship. The target audience, the medium, the desired response and the timing should be identified.
3. Strategy and plan. Decide on level of measurement. Output measures how the message went out and who it reached. Out-take measures to what extent the message was remembered and understood. Outcome measures to what degree PR activity changed opinions, behavior or attitudes.
4. Measurement and evaluation. Measures the direction of activities. Are we getting there, and if so, do we stay on course? If not, should we adjust tactics, strategy or objectives?
5. Result. A review of result against the previously stated objectives: what did we learn that can be fed back into the planning loop? What worked and what did not? What can we re-use next time?

Lages & Simkin (2003) further support the importance of utilizing overall planning, execution and evaluation of an organization's PR communication with both external and internal publics.

PR: EFFECTIVENESS AND EVALUATION

As in advertising, PR effectiveness and evaluation is based on setting measurable objectives in the beginning of the planning (Wells et.al. 2003). The ability to monitor, measure, evaluate and plan content in its relevant context thereafter becomes critical for most PR practice as a ground of competitive advantage (Phillips, 2001). Schmitz (2004) states that it is as important to follow-up measure and evaluate PR activities as in fact to implement them. Xavier et.al (2005) put forward that there is no general method for measuring effectiveness, instead practitioners select among an array of different methods and models to demonstrate the effectiveness of PR activities.

Evaluation models can be categorized into those focusing on a specific process of PR or those accommodating an integrated planning approach (ibid.).

According to Wells (2003) PR practitioners must track the impact of a campaign in terms of output, how many news releases lead to stories or mentions in news, and outcome like attitude or behaviour change. Such tracking is done to prove the effectiveness of PR programs and to learn from it to be able to fine-tune further PR activities (ibid.). Evidently there is a lack of knowledge on how much evaluation techniques there are, and how much it is worth to utilize them in order to provide the organization with good evaluative information (Phillips, 2001). To measure and evaluate PR activities initiated by the organization, Schmitz (2004) provides two general ways to do it: Do it yourself by reading newspapers and magazines, relevant websites, check out what is mentioned about your organization in radio and TV. This is a very time consuming activity and therefore it can be more effective to outsource this activity to a media-monitoring agency. Further, it is recommended to mix own monitoring, and media-monitoring agencies to get out as much valuable information as possible (ibid.).

Following is a guideline provided by Wells et.al (2003) with common types of evaluation measures used in PR:

- *Output Production.* Numbers of PR products, such as news releases or event activities generated.
- *Distribution.* Number of media outlets (TV stations, newspapers) receiving PR products.
- *Coverage.* Number and size of clips, column inches, seconds, or minutes of time or space.
- *Impressions.* Media placements multiplied by circulation or broadcast reach.
- *Advertising value.* Equivalent ad cost for time or space.
- *Systematic Content Analysis.* Positive or valence (whether the story or mention seems to be more positive or negative), key messages (the idea in the story), sources, and prominence.

Outcome Objectives achieved:

- *Awareness*. Aided and unaided to recall the target audience.
- *Attitudes*. Perceptions and preference or intent to buy.
- *Behaviour*. Did they do what you wanted them to?

According to Beavers-Moss (2001) it is important for the bank to identify what gain is expected from the PR activities. If the goals are defined explicitly and measurably, they are easier to achieve.

The Effectiveness Yardstick Model

To simplify the process of measuring effectiveness in PR activities Lindenmann (1993) has developed a straightforward set of guidelines or standards that PR practitioners can follow to measure PR effectiveness. The guideline is called the "Public Relations Effectiveness Yardstick" and involves a two-step process: first, setting PR objectives, and then determining at what levels to measure PR effectiveness.

Step One: Setting Objectives

What are the goals or objectives of your PR program? What is your PR program or activity seeking to accomplish?

In PR, what you try to accomplish usually falls into one of these four categories:

1. You, or your organization, are trying to get out certain messages, themes or ideas.
2. You would like these messages or ideas distributed to certain key or target audience groups.
3. Your envision distributing these messages to your target audiences via certain pre-selected or specific communications channels.
4. For what you say, for how you say it, and to whom, there are certain short-term or long-term "ends" or objectives you are interested in accomplishing. Based on how and what you say and do, you would like those you reach to respond in a certain way.

Step Two: Determining Levels of PR Measurement

After setting the PR objectives, then you have to decide what exactly you want to measure. In this guideline there are three different measures of PR effectiveness.

Level 1: Basic Level

It measures PR "outputs". It examines how well PR people present themselves, how they handle given activities or events. At this level, PR practitioners measure the amount of exposure their organization received in media, the total number of placements, the total number of impressions, and/or the likelihood of having reached specific target audience groups. To measure "outputs," PR practitioners often use content analysis techniques to track or measure publicity placements. Or, conduct simple public opinion polls to find out if targeted groups have been exposed to certain messages.

Level 2: Intermediate Level

This level is more sophisticated. At this level, PR practitioners measure whether or not target audience groups actually received the messages directed at them: whether or not they paid attention to the messages, whether or not they understood the messages, and whether or not they have retained those messages in any shape or form. To measure "outgrowths," practitioners usually rely on a mix of qualitative and quantitative data collection techniques, using such methodologies as focus groups, depth interviews with opinion-leader groups, and extensive polling of key target audience groups either by telephone, face-to-face, or through mail.

Level 3: Advanced Level

This level is the most advanced PR measurement level. When one reaches this higher end of the Effectiveness Yardstick, the "outcomes", such as opinion, attitude, and behaviour change are measured. To measure "outcomes", the PR practitioner needs to rely on: techniques such as before-and-after polls; the development and use of experimental and quasi-experimental research designs; use of unobtrusive data collection methods such as observation, participation, and role-playing; the use of advanced data analysis techniques (such as perceptual mapping, psychographic analysis, factor and cluster analysis, and conjoint analysis); or the conducting of comprehensive, multi-faceted communications audits. (ibid.).

Corporate reputation and PR

When reviewing the existing literature in the areas of trust, credibility, and corporate reputation gained by PR, it can be found that the area is not thoroughly researched. Therefore models and theories from existing literature are hard to find. Provided below are theories relevant to answer our research questions.

Trust and Credibility

Seal (1998) suggests that trust is based on personal knowledge of the other part in a relationship. However trust goes beyond possessing information about each other. Possession of information about someone does not directly correspond to trust. Trust needs history as a reliable background and is therefore enacted in dependent relationships. Saparito et.al. (2004) describe the concept of trust as; the trusting party must perceive the trusted party to be acting out of a commitment to the relationship that goes beyond instrumental motive of advancing self-interest.

Seal (1998) describes three types of trust in the organizational setting;

- Contractual trust means that partners keep their promises whether or not they are based on written agreements.
- Competence trust is when you have the business ability to fulfil obligations. If you for example are unable to fulfil your promises to repay loans because you lack in funding, you break the competence trust.
- Goodwill trust is when the company can act on the behalf of its clients without detailed instructions.

Credibility is defined as the capability to influence because of the perceived knowledge or skills one has or is presumed to have

(Budd, 1995). The collective outcome of building trust and gaining credibility is reputation (Budd, 2001). According to Beavers-Moss (2001) PR serve to enhance demand for products and services through building credibility. Managers in service industries that are not well-differentiated in terms of basic services should recognize that well-structured and valuable communication has a strong effect on consumer perceptions. It leads to trust, satisfaction, and loyalty. These communications should be used as relationship-enhancers, offering the customer useful and needed advice and information, packaged in such a way that the customer finds it easy to understand and pleasant to absorb. (Ball et.al. 2004).

Corporate Reputation

According to Budd (2001) the managing of corporate reputation is a very delicate and sensitive process. You are not dealing with a tangible product but with a judgement, an attitude, a sense, a feeling rooted in a persons mind. Good reputation is hard to build and cannot be bought. It is also very fragile, and easy to loose. Hutton et.al. (2001) argue that companies with extensive corporate communication strategies were more likely to have strong reputations. Specifically, the more companies focused on "managing relationships" with non-customer publics or "reputation management" as their guiding communication philosophy, the more likely they were to have a strong reputation.

Dolphin (2004) argues that any communication that makes an organization more transparent enables stakeholders to appreciate its operations more clearly, facilitating a better reputation. The intangible equity in a corporate reputation is an organization's most enduring and lasting asset. The reputation also wins a competitive advantage for the organization in an increasingly crowded marketplace. Therefore a good corporate reputation is an asset of immense value. However, it is intangible and both difficult to measure and difficult to replicate by other companies. The reputation is a highly visible signal of an organization's capabilities and reliability providing information about future performance (ibid.).

Research has shown that a positive reputation does contribute to corporate success. This has been recognized and utilized by senior managers since the mid-1980s, to build and sustain favourable corporate reputation. The management of reputation has also developed into a major tool for the communication strategist, with the focus on the role of gaining the support and approval of important audiences. This is a value creating strategy in one way or another. Today there is no doubt that corporate reputation is given more attention than ever before since marketers and communicators are concerned about their companies' reputations and advantages brought by good reputation (Dolphin, 2004). The loss of reputation is also seen as a larger problem than loosing money for an organization (Hutton et.al. 2001).

Dolphin (2004) states some clear differences between corporate reputation and corporate identity that is often used interchangeably by both management and scholars, which causes confusion. Reputation is gained over time and may not be that open for rapid manipulation, an image can, unlike from reputation, clearly be created and manipulated in a short period of time. Budd (1995) also confirms that corporate reputation may not be easy to change within a short period of time even though extensive communications with the public is utilized.

Hutton et.al. (2001) define reputation management as an emerging business function, resting on the foundations of what traditionally is termed as "public relations", clearly relating the two activities to each other. Advocates of reputation management state that the new term will act as a galvanizing concept that will enhance public relations' stature, perceived value and centrality within organizations.

Reputation management is a general phenomenon that does not need to occur in response to a reputation problem. Organizations with poor reputations may engage in actions that enhance its reputation, but also organizations with a favorable reputation may engage in actions designed to sustain or enhance its reputational standing (Weiss et.al. 1999). According to Nakra (2000) public relations practitioners must develop the ability to manage corporate reputation by taking a "360 degree" view and communicate well with all stakeholders with a unified message.

With today's ongoing globalization and increasing competition, bank marketers must know how to protect and uphold their reputation. Considering the intangible nature of bank products and services, credibility and value are gained mainly from the organization's established reputation. Good PR can enhance a banks marketing and improve the institutions overall competitiveness (Beavers-Moss, 2001). The corporate reputation is especially important when acting on a market where the products and pricing is highly similar and hard to differentiate. A sound reputation must be the foundation on which to position an undifferentiated product. An international bank comments that, "banking is a reputation business", which indicates the importance of reputation in the specific industry. The communicator at this bank had clearly understood his role as one of guarding the reputation of the organization (Dolphin, 2004).

Dolphin (2004) also describes a case from a large international bank, which was identified as using a hard-nosed strategy, when not writing of third world debts, with bad reputation for the bank as a direct result.

The management of the bank instead utilized PR activities with extensive sponsorship programmes to repair damages in the corporate reputation. Image and reputation is described as one of the most important factors when analyzing customer perception of service quality in the banking industry. Trustworthiness, tradition and reliability can build a favourable image that can positively influence the perception of quality, value and satisfaction (Kangis & Voukelatos, 1997). These factors helps to influence customer loyalty, which is critical to banks and service firms because customer defections can have more to do with a service company's profits than scale, market share, and many other factors usually associated with competitive advantage (Saparito et.al. 2004). Beavers-Moss (2001) also discusses the importance of public relations when managing customer loyalty aspects.

Conceptual Framework

The purpose of this section is to display a conceptualization for this thesis in order to assist answering the research questions. This conceptual framework is founded on a selection of models and theories that best fit to address the research topic. The conceptualization will serve as the basis for the interview guide which is developed in order to collect relevant data for this thesis.

ROLE AND OBJECTIVES OF PR

Definitions

The area of PR is vast with numbers of definitions; therefore it is hard to give a concrete definition of PR. We will not narrow it down just using one definition. Instead this study will compare the collected data against different definitions, provided by Hutton (1999), Lages & Simkin (2003) and Jefkins (1978), to find out if there are similarities or differences between the collected data and selected definitions.

Objectives and Strategies

Research has found that there is a tremendous variability in organizations explanation of goals and objectives of PR (Hon, 1998). According to Wells et.al. (2003) there are numerous objectives with the PR-strategies. Usually these objectives focus on creating credibility, delivering information, and building positive images.

According to Dolphin & Fan (2000) a communication strategy is essential for any organization. It needs to be managed and formulated by the information director in close cooperation with the executive team (Dolphin & Fan,2000; Nakra, 2000). Many organization have written quantifiable goals and objectives that are tied directly to the organizations overall goals and objectives (Hon, 1998). Different philosophies are often appropriate for different companies or industries (Hutton et.al. 2001).

Jefkins (2000) describes the ideal organizational structure with the PR department as independent, directly responsible in front of the CEO. However if the PR executive instead is positioned in the marketing, advertising or sales promotion department, the use of PR is strictly limited. According to Lages & Simkin (2003) PR as a management discipline is much wider than a communication technique or an specialized program, such as media relations. Most organizations realize the importance of effective communications with its publics (Wells & Spinks (1999). This communication can increase value through creating brand awareness in the community (Lynn, 1999).

The public opinion is highly dynamic and therefore the PR responses utilized by companies should be actively managed. (Wells & Spinks, 1999; Worcester, 1997).

Defining Publics

The importance of identifying the organizations publics is emphasized by Worcester (1997). Schultz & Barnes (1999) point out that specific publics should be targeted. Thereafter segmentation with traditional methods can be conducted. Wells & Spinks (1999) recommend establishment of PR activities with the community in hole.

Proactive PR versus Reactive PR

Public relations can be characterized either as proactive or reactive. Proactive PR is offensive and opportunity seeking, mainly used to promote products and services. Reactive PR is defensively oriented and problem solving. It is undertaken as a result of external pressure. (Shimp, 2000).

HUTTONS FRAMEWORK FOR DEFINING PUBLIC RELATIONS

The framework of Hutton (1999) is going to be used to analyze PR practices of organizations. In this way it is possible to identify the organizations role in PR, as one of the following:

- Persuasion
- Advocacy

- Public information
- Cause-related public relations
- Image/reputation management
- Relationship management

HUTTON'S HIERARCHY OF PUBLIC RELATIONS

The hierarchy of PR, a framework constructed by Hutton (1999), is a helpful instrument when defining primary purposes and objectives of PR in a given context. It provides an overall picture of PR from the definition to the actual tools utilized. It also merges into other theories and models in the area and supports the overall view of the topic.

FUNCTIONS AND TOOLS IN PR

Types of PR

In PR there are different types of relations which all refer to relationships with various stakeholders. We will use the types provided by Wells et.al. (2003) to describe the different types of PR:

- Media relations
- Employee relations
- Financial relations
- Corporate relations
- Public affairs
- The PR toolkit

We will use the five step framework developed by Phillips (2001) on how to set up PR activities and how to evaluate them. The five steps involved are:

- Audit research
- Objectives
- Strategy and plan
- Measurement and evaluation
- Result

PR Tools

To be able to differentiate the tools used within PR we will utilize the model stated by Wells et.al. (2003). There are three types, controlled, uncontrolled and, semi-controlled types of PR tools.

Effectiveness and Evaluation of PR

To be able to measure the effectiveness of the PR activities initiated by the organization, evaluation have to be done. According to Schmitz (2004) it is as important to follow up, measure, and evaluate the PR activities as in fact to implement them. There is also evidence of a lack in knowledge on how much evaluation techniques there are, and what can be worth to evaluate (Phillips, 2001). There is no general evaluation method, instead a variety of methods are used to measure effectiveness (Xavier et.al. 2005). A framework by Wells et.al. (2003) with common types of evaluation measures will help to answer how awareness, attitudes, and behaviours have been affected by the PR activities. The "Public Relations Effectiveness Yardstick" framework by Lindenmann (1993) will help to explain how effectiveness is measured.

CORPORATE REPUTATION AND TRUST

Trust and Credibility

The trusting party must perceive that the trusted party is acting out of commitment that is going beyond motives of self-interest. (Saparito et.al. 2004). Well structured communications has strong effect on consumer perception, and leads to trust, satisfaction and loyalty. Corporate communications should be used as relationship-enhancers offering the customers advice and information. (Ball et.al. 2004).

Corporate Reputation

Corporate reputation can win competitive advantages for an organization in a crowded marketplace. It is a visible signal of an organization's capabilities and information about future performance (Dolphin, 2000). Management of reputation has developed into an important tool for communication strategists (Dolphin, 2004). The loss of organizational reputation is seen as a larger problem than a short term loss of money (Hutton et.al. 2001). Corporate identity and corporate reputation should not be mixed up and used interchangeably (Dolphin, 2004). Reputation is gained over time and not easily changed. An image is unlike from reputation easy to create and manipulate in short time (Budd, 1995). Reputation management, resting on the foundations of PR, is an emerging business function that gains importance in organizations (Hutton et.al. 2001). It does not need to occur in response to a reputation problem, it can be both reactive and proactive (Weiss et.al. 1999). Bank marketers must know how to protect and uphold their reputation, since credibility and value is to a high degree gained from it (Beavers-Moss, 2001). Trustworthiness can positively influence the perception of quality, and influence loyalty (Kangis & Voukelatos, 1997).

7

Methodology

In this chapter the methodology of the thesis is presented. The selections and implications of the research methods are explained together with justifications of the choices. The chapter ends with a conceptualized summary of the methodology process.

RESEARCH PURPOSE

Yin (2003) distinguishes three types of research: Exploratory, descriptive, and explanatory. Exploratory research is applied when a problem is difficult and you have little knowledge about the area you are studying (Eriksson & Wiedesheim-Paul, 2001). It can be seen as a pilot study, in which the researcher creates a base of understanding to formulate more precise questions or a testable hypothesis (Gummesson, 1991). According to Wallén (1996) it gives a basic understanding of the problem and its context. According to Patel & Davidson (1994) the purpose of exploratory research is to collect as much information as possible about a specific subject. It is suitable as a base, when formulating interesting questions for future research.

Descriptive studies are focusing on illustrating characteristics for the research object and are consisting of gathering and systemizing existing data (Wallén, 1996). Description is compared to prediction and prescription; which grants possibilities to deduce and recommend (Gummesson, 1991). The descriptive research is used when the goal is to develop a careful description of different patterns that were expected during the exploratory stage. The objective is to describe how something is without explaining why (Yin, 2003).

Explanatory research is used when the researcher is searching for a cause and effect relationship, to be able to create theory that can be used to explain empirical generalizations (Eriksson & Wiedesheim-Paul, 2001). Explanation is the superlative of understanding in a learning environment (Gomm et.al. 2000).

The previously stated problem discussion and the formulation of our research questions, combined with the above definitions of research purposes will help us to decide what methodology structure is appropriate. The conclusion is that this study could be classified as descriptive and to some extent exploratory.

Research Approach

A basic distinction can be made between a quantitative and a qualitative research method. In most situations, numbers describe the quantitative data, and words describe the qualitative data (Blaxter et.al. 2001). Qualitative research tends to offer more detail about the subject, with data in large scale, which is often perceived as "facts". On the other hand quantitative research is concerned with collecting and analyzing information in many forms. It tends to focus on exploring in detail, which provides more precision (ibid).

The purpose of this thesis is to describe the various aspects of PR in organizations. Since these factors need to be studied in detail to be able to gain a better understanding, it is appropriate to use a qualitative research method.

There are two ways of drawing conclusions, inductive and deductive. The inductive way to draw conclusions is founded on empirical data. The researcher establishes theories and models that are based on different phenomena in reality. The deductive approach means that the researcher is using existing theories and investigates these empirically with different methods. (Eriksson & Wiedesheim-Paul, 2001). The frame of reference in this study is based on existing theories and therefore the approach is deductive.

Research Strategy

According to Yin (2003) there are five different strategies for research. These research strategies are; Experiments, surveys, Archival analysis, history and case studies. Some of these strategies are better suited than others for dealing with specific issues, and a crucial thing for good research is that strategy choices are done rationally.

The case study is ideally suited to the needs and resources of a small-scale researcher, because it allows for a focus on one or few examples. Data in case studies are drawn from people's experiences, which allow the researcher to show the complexity of real life circumstances.

(Blaxter et.al. 2001). Relationships and processes within a social setting tend to connect and relate. To understand one factor, it is important to understand many others, to be able to see how different parts are linked together. The case study approach offers a good chance to review the complexities of a given situation. When concentrating efforts on one case rather than many, there can be insights gained from the individual situation, which had not been discovered through the use of a broader research strategy (Denscombe, 2003). Since the research approach chosen in this thesis is qualitative, and the focus lays on providing a better understanding of processes and relations within a specific company utilizing PR, the best suited research strategy is the case study. As above stated by Denscombe (2003), the case study is the best way to penetrate and investigate a single or few complex situations, which is the purpose of this study. According to Yin (2003) evidence from multiple cases is more convincing since you get a larger amount of data to support the solidness of the study. Therefore we have conducted case studies at two Swedish banks, SEB and Handelsbanken.

DATA COLLECTION METHOD

According to Yin (2003) the field of qualitative research has six forms of sources of evidence for collecting data. These six forms are: documentation, archival records, interviews, direct observations, participant observations and physical artifacts.

Documentation is important for almost every case study. Documents can be letters, memoranda, agendas, newspapers clippings or other articles in mass media or community newsletters. In case studies documentation is best used to confirm and argument evidence from other sources (Yin, 2003). General information about the companies has been found at their web pages and in printed material such as annual reports.

Interviews are a narrative method of collecting data. The interview consists of two or more participants that engage in a conversation that constitutes a learning process (Blaxter et.al. 2001). To better grasp the research purpose, interviews provides a more in-depth insight into the research area. By interviewing the research is limited to fewer informants with rich information sharing (Denscombe, 2003). According to Yin (2003) the interview is the most important source when it comes to obtaining information within a case study. There are three different kinds of interviews: open-ended interviews, focused interviews and survey interviews. The most common interview is the open-ended, where the researcher asks questions about a certain issue as well as letting the respondent to propose his or her own insights and opinions about the matter. A focused interview can be open-ended but the interview is often done faster. The researcher is also most likely following pre-made questions. A survey interview is structured in the way that the researcher is following a more strict form of questions, similar to formal survey. It is focused on collecting quantitative data. (Yin, 2003).

Due to the nature of the research we have used a mix of open-ended and focused interviews. With an interview guide as a foundation, the respondents were able to talk freely about the aspects surrounding the questions.

According to Eriksson & Wiedersheim-Paul (2001) there are two kinds of data, primary and secondary data. Primary data is gathered directly by the researcher with a specific purpose in mind. Secondary data is what past researchers already have gathered for their own various purposes. The interview is our primary data and the documentation is our secondary data.

Sample Selection

After selecting a suitable research strategy, we chose companies to take part in our study. After initial phone-calls to organizations in the banking industry, we found two nation-wide banks that where interested to participate and also could provide interesting cases for our research. Those were Handelsbanken and SEB. The particular banks where chosen due to the understanding that large organizations, especially in the banking industry, were most likely to have researchable PR-activities. A problem when conducting research on larger organizations is to get access to right persons and departments. During the preliminary phone-calls we were able to book interviews with the right respondents at the banks information and communication departments. We interviewed Mr Sten Törnsten, Head of communications at SEB, and Mrs Elisa Saarinen, corporate communications director at Handelsbanken. To get insight in the local activities at the banks, we met for an interview with Mr Jan Persson, branch office manager at Handelsbanken in Luleå. We also had a telephone interview with Mr Markus Isaksson, branch manager at SEB in Piteå. Since all persons interviewed are directly involved in communication and information issues at key level, they could provide relevant data for our research.

The interviews with Sten Törnsten and Elisa Saarinen were conducted by telephone since they were stationed at the bank headquarters in Stockholm. Our research was conducted from Luleå University of Technology. Also Markus Isaksson in Piteå was interviewed by telephone. The interviews were recorded after approval from the respondents to complement our own notes taken during the interview. In this way we could return to the recorded material at any time if needed. The interview with Jan Persson was conducted face to face at Handelsbanken's office in Luleå.

Analysis of Data

A case study should start with a general analytical strategy that provides the basis for what to analyze and why. There are three different general analytical methods: Relying on theoretical propositions, thinking about rival explanations, or developing a case description. Yin (2003) says that without a general analytic strategy, a case study analysis will be difficult to carry out.

According to Yin (2003) the first strategy, relying on theoretical propositions, is the most preferred. It means that you are following the theoretical propositions that led to your case study. The original objectives and design of the case study presumably were based on such propositions, which in return reflected a set of research questions, review of the literature, and new hypotheses or propositions.

Thinking about rival explanations tries to define and test rival explanations; this can also be related to the first strategy. The final strategy is developing a case description; this is according to Yin the least preferred, but it can be used when you have problems making either of the other approaches work.

In this thesis we have used the method of relying on theoretical propositions. The research questions are developed and built on the basis of previous studies, and the findings are compared to the previous research conclusion. We started to analyze the collected data using within-case analysis, comparing existing theories to our empirical findings. After the single cases where analyzed, a cross-case analysis was made to distinguish similarities and differences and to draw conclusions based on the analysis between the banks (Yin, 2003).

Validity & Reliability

In all research, the methods and conclusions need to be justified. This justification has to demonstrate the nature of the decisions taken during the research, and on which ground the decisions are reasonable for the reader (Denscombe, 2003).

Reliability

Reliability is concerned with how reliable and accurate the research methods and techniques for collecting data are. The reliability is a way of measuring how well a method provides a researcher with the same results, if the method were to be repeated under the same circumstances. If a method is not reliable, it also lacks validity, but high reliability does not automatically mean high validity. It is possible to use a method that would provide the researcher with the exact same results under different occasions, without actually measuring what was intended to measure (Yin, 2003). According to Denscombe (2003) the meaning of reliability is whether research instruments are neutral, and if doing a similar study, same results will be achieved.

We have tried to be as objective as possible when handling and evaluating the collected data. A digital-recorder was used during the telephone interviews. By using a digital-recorder others can review the interview answers, and we can also double-check the material afterwards. We also tried to avoid biasing the respondents' answers by asking leading questions. The interviews where conducted in Swedish and thereafter translated into English, therefore some minor translation errors can have occurred, which can affect the reliability.

Validity

The meaning of validity is whether your methods, approaches and techniques actually measure and relate to the problem that has been explored (Blaxter et.al. 2001). Validity is defined as an instrument's ability to measure exactly what it is supposed to measure (Eriksson & Wiedesheim-Paul, 2001). There are according to Yin (2003) three forms of validity, construct-, internal-, and external validity. When establishing construct validity the researcher makes sure that the correct operational measures are utilized for the concepts being studied, and that objective judgment is used to collect data. Internal validity is only of relevance if conducting an explanatory study, and since we are not conducting an explanatory study this is of no relevance. Finally, external validity refers to establishing of the domain to which the findings to a study can be generalized. Since our sample is small, and the study qualitative, we are not aiming to generalize (Yin, 2003).

Two or more methods are used in order to complement each other. Combined they can produce differing but supporting ways of collecting data with increased validity as a result (Denscombe, 2003). By using interviews and documentation, the construct validity of this study was increased. To further increase the validity, a simplified outline of the interview guide was sent to the respondents in advance. This gave our respondents the possibility to prepare for the interview and to obtain the correct information. After the interviews were documented, they were sent to the respondents for corrective reading.

According to Denscombe (2003) direct contact at the interview enables that data can be checked for accuracy and relevance, as it is collected. When interviewing by telephone we were not able to see the facial reactions of the respondents, but were are able to get back to any issues and ask them directly if there was anything left unclear.

8

Empirical Data

This chapter will present the empirical data which consist of case studies of two banks, namely SEB and Handelsbanken. First we will present a background of the companies followed by the data collected through the interviews. The data for the case of SEB is based on the interview with Sten Törnsten, head of communications, and Markus Isaksson, local branch manager in Piteå. In the case of Handelsbanken, the data is based on the interview conducted with Elisa Saarinen, head of corporate communications, and Jan Persson, local branch manager in Luleå.

CASE ONE: SEB

Introduction

The SEB Group is a North European financial group for corporate customers, institutions and private individuals with ten home markets in the Nordic and Baltic countries, Germany, Poland and Ukraine. As a financial partner for companies, institutions and private individuals, SEB Group operates within retail and private banking, merchant banking, investment banking, asset management and life insurance. SEB Group has 680 branch offices and five million customers, of whom about 2 million use the Internet for their banking transactions. The SEB Group is represented in 20 countries around the world with about 20,000 employees and an annual net income of SEK 28 billions. The main competitors of SEB are large national banks with similar products and services:

Föreningssparbanken, Handelsbanken, Länsförsäkringar Bank, Nordea, and Skandiabanken.

The SEB Group is noted at Stockholm Stock Exchange with about 300 000 shareholders such as institutions, mutual funds and private individuals. Foreign shareholders count for 25 percent of the shares, and Swedish owners for 75 percent. The two largest Swedish shareholders are Investor and Trygg-foundation, with 28 percent of the total shares. In Sweden the SEB Group has about 200 branches all over the country which serves both private individuals and company customers. This division is called Nordic Retail & Private Banking with about 4700 employees and an annual net income of SEK 8.5 billions. From now on SEB Nordic Retail & Private Banking is named just as SEB, while SEB Group with all divisions is named SEB Group.

For private individuals SEB offers solutions regarding everything from paying bills to share-trading and financing for accommodation. As far as your savings are concerned, SEB has both expertise and solutions, regardless of whether you want to save for a summerhouse or for your pension. Through Internet services, telephone banking and mobile banking services, SEB is available to the customers regardless of time and place. With in-depth knowledge of the Swedish corporate market and a range of services for all types of companies and businesses, SEB has the ability to support companies with the services needed.

Roles and Objectives at SEB

In late 70s and early 80s PR started to have a more active role within SEB. Back then, the first employees with PR competence were hired to the company and were given resources from top management to actively start working with PR activities. During the recent ten years, much has happened regarding communication both within SEB, and in the banking industry in general.

There is no general definition of the term PR that is utilized within the SEB Group. PR is used in a structured way in the whole organization and the definition can vary between top management level at headquarter and local level at some of the 200 branches. The definition of PR varies depending on what is involved in it. From an overall perspective at central level SEB defines PR as: "All contacts with media initiated by the bank itself, and media publicity as a result of other activities initiated by the bank".

According to Sten Törnsten: "Everything that is a result of direct or indirect activities by the bank that leads to publicity is defined as PR".

At SEB there is a view of PR as the activities that lead to publicity in media. The company works with communication towards other target groups than public media, but this is not by SEB defined as PR as it is in general theories. Communication directed to internal target groups falls under the definition "internal communication" and the communication process with existing and potential customers goes into the field of marketing. From now on in the case when mentioning the term of PR, it involves all of SEBs communication activities that falls into a broader definition of PR.

SEB has a broad definition of its "publics", in other words which groups are included in the target group. These are: customers, potential customers, employees, the rest of the community including citizens and companies that today are not customers of SEB, public media, authorities and other decision makers. In principle, all of the groups mentioned above are involved in the target group of the company. SEB works differently with the various target groups, depending on the ambition and importance of the relation.

The overall objectives with PR activities at SEB are to confirm existing customers that they have chosen the "right" bank, and that SEB wants to keep them as customers. The objectives are also to reach out to new and potential customers with offers, and to reinforce the brand and the image of the organization. These objectives are then split up into the different target groups for further development. The SEB Group has formulated an overall objective in the communication policy at top management level. The policy has no end in it self, it is stated to secure that SEB Group in its daily business can reach the goals that are set, which are; to have satisfied customers, good result, profitability from the business, and to get employees motivated. The overall communication policy is a steering document which is revised annually. Based on the overall communication policy, strategies and goals of different target groups are set and further developed into goals of specific PR activities. The top management is highly involved in the communication strategies of the SEB Group. The overall communication policy, which controls the image, and how to behave and act within the organization, comes to decision in the group executive committee. The communication policy has a long time perspective but is readjusted annually. An annuall operative communication plan is also developed by the group executive committee which controls more in detail how different activities will be held and managed. Separate plans are created for the information departments and marketing departments. These operative plans act as frameworks at divisional level on how to operate, and are implemented down to branch level to coordinate how to communicate in sales and customer activities.

At the division of Nordic Retail & Private Banking, there is an information department and a marketing department, both highly involved in PR activities. This type of structure is the same through the entire organization, from highest group level to underlying divisional level, with the main focus and the "engine" of PR activities at the information department. Most of the employees involved in PR activities are located at the information departments, and often also the marketing department is involved in different projects in cooperation with the information department. The PR activities are included both in the information and marketing plan, with an overlap between the areas. When designing media activities, SEB cooperates with advertising agencies and media agencies to get professional assistance. When designing PR activities, PR agencies are used at rare occasions in specific projects. Mostly SEB rely on its internal PR resources within the information and marketing departments.

The policy documents initiated by top management are not measurable; in fact they should be seen as frameworks for the entire organization. On the other hand, in yearly operative plans, SEB tries to set measurable goals to be able to follow up the results of specific activities such as projects, advertisements, press releases and channels like the intranet and the Internet website. At lower level, SEB always tries to set up measurable goals for the PR activities. According to SEB, PR activities are important because they create value for the organization, through keeping the customers satisfied and loyal. By the nature of the intangible bank services and the fact that increasing amounts of customers do their bank transactions on the Internet, PR is an important tool for the organization when communicating and maintaining relations with the customers.

SEB knows a great deal of the public opinion about their organization, and what customers feel and think about the bank. This is done by regular and careful measurements by the bank itself, and also by external surveys done by research agencies which examine how customers perceive their bank. Today SEB can observe a positive trend in how customers perceive trust toward the bank. The amount of trust is about the same as before the Swedish bank crisis during early 1990. In general, Swedish bank customers are loyal to their banks and the opinions of the banks are positively increasing. The public opinion of banks is dynamic, especially connected to some products or services during a quick raise or fall at the capital market. This often leads to a question; if the service or advice given by the bank was correct.

It is relatively easy to switch bank in Sweden, even though most of the customers are loyal. By utilizing PR activities, SEB believe that they can change the view and opinion about themselves in the mind of the publics. It is important to really stand up for what you say, and to deliver high quality services, attractive offers, and have competent employees. By doing the right things at the right time, one can improve the picture of the provided message with PR. SEB has flexibility in the PR activities to be able to encounter changes in the public opinion, and the bank has been fairly quick to adapt their PR activities to public opinion overtime. Even though, the time of adapting to a change can be improved.

Within SEB, PR activities are used both to build an image of the organization and to inform and educate about products and services. The recent years, SEB have put extra effort in PR activities that informs and educates about advice services provided by the bank. This is done because bank advice services are becoming increasingly important for the customers. Therefore specialists and experts in different areas inside the bank have been highlighted in the communication to provide their view and recommendations about specific issues of interest to the customers. This is done to give the high competence inside the bank a face in front of the publics. SEB consider that until a couple of years ago, not enough image building activities had been done. Today, SEB have improved with more focus on image building activities.

In PR activities, SEB consider them self as not so proactive as they want to be. Often SEB is more reactive than proactive in their actions. The ambition is to be more proactive and actively shape the image of the organization, instead of using PR to act when questions arise from outside.

Functions and Tools used by SEB

When communicating with different target groups, SEB use PR to reach out and build a relation with customers and publics. The most important relation is between SEB and their customers, followed by media relations. Media publicity is not a goal in itself; instead it should be seen as a medium to reach customers or potential customers. Employee relations called "Internal information" is also an important relation, where PR is utilized actively to inform and stimulate employees. In financial relations PR is also used to get editorial space in the media to influence and inform potential investors and stakeholders. The least dominant, but still important relation in SEB's communication strategy is the public affairs, the communication with various governmental institutions and decision makers. It is least important since the Swedish Bankers' Association usually manages this relation commissioned by the member banks of the association.

The most common PR tools used by SEB are image building activities like press releases, regular reports and speeches. SEB puts great focus on the personal contact with the customers. Therefore at branch level, the personal contact is an important tool. The company website is another important PR tool which SEB put much effort on. Almost fifty per cent of the customers use Internet services to do their bank transactions. Therefore this channel is useful to inform, educate and build relations with the customers. The least important tool used by SEB is publications. They have a great amount of printed publications and brochures, but today more effort is instead put on e-activities such as the website and the Internet bank.

On local level, the branch manager is responsible of marketing activities such as advertising and PR. Regarding advertising, the branches are highly regulated through a common graphical profile and platform of messages on how to act in media. There are clear guidelines on what to do or not. When dealing with PR activities the freedom of action is higher. It is the branch manager's responsibility to take care of the in-house resources available at local level, and to utilize the resources from central level in best way with activities suited at branch level. Tools are utilized both to maintain existing customers and obtain new customers. These tools include for example; local events, editorial space about savings and transactions in local magazines and customized product packages at local festivals or events. The intention to act at local level is to provide genuine knowledge held within SEB to develop a relationship between the bank and its customers. There is a plan at SEB to create extended guidelines for PR to help the branch managers to act more effectively. Today the branch manager must act both as a marketing and information manager when dealing with local activities concerning advertising and PR.

When working with media activities at the Information department, SEB have no structured framework for planning, implementation and follow-up of activities that generate publicity. They work on a daily basis in a structured way, but with no documented strategies. When dealing with other PR tools, SEB have a well-structured framework and strategy for planning, implementing and follow-up to secure the results of the activities. There is no general framework for all activities; instead every activity has its own framework or model developed for its specific function. For the executives there is an evaluation toolbox available for measuring of PR activities.

SEB's bank services contains intensive customer relations through face to face meetings at branches, by regular phone calls, self-service phones, the webpage, internet banking transactions and ATMs. Over time, the non-personal contacts have become increasingly important. In the marketing mix, SEB believes that PR, and especially personal relationships are the most important parts, followed by other components such as advertising.

Evaluation of PR activities is done at different levels at SEB. There is an intention to measure what is measurable, how many have seen the activity, and what the public think about it. This is done through interviews and surveys. SEB also measure the customers' opinion and the public opinion to see how the bank is perceived. This is done by regular weekly surveys performed by a research agency. Together with other infrequent external reports regarding customers and target groups, this gives a comprehensive picture of the penetration of the initiated activities, the public opinion about the bank and how the opinion changes over time.

Today, these activities are important to get a complete knowledge base for decision making. Media tracking is done on a daily basis by internal resources. External reports are also purchased quarterly from Observer, a tracking agency, which measure how SEB have figured in media and the characteristics of the publicity, if it is positive or negative. SEB also purchase annual reports that provide information about the view and opinion expressed by journalists about SEB including top management. At SEB, measuring, follow-ups and evaluation, has been improved and made more effective the recent ten years.

Trust and Reputation at SEB

In SEB the most important trust building activity is the contact with customers whenever it is physical, by phone or at Internet. One of the greatest advantages with good PR, if used in right way, is that it can strengthen positive values and trends amongst the publics. It is harder to handle and manage negative issues with PR. The effects of negative issues can be toned down but not eliminated by using PR. Activities regarding PR should first of all be used to handle positive issues, but can also if needed be used to fend of negative issues. External reports have said that PR activities initiated by SEB develop trust with their customers. There is a positive development in the customers' attitudes towards trusting the bank. Even though, SEB can be more effective in the communication and PR activities with their customers. If more emphasis is put on pro-activity and higher integration with the target groups, trust and reputation would be easier to develop. The trust and reputation developed by PR activities can be seen as a complement to the concrete face-to-face customer relation when creating loyalty and customer satisfaction. SEB also believes that active initiative with PR activities can change corporate reputation in a short period of time.

It is few industries where reputation and trust is of such high importance as it is in the banking industry. It is a result of the banks intangible products and services, which includes managing of the entire economy of private and corporate customers. By developing trust and reputation, SEB can achieve competitive advantages against their competitors, which can help generating new customers. Already existing loyal customers can be seen as a receipt of appreciation of the activities in the bank, and the developed trust and reputation influences this appreciation positively. Managed correctly, trust and reputation developed between SEB and their customers, mediate signals about the bank as a trustable and credible partner also in the future.

The importance of protecting and upholding corporate reputation will be increasing in importance for years ahead. Seen over time, corporate reputation at SEB has become more important and has involved the group executive committee in higher degree. Another development seen over time, past ten to fifteen years, is the integration of communication strategies throughout the entire organization, and the integration of communication strategies in the daily work at all levels within the SEB Group.

CASE TWO: HANDELSBANKEN

Handelsbanken is one of the major Swedish banks with approximately 9 400 employees and an annual net income 2004 of SEK 13.1 billion. With 455 branches in Sweden, they have a strong position on the Swedish bank market. Over the past 15 years, banking operations has been developed in the Nordic countries, making Handelsbanken to one of the largest Nordic banks. In addition Handelsbanken also operates in Great Britain and 13 other countries. Handelsbanken's competitors are all the major banks in Sweden and the Nordic countries; SEB, Föreningssparbanken, Nordea, Länsförsäkringar Bank and Skandiabanken. Handelsbanken is noted at the Stockholm Stock Exchange, with approximately 115 000 shareholders, most of them private individuals. About 50 percent of the shares are owned by Swedish institutional holders, such as insurance and investment companies.

Handelsbanken is delivering complete universal banking services, in other words they provide services in the whole banking sector. Their goal is to do so with better service and lower costs than their competitors. In general, the profitability should be kept higher than the industry average. Handelsbanken's cost effective strategy have shown results; the past 33 years they have had higher profitability than their average competitors, they have been the most cost effective bank in Europe for many years, and they have been ranked having constantly high levels of customer satisfaction for the past 15 years.

To be able to understand Handelsbanken's corporate philosophy one has to review the history of the bank. In the 1970s the bank did undergo a large change moving towards a strong decentralized strategy, where the local branches got plenty of responsibility. It is the local branches that decide what to communicate and market to the customers, leaving no room for a central marketing department. This is a unique concept in the bank market where organizations generally are strongly centralized. The decentralized way of thinking results in the organizations lead philosophy; the branch office is the bank, and the bank is the branch office.

Roles and Objectives at Handelsbanken

At Handelsbanken there is a strong belief that the local offices, working close to local market, have the best knowledge of what products and services are needed, and in what way it is proper to encounter the important publics of that area. This is a unique way of working that cannot be seen in many companies. Working in this way, there is no central control over what is to be communicated, it is the local branches that have total responsibility to decide how and when to communicate, and market their services to the publics. The local managers decide what actions to take when contacting local press, local authorities and other local organizations. The local manager also plans the future of the branch office. At Handelsbanken there is no requirement for a homogenous design of the local offices as demanded in many other organizations. Instead it is encouraged to be different and find new ways to reach the overall objectives. The branch office is supposed to resemble the branch manager and his employees.

At central level contacts with central authorities, interest groups, organizations and nation wide media are handled. International PR contacts are also handled at central level. The central communication department is working as a supporting function for local branches, handling general issues. But all local events and happenings are handled by local managers, even if it would be national TV, looking into the activities of a local branch office. Handelsbanken's objectives with PR are to market the bank in best possible way, and to develop a strong and lasting long-term relationship with the publics.

The way of organizing utilized by Handelsbanken, leaves little work for the central communications department at the local field where products and services actually are sold. One of the main tasks of the communication department is actually to keep on encouraging decentralization and preventing things from being centralized. Responsibility is in this way pushed out to branch level of the organization. It is a task that has taken 35 years to establish in the organization, but can according to Handelsbanken be ruined during a coffee-break.

At Handelsbanken it is believed that the names or the structure of the departments does not decide how important PR is for an organization. The important part is that you reach out to the publics with your message in one way or another. This is a unique concept regarding the PR activities. Therefore at central level of Handelsbanken, there is no particular department or person responsible for PR activities. Instead it is seen as an unwritten responsibility of the entire head of management. The closest department, handling issues nearly related to PR is the corporate communication department. The group executive managers are highly involved in national level and international PR activities, especially regarding national authority contacts. To some extent all of the departments are involved in different PR situations when meeting and working with people outside the bank. When developing Handelsbanken's PR and communication strategies, the board of directors is not involved. The strategies are created by top management in close cooperation with the CEO. The communication strategies provide general communication guidelines that are passed down in the organization. These describe how to act, and explain what parts are important to handle regarding internal and external communication. There are no written objectives for PR at central level. Instead there is what is very closely related, communication guidelines. Every local branch office is free to develop their own written objectives for PR activities, within the general guidelines.

Handelsbanken has no centrally managed marketing or advertising. There is a belief that a central management cannot have knowledge of an entire market, and therefore there is no purpose of having any central marketing or marketing department. It is the local offices working closely to the customers, that knows how, and when to market, and therefore marketing has become entirely their responsibility. Customers in different geographical areas has interest in diverse services and products during different times, which encourages that all marketing efforts should be carried out locally.

According to Handelsbanken PR activities are bringing value by resulting in strong and good relationships with various publics. These relationships are important to maintain, but does not always result in the outcome that Handelsbanken wish for. For example relations with media can be fine, but does not stop the newspaper from writing an article with negative bias if they have the possibility to do so. The newspaper is also doing their job, filling their pages with exciting news. Therefore bad publicity does not necessary need to be the result of a poorly maintained relationship with the media.

Handelsbanken believes that the view and attitude of the organization can be changed with PR, and since Handelsbanken is perceived by the publics as very local, this is best done locally. Since there is no top-down management in Handelsbanken's organization, there is a large flexibility at local level to adjust PR activities to meet the publics' opinions in best possible way.

Handelsbanken defines their publics as very broad; it contains existing customers, future customers and everyone that could be interested in the banks' services in the future. The most important of these groups is existing customers. The relationship with them is mainly maintained with PR activities, such as personal relations.

Handelsbanken experience benefits from other banks TV-advertising campaigns. Internal investigations show that customers of Handelsbanken mix up the names of large banks that conducts TV-advertising, and believes that they have seen Handelsbanken in TV-advertising even though they have none. According to Handelsbanken the large banks are to such a high degree similar, that customers do not always register the differences. This is a strong motivation to not use national advertising. Handelsbanken does not utilize PR image campaigns in general aspect, but the central PR is to a large degree an image building activity towards different national interest groups. The central activities are aiming towards building an image in the central community. The local PR-activities are to a larger degree related to informing and educating about products and services. But also image building elements can be found locally with speeches, special events, and meetings with local decision makers.

In the aspect of being proactive versus reactive in PR activities, Handelsbanken is to a high degree utilizing a proactive strategy. Even though the bank acts reactively when needed for example to fend of rumours in a publicity situation, the majority of their activities are proactive in their nature, such as informing and building relationships at local level.

Functions and Tools used by Handelsbanken

All relations that involve the organizations customers are very important for Handelsbanken. Also internal relations are described as very important when considering the fact that Handelsbanken is a large organization with approximately 9 400 employees. Extensive effort is spent in internal employee relations, to be able to build shared values inside the organization. In opposite, public affair relations are not given as much time and energy as customer and internal relations. This reveals that not all of the interest groups are as important in the PR activities. And naturally the same energy is not put in all of them.

Handelsbanken emphasize the importance of utilizing every possible tool in their PR activities. If there is a tool that can provide value in the PR activities, it should be utilized. This is with exception of corporate image campaigns, which are not frequently utilized by Handelsbanken. It can generally not be said that any of the tools are more usual than the other. What tools are used at what time varies between different branch offices, since most decisions are taken at local level to best meet the local customers' needs. At central level, Handelsbanken has an in-house advertising department, which help the branches to carry out locally planned marketing and PR activities. This function is seen as a support for the local branches that not always hold advertising knowledge and competence locally. At Handelsbanken there is no framework at central level used for planning and implementing the overall PR activities. It is the local branches that are working with the actual activities that can utilize these kinds of structures if it is found necessary. At central level there is no evaluation framework that is used to evaluate PR efforts. It is once again the responsibility of the local branches to evaluate their own PR-activities if it is a priority. In other hand revenue and efficiency of the local offices are evaluated centrally. There is an idea that the economic figures can give good signals of how well the branch offices are managed. With good economic results and high efficiency, local managers are also probably managing PR activities successfully, and therefore no further evaluation is necessary. The PR activities are seen as one of the means of delivering a good result. But there is no interest of evaluation the PR or communication itself. According to Jan Persson, local activities are evaluated only from an efficiency perspective. The outcome of effective PR-activities can according to Handelsbanken be seen in the increasing amount of customers, or in an increased amount of services that existing customers are utilizing. Therefore there is no specific evaluation of PR at local level.

Jan Persson at the local branch in Luleå describes their PR activities as highly customer focused. The most important part in PR, where Jan Persson has laid main focus, is in building and maintaining personal relationships. The staff is organized in small units and thereafter stimulated and encouraged to establish customer contacts. There is an intentional strategy with events and personal relations as the most important parts. These categories include for example; breakfast meetings, share and investment information meetings, real estate displays, and local events such as industry trade shows or special event days at the university. PR activities are utilized both to maintain existing customer relations and to interest new customers from the publics. To acquire new corporate customers, the branch office in Luleå is utilizing an ambassador program. In this program existing corporate customers are chosen to be ambassadors and promote Handelsbanken to other companies in various settings. Even though the local office is not utilizing publicity as a frequent tool, it is very important to maintain good relations with local media. Jan Persson further explains that PR through the local website is gaining more importance for the bank. This area is under constant improvement since a large and constantly increasing amount of customers integrates with the bank through the website. At local level all the branches have their own websites that they can utilize in the communication with local customers.

As a part of the marketing mix, PR is a very important element for Handelsbanken. The importance of the PR function is pointed out, when saying that it is something utilized by all branch managers at more than 600 offices, all the time. Only because Handelsbanken does not put emphasize at central management of PR, it does not get less important. The PR function can also be seen as more important since Handelsbanken does not have any traditional marketing department. The traditional marketing tasks are instead handled locally. The importance for Handelsbanken to be visible and to constantly communicate in the local society is imposed with great importance. The focus of the entire organizations activities actually lays on personal relations and communication with the local publics. The entire concept and success of Handelsbanken builds on the belief of importance in local relations. Handelsbanken has a model of how to work with publicity. At occasions PR agencies can be hired to do some PR work. Handelsbanken is also using tracking services from external agencies to track publicity in traditional newspapers, on-line newspapers, Television and radio. Handelsbanken sees no further need for having in-house personnel for working with evaluation of the publicity since the bank's efficiency is measured through economic results. After the publicity has been tracked it is reviewed by the corporate communication department, and the head of corporate communications, mainly to build a knowledge base of where publicity of Handelsbanken has appeared, and in what purpose. In rare occasions there is need for taking further actions after receiving publicity.

Trust and Reputation at Handelsbanken

Handelsbanken believes that the most central part of PR, when developing a base of trust with the publics, is the personal relationship. To have a person representing the organization in a confidence-inspiring way in different situations and settings is very important. At Handelsbanken there is a belief that trust is not always developed buy how much you are seen in public occasions, but how you are appearing when doing so. When trust is developed with customers, their loyalty and satisfaction is also increased. Handelsbanken has seen support of the relation of trust and loyalty in different opinion polls since 1989. In these opinion polls, Handelsbanken has been ranked at a constantly high level, confirming their success in communicating at local level.

When considering the building of corporate reputation, Handelsbanken believes that a large part of it lies within the PR activities. Some importance also lies in the concept of not being visible in all situations. To not be the most modern and active organization can be a PR goal in itself. Since many people and stakeholders understand the concept of Handelsbanken, they also know what is delivering value in the bank's services and products. The customers expect that Handelsbanken continues to act locally in a small scale. The continuity and recognition of the concept in the communication and PR, is what develops trust. There is actually an objective at Handelsbanken to create as little news publicity as possible, since news creation is not seen as a trust developing tool. Handelsbanken views trust as something that can be created during a relatively short period of time. Especially when managing new customers that does not know that much about the organizations way of working.

Good reputation is extremely important when selling financial products and services. A bank needs to develop trust when selling their products and services since money, loans and savings, is a sensitive matter for private customers and companies. A good reputation is not possible to build if not top management works towards the same objectives and avoid scandals. Good reputation can only be developed if no scandals have occurred for many years. According to Handelsbanken organizations often have a belief that PR can make everything right again, no matter what scandal have occurred, but this is not always the case. The importance of managing an organizations reputation has according to Handelsbanken had a constant and stable importance over the long-run. Corporate reputation is not seen as something that has gained in importance since past time, or will probably not gain further importance in the future. There can possibly be some differences in the importance of corporate reputation during a business cycle, affecting people's behaviour. During good times, reputation is not that important, but when turning into a recession, the reputation gains in importance.

According to Handelsbanken there is a risk with being a stable company. During calm times one can get accused for being a boring organization. Elisa Saarinen says that "Stable can be boring, but a bank should not be such an adventure either." Since Handelsbanken is not changing extensively, and stays stable in the long-run, it is believed that they are succeeding to send signals to the publics, that they are going to be a reliable supplier also in the future. The reputation of an organization is measured during a long period of time, and since Handelsbanken works with a long-term perspective in mind, they succeed with doing this. Since succeeding in building a strong and stable corporate reputation, Handelsbanken definitely believes that they get advantages against their competitors.

9

Data Analysis

In this chapter the empirical data presented in chapter four will be analysed and compared to the theories brought up in the conceptual framework based on the literature review. First a within-case analysis will be conducted of the two cases. Further a cross-case analysis will be made to compare the two cases with each other.

WITHIN CASE ANALYSIS OF SEB

Roles and Objectives

Definitions

At SEB top management level PR is defined as: "All contacts with media initiated by the bank itself, and media publicity as a result of other activities initiated by the bank". In other words: "Everything that is a result of direct or indirect activities by the bank that leads to publicity is defined as PR". This definition is not direct in line with definitions stated in theory, but not that far away either. Partly, it is in line with the statement "using communications to build and hold goodwill" provided by Hutton (1999).

Lages & Simkin (2003) state that it is hard to define the content of PR, and what it actually involves. At SEB PR is viewed as activities that lead to publicity in media. The company works also with communication toward other target groups than public media, but this is not by SEB defined as PR as it is in general theories. This supports the theories that PR is hard to define.

Objectives and Strategies

According to Dolphin & Fan (2000) a communication strategy is essential for any organization. It needs to be managed and formulated by the information director in close cooperation with the executive team. The role of the information director is to act as a bridge between his organization and its audiences, and in this way help to create or sustain the corporate image or reputation. The SEB Group have formulated an overall goal in their communication policy at top management level. The policy is developed by the head of the communication department in cooperation with top management. The policy is used as a framework to reach the goals of the organization in the daily operations. SEB is therefore partly in line with theory.

Dolphin & Fan (2000) and Nakra (2000) state that when shaping the PR strategy, considerations must be given to the nature of the organization; to its vision, mission and to its key audiences. PR activities must also be involved early in developing strategies for building and maintaining the corporate image and reputation. Within SEB this can be seen through the development of the communication policy which regulates the PR activities at lower levels in the organization. Consideration is given to the vision and key audiences when developing the policy documents, and therefore SEB support theory.

PR has a key role in the strategic planning of an organization, and should therefore be closely linked to the organizations board room through an information director (Dolphin & Fan, 2001). In line with theory, at SEB, the top management and the board of directors are to a great extent involved in the strategic communication decisions. Jefkins (2000) describes the ideal structure of the PR department as independent and directly responsible to the CEO. However if the PR executive instead is positioned in the marketing, advertising or sales promotion department, the use of PR is strictly limited. At SEB the information (PR) department is located directly under top management. Mainly, the PR functions are located at the information department, but some of the functions are located at the marketing department that is in close cooperation with the information department. SEB disagrees with theory since cooperation between the departments does not strictly limit the PR activities.

According to Lages & Simkin (2003) PR as a management discipline is much wider than a communication technique or a specialized program, such as media relations. It is also important if you master the technical skill to know why and when to use them. SEB is developing and implementing the strategic goals at different levels making PR to a management discipline. From top management down to branch level it is secured that the right tool or activity is used at right time and place. Therefore it can be found that SEB is in line with theory.

Most organizations realize the importance of effective communications with its publics. Establishment of ongoing, reliable and respected external communication processes should be a priority (Wells & Spinks, 1999). SEB agrees with theory, and believe that PR is an important tool when building and maintaining communications. It also creates value to the organization, because it generates satisfied and loyal customers. Further SEB agrees with Lynn (1999) that communication can increase value through creating brand awareness in the community.

Hon (1998) points out that there is a tremendous variability in organizations explanations of public relations goals and objectives, perhaps reflecting the diversity of organizations represented. Each department divides its responsibilities differently, and not surprisingly, priorities tend to reflect the mission of the organization. This is in line with SEB where strategies and goals with PR activities change dependent on organizational level and function within the organization.

Hon (1998) discusses further that PR goals and objectives have to be "strategic", meaning that PR goals and objectives must be tied directly to organizational goals and objectives. This is in line with how SEB strategically work with PR. At lower levels the communication guidelines and policy documents helps to develop written, quantifiable goals and objectives for the PR activities. By using these guidelines and policy documents SEB can secure that the PR activities are tied directly to the organizational goals.

According to Wells et.al. (2003) there are numerous objectives with PR strategies. Usually these objectives focus on creating credibility, delivering information, and building positive images. SEBs objectives of building relationships, find new customers, and to build a positive image fits into this theory. Worcester (1997) describes the attributes of the bank image in the eyes of the public as highly dynamic and never static. Even if it looks static, it is hardly ever so. Wells & Spinks (1999) state that the public opinion is highly dynamic and therefore the PR responses utilized by companies should be actively managed. By using PR activities SEB think that they can change the view and opinion about themselves in the mind of the publics. By utilizing right PR activities at the right moment, SEB is flexible when meeting changes in the public opinion. When looking backwards, great changes have been made within the organization.

SEB have been fairly quick to adapt their PR activities to the public opinion over time, it can therefore be said that they are to in line with theory.

Defining Publics

Schultz & Barnes (1999) and Worcester (1997) emphasize that specific publics should be targeted. Thereafter segmentation with traditional methods can be conducted. SEB has a broad definition of their publics, but specific publics are segmented and targeted in order of importance, with the customer segment as priority, therefore SEBs strategy is partly in line with theory.

Wells & Spinks (1999) recommend establishment of PR activities with the community in hole. SEB partly agrees with this theory. Even though the community is not the most important target group, some PR activities are directed to the entire community.

Proactive PR versus Reactive PR

Public relations can be characterized either as proactive or reactive. Proactive PR is offensive and opportunity seeking to promote products and services. Reactive PR is defensively oriented and problem solving. It is undertaken as a result of external pressure (Shimp, 2000). In the tactics and strategies utilized by SEB, it can be observed that they are somewhere between proactive and reactive with more emphasizing on pro-activity. SEB consider them self not as proactive as they want to. And they are focusing on being more proactive in their future approach.

HUTTON'S FRAMEWORK FOR DEFINING PUBLIC RELATIONS

To be able to define SEBs role in PR, and to be able to plot the bank in Hutton's three dimensional cube we identified where the bank was located in the three dimensions of; initiative, image and interest.

Initiative

SEB is somewhere between proactive and reactive with more emphasis on pro-activity in their PR activities. Therefore SEB can be placed in the middle of the scale between proactive and reactive a little closer to the proactive side.

Image

At SEB the PR activities are used both to build an image of the organization and to inform and educate about products and services. Since the focus today is to inform and educate about the genuine knowledge within the bank, SEB can be placed at the reality side in the image category.

Interest

When examining SEBs main interest as public or client focused, it can be seen that both existing customers and the general publics with future potential customers are in focus. The main emphasize is on existing customers, and therefore SEB can be seen with a slightly stronger focus on the clients than the publics in the interest category.

When plotting the characteristics of SEB into the three dimensional cube, it can be observed that that the nearest role in the framework is role number six, the relationship management role. Hutton (1999) describes the relationship management role as seeking conformance with the clients and publics. The publics support is vital for the organization in its long-term objectives. Emphasize is on mutual trust, cooperation and whenever possible, a win-win situation between the client-organization and the customer. This matches to a great extent the objectives and way of working at SEB.

HUTTON'S HIERARCHY OF PR

When roles, functions and tools of SEB are put into Hutton's hierarchy of PR the following can be observed as an overview of the organization to distinguish different characteristics.

FUNCTIONS AND TOOLS

Types of PR

Wells et.al. (2003) has developed a framework to describe the five different types of PR that refer to relationships with various stakeholders;

- Media relations
- Employee relations
- Financial relations
- Corporate relations
- Public affairs

When observing the relationships of SEB it can be seen that the most important relation is the one between SEB and their customers. This category can be found in media relations, financial relations and corporate relations. Secondly by priority, SEB place media relations. This is not a goal in itself; instead it is a medium to reach their customers and stakeholders. Employee relations are also of high importance within SEB where it is used to stimulate and to motivate employees. The least important relation is public affairs, since the Swedish Banker's Association manages this issue for its members. It can be seen that SEB identifies the same relation categories as described in theory.

The PR Toolkit

The PR toolkit is a five step framework by Phillips (2001) on how to set up PR activities and how to evaluate them. The five steps involved are:

- Audit research
- Objectives
- Strategy and plan
- Measurement and evaluation
- Result

When observing the methods utilized by SEB in setting up PR activities, one can see that some of the steps can be identified in the framework by Phillips (2001). According to Phillips (2001) the objectives must reflect the business goals of an organization. This is observed within SEB through their communication policy and marketing policy at top management level. The policies go further down to develop objectives on local level. PR activities should also be coordinated with the marketing function, which also is the case within SEB. Decisions on levels of measurements must be done to develop a strategy and plan. This is also done by SEB in their planning of PR activities, especially at lower level where the PR activities will be utilized. At SEB things that are measurable are measured and evaluated through surveys and polls, both by internal resources and external agencies to follow up the results of the initiated PR activities.

Disagreeing with theory, SEB state that there is no general toolkit or framework for how to plan, implement and follow up PR activities. Instead every activity has its own framework, quite similar to the PR toolkit by Phillips (2001), developed for its specific function.

PR Tools

Wells et.al. (2003) state that there are three types of PR tools; controlled, uncontrolled and, semi-controlled. SEB explains that they are utilizing most of the tools from the categories. The most common tool for image building activities at SEB are press releases, regular reports and speeches. Interpersonal communication is of high importance at SEB, especially at branch level. This can be seen through the daily personal communication with customers, through events and through customized product packages. Editorial space in local magazines is also used at branch levels. Another important tool is the webpage and foremost the internet bank office where SEB inform, educate and build relations with their customers during their bank transaction visits. The least important tool used by SEB is publications. SEB utilize most of the tools provided in theory.

Effectiveness and Evaluation of PR

To be able to measure the effectiveness of PR activities initiated by the organization, evaluation have to be done. According to Schmitz (2004) it is as important to follow up, measure, and evaluate the PR activities as in fact to implement them. At SEB, evaluation is done at different levels with an intention to measure what is measurable.

It is also stated in theory (Xavier et.al. 2005) and strengthened by SEB that there is no general evaluation method applicable in all situations, instead a variety of methods are used to measure effectiveness within the organization.

A framework developed by Wells et.al. (2003) with common types of evaluation measures helps to answer how awareness, attitudes, and behaviours of the publics have been affected by the PR activities. Most of the evaluation measures in the framework are utilized by SEB and therefore partly in line with theory. Output production, distribution and coverage are measured by interviews, polls and surveys by the bank itself and also by external reports. Systematic content analysis, measures whether articles are positive or negative in their content. These are measured annually by external agents. Regular measuring of awareness, attitudes and behaviours is done both by the bank itself and by external research agencies.

According to Beavers-Moss (2001) it is important for the bank to identify what gain is expected from the PR activities. If the goals are defined explicitly and measurably, they are easier to achieve. The trend today at SEB is to develop extended guidelines for PR to help branch managers to act more effectively to reach the objectives and goals set on higher levels, and therefore SEB support this theory.

The PR effectiveness measurements initiated by banks can be analyzed by using the "Public Relations Effectiveness Yardstick" framework by Lindenmann (1993). This model involves a two-step framework when setting objectives and determining at what level to measure PR effectiveness. The effectiveness is then measured on a three level basis. SEB utilizes frameworks for follow-up and evaluation of the PR activities. SEB has no general model that fits into the theory by Lindenmann (1993). Instead a variety of internally developed methods are used dependent on the PR tool and what is to be measured.

TRUST AND REPUTATION

Trust and Credibility

Saparito et.al. (2004) state that the trusting party must perceive the trusted party as acting out of commitment, which is going beyond the motive of self-interest. To achieve such trust, SEB see the contact with the customers as an important possibility for showing dedication, whether it is in person, by telephone or by the Internet, and therefore SEB is partly in line with theory. According to Kangis & Voukelatos (1997) trustworthiness can positively influence perception of quality, and influence loyalty. Ball et.al. (2004) explain that well structured communications has a strong effect on consumer perception, and leads to trust, satisfaction and loyalty. At SEB the trust developed by PR activities can be seen as a complement to the meetings with customers in various settings when creating customer loyalty and satisfaction. SEB has also recently developed their advice and information services for their customers. The bank has realized that when selling financial services, professional advice and information can enhance the relationship with the customer. SEB has understood the importance of trustworthiness, and is therefore consistent with theory.

Corporate Reputation

Dolphin (2000) explains that corporate reputation can win competitive advantages for an organization in a crowded marketplace. It is a visible signal of an organization's capabilities. SEB explains that there are few industries where reputation is of such importance as in the banking industry. By managing the organization reputation, SEB can achieve competitive advantages against their competitors. This is in line with the theory. Bank marketers must know how to protect and uphold their reputation, since credibility and value is to a high degree gained from it (Beavers-Moss, 2001). According to Hutton et.al. (2001) the loss of organizational reputation is seen as a large problem. SEB agrees in these statements and emphasizes the importance of reputation when selling such intangible products as financial services.

Budd (1995) explains that corporate reputation is gained over time and is not easily changed. SEB does not support this theory and believes that the corporate reputation can be changed in the view of the publics in a relatively short period of time with active PR management.

According to Hutton et.al. (2001) reputation management is an emerging business function that gains importance in organizations. According to Dolphin (2004) the management of reputation has developed into an important tool for communication strategists. According to Weiss et.al. (1999) it does not need to occur in response to a reputation problem, it can be both reactive and proactive. According to SEB, the importance of reputation management has increased in the present time and it is involving the group executive committee in higher degree. The focus has moved more into a proactive strategy even though also reactive responses still are important. The last ten to fifteen years there can also bee observed an evolvement at SEB, where the importance of integration of the PR activities in reputation management throughout the entire organization has increased, and therefore it can be said that SEB agrees with theory.

WITHIN CASE ANALYSIS OF HANDELSBANKEN

Roles and Objectives

Definition

Lages & Simkin (2003) explain the difficulty of defining PR since organizations often describes it differently. This theory is supported by Handelsbanken where PR is not defined. Handelsbanken has not stated any overall definition of their PR activities. This can probably be the result of the bank not putting any significant importance in the term PR. Even though the bank does not actively define PR, they put great importance in the actual activities within the area. The activities at Handelsbanken traditionally known as PR are mainly called corporate communication.

Objectives and Strategies

Dolphin & Fan (2000) explain that a communication strategy is essential for any organization. It needs to be managed and formulated by the information director in close cooperation with the executive team and the board (Dolphin & Fan, 2000; Nakra, 2000). In this point Handelsbanken has understood the importance of creating and managing a communication strategy, and is therefore in line with theory. At Handelsbanken the strategy is formulated by the information director and top management in close cooperation with the CEO, though the organization board is not involved in the communication strategy development. Hon (1998) states that organization should have written, strategic, quantifiable goals and objectives tied directly to the organizations overall goals and objectives.

Handelsbanken is in line with theory and has written overall communication goals and guidelines that are tied directly to the organizations overall objectives. These are no direct PR goals but can be seen as a closely related guideline for PR activities.

Hutton et.al. (2001) explain that different philosophies are often appropriate for different companies. This way of thinking leaves room for Handelsbanken's decentralized strategy when managing PR.

According to Lages & Simkin (2003) PR as a management discipline is wider than a communication technique or a specialized program, such as media relations. This is in line with Handelsbanken's broad view of PR as something utilized throughout the entire organization.

Most organizations realize the importance of effective communications with its publics (Wells & Spinks (1999). This statement matches well with the concept of the bank. Handelsbanken describe effective communication and building relationships with the publics as vital. Lynn (1999) states that effective communication can create brand awareness in the community. Handelsbanken agrees with this theory, and since they do not utilize nation wide marketing in the same way as competitors, their PR activities get more important when building awareness.

The public opinion is highly dynamic, and therefore PR responses utilized by companies should be actively managed (Wells & Spinks, 1999; Worcester, 1997). Handelsbanken has understood the importance of being flexible in their PR activities that are managed close to the customers at local markets. Large flexibility in PR activities is possible since there is no traditional centralized top-down management at Handelsbanken. As observed, Handelsbanken is in line with this theory.

According to Wells et.al. (2003) there are numerous objectives with the PR strategies. Usually these objectives focus on creating credibility, delivering information, and building positive images. Handelsbanken's objectives with PR is to market the bank in best possible way to develop lasting long-term relationships with the customers and other publics, and therefore Handelsbanken's objectives are in line with this theory.

Defining Publics

Schultz & Barnes (1999) and Worcester (1997) emphasize that specific publics should be targeted. Thereafter segmentation with traditional methods can be conducted. Handelsbanken's strategy is in line with this theory. Specific publics are targeted and segmented into groups in order of importance. The target publics are defined broadly with existing customers as priority. Wells & Spinks (1999) recommend establishment of PR activities with the community in hole. Handelsbanken's activities are to some degree consistent with this theory. Even though the community in hole is not the most important target, some PR activities aim at the entire community.

PROACTIVE PR VERSUS REACTIVE PR

PR can be characterized either as proactive or reactive. Proactive PR is offensive and opportunity seeking, mainly used to promote products and services. Reactive PR is defensively oriented and problem solving. It is undertaken as a result of external pressure (Shimp, 2000). As observed from the tactics of PR at Handelsbanken, the bank is obviously to a higher degree proactive than reactive in their activities. The main focus is laid on building strong relationships.

HUTTON'S FRAMEWORK FOR DEFINING PUBLIC RELATIONS

To be able to define the role of PR at Handelsbanken, and to be able to plot the bank in Hutton's framework, we identified where the bank should be located in the three dimensions of; initiative, image and interest.

Initiative

Handelsbanken is mainly proactive in their PR activities, even though the bank acts reactively when needed. Therefore the bank can be placed as fairly proactive in the initiative category in Hutton's framework.

Image

At Handelsbanken the central PR activities are more focused on image building than the local activities, which have more focus on informing and educating.

Since focus in the organization is put on the local activities, and the central tasks are only a supportive function for the local activities, Handelsbanken can be placed at the reality side in the category of image.

Interest

When examining Handelsbanken's main interest as public or client focused, a clear emphasis at the existing clients of the organization can be observed. Also the general publics with future potential customers are important, but not with the same significance. Therefore Handelsbanken can be seen as more client focused in the category of interest.

With the characteristics of Handelsbanken plotted into Hutton's framework, it can be observed that the bank is very close to role number six, relationship management, in all the dimension categories. Therefore Handelsbanken can be described as having relationship management as the main role in their PR activities.

Hutton (1999) describes the relationship management approach as seeking conformance with the clients and publics. The publics support is vital for the organization in achieving its long-term objectives. Emphasize is on mutual trust, cooperation and if possible, win-win situations. This view of PR, match to a great deal with the objectives and concept of Handelsbanken.

HUTTON'S HIERARCHY OF PUBLIC RELATIONS

When the aspects of Handelsbanken's PR activities are placed into Hutton's (1999) hierarchy framework of PR, the various characteristics of PR in the bank can be observed.

FUNCTIONS AND TOOLS

Types of PR

Wells et.al. (2003) describe the different types of PR that refer to relationships with various stakeholders;

- Media relations
- Employee relations
- Financial relations
- Corporate relations
- Public affairs

From the case of Handelsbanken it can be seen that relations involving existing and future customers is of priority in the PR activities, customer contact relations can be found in media, financial and corporate relations categories. Also employee relations are of very high importance in such a large organization. The relation given least importance in Handelsbanken is public affairs. All the relations described in theory can be found in the PR activities of Handelsbanken.

The PR Toolkit

Phillips (2001) has developed a framework on how to set up and evaluate PR activities. Since Handelsbanken does not utilize any specific framework of this kind when developing their PR activities the bank cannot be measured against this theory.

PR Tools

Wells et.al. (2003) has presented a model with three types of PR tools, controlled, uncontrolled and, semi-controlled. Handelsbanken stated that they are utilizing all possible tools from the categories with the purpose of building relationships and trust with customers and potential customers. Not all the tools are used at all branches; local managers have the ability to utilize the tools they best believe will reach the public. For example the local manager at the Luleå branch explained that focus of their PR-activities is to build personal relations. Therefore personal contacts and events where the bank is meeting people were of great importance. Also the local web-site had gained in importance the past time. The only tool that hardly ever is used is general image campaigns.

Effectiveness and Evaluation of PR

According to Schmitz (2004) it is as important to follow up, measure, and evaluate the PR activities as in fact to implement them. Handelsbanken is not measuring or evaluating their PR activities at all. There is a belief that there is no value in itself to evaluate communication and PR activities. Instead all the evaluation is done on economic results and outcomes. If the branch is delivering good results, it is believed at central level that also the communication and PR activities are handled with success.

The communication and PR is only seen as tools to reach the objective; profitability, and is therefore not evaluated if the final results are satisfying. One tool at Handelsbanken that in some way is evaluated is publicity. The publicity is tracked down by external agents, and then reviewed by the corporate communication department, mainly for the knowledge of when, and in what purpose the organization has gained publicity. Regarding follow up, measuring and evaluation, Handelsbanken is not in line with theory.

TRUST AND REPUTATION

Trust and Credibility

The trusting party must perceive that the trusted party is acting out of commitment that is going beyond the motive of self-interest (Saparito et.al. 2004). With this fact in mind, Handelsbanken agrees with theory and tries to build a base of trust with the publics, mainly through utilizing personal relations at local level. Handelsbanken believes that personal relations is the main tool when developing trust with the publics. At the bank, trust is viewed as something that can be developed in a relatively short period of time, especially if handling new customers that does not know much about the organization.

Ball et.al. (2004) state that well structured communications has a strong effect on consumer perception, and leads to trust, satisfaction and loyalty. Corporate communications should be used as relationship-enhancers offering the customers advice and information. Handelsbanken is in line with theory, and has understood the importance of communication when establishing and maintaining relationships with customers and other publics. The bank has been able to observe a strong customer satisfaction and high customer loyalty as a direct result of their relationship-building in PR and communication activities.

Kangis & Voukelatos (1997) state that trustworthiness can be positively influencing the perception of service quality, and therefore also increase customer loyalty. Handelsbanken agree with theory, and understand the importance of trustworthiness and explains that the organization's reputation is extremely important when selling financial products and services. Since the bank is handling such a sensitive matter as private individuals and entire economies of companies, a large part of the impression is mediated through trustworthiness. Handelsbanken points out that when succeeding to develop trustworthiness, the customer loyalty can be kept high.

Corporate Reputation

According to Dolphin & Fan (2000) the corporate reputation can win a competitive advantage for an organization in a crowded marketplace. It is a visible signal of an organization's capability and information about future performance. Handelsbanken agree with theory, and believe that a large part of their reputation is a result of their stable communication and PR concept. The stability and recognition that can be perceived by the customers as a result of the concept, gives Handelsbanken competitive advantages and informs customers about their future performance capability.

According to Dolphin (2004) management of reputation has developed into an important tool for communication strategists. Beavers-Moss (2001) argues that bank marketers must know how to protect and uphold their reputation, since credibility and value is to a high degree gained from it. Hutton et.al. (2001) describe the loss of organizational reputation as a large problem. Budd (1995) explains that reputation is gained over time and is not easily changed. At Handelsbanken the reputation is seen as extremely important and the preserving of it is a priority. The reputation development is emphasized in the entire organization and especially at top management and board level. Scandals at top level are seen as a great threat to the organizations reputation. A ruined reputation is according to Handelsbanken not possible to repair only with PR, and therefore the important part is to avoid the loss of reputation from the beginning. Handelsbanken is in line with the theories about reputation management. Reputation management, resting on the foundations of PR, is an emerging business function that gains importance in organizations (Hutton et.al. 2001). This theory is not supported by Handelsbanken. The bank has not seen any movement in the past to a greater importance of reputation management. It is also not believed that it will become increasingly important in the near future. Handelsbanken instead believes that the importance of an organizations reputation is dependent of the business cycle. During good times corporate reputation gets less important than during recession.

Cross-case Analysis

In this part of the analysis the two cases of SEB and Handelsbanken are compared with each other. The cross-case analysis of the banks is going to be conducted one research questions at a time.

Roles and Objectives of PR

- Understands the importance of an overall communication strategy.
- Top management is formulating the communication strategy.
- Board is involved in developing the communication strategy.
- Communication objectives are written and tied to the banks overall objectives.

- Overall communication objectives are measurable.
- Overall PR responsibility falls under the departments;
- PR strategies are centralized versus decentralized.
- Responsibility of PR is mainly at local level.
- Understands PR as something to be utilized in the entire organization.
- Communication and PR is understood as vital for the organization.
- PR is believed to build brand awareness for the bank.
- Believes that the public opinion can be changed with PR.
- There is flexibility in PR-activities.
- Build Relationships,
- Reach new customers,
- Strengthen the image
- Marketing & Information Centralized
- Partly flexible
- Build Relationships,
- Market the bank
- Corporate Communications Decentralized
- Highly flexible.

From the cross-case analysis it can be observed that both banks are quite similar in the objectives and management of overall communication strategies. The point where the organizations differ in high degree is in the centralization versus decentralization of PR strategies. When most PR activities are utilized and controlled at local level at Handelsbanken, SEB has to a higher degree control over the PR activities at central level. The cases make it obvious that both of the organizations put great importance in corporate communication and PR strategies. The main objectives of PR at both organizations are quite similar. The relationship building function can be identified as a common ground, with priority at both of the banks. In addition to the relationship objectives, both banks have other goals that differ slightly from each other.

HUTTON'S FRAMEWORK FOR DEFINING PR

When comparing Handelsbanken and SEB in Hutton's framework it is easy to observe the strong similarities between them. Both banks have a reality orientation in image building activities. The banks are more focused in their clients than the general publics, in the interest dimension. Finally both organizations have a stronger orientation towards pro-activity than reactivity in their PR initiative. With these characteristics, both organizations can to a high degree be identified with role number six, relationship management.

Hutton's Hierarchy of PR

Also in Hutton's hierarchy of PR it is easy to observe the similarities between the banks when analyzing them toward each other. It can be seen that both of the organizations have similar situational roles, and also similar primary functions performed. Many of the PR tools utilized are also to a high degree similar.

Defining Publics

Both organizations define their publics broadly and see the community in hole as having some importance when directing PR efforts. There are some differencies between the banks considering their orientation as proactive or reactive. Handelsbanken is today already a highly proactive bank. At the moment, SEB is fairly proactive with the intention to work further with their pro-activity.

FUNCTIONS AND TOOLS UTILIZED IN PR

- Considers relation with customers, involving media, financial, and corporate relations as the most important.
- Considers employee relations as important.
- Least important relation is public affairs.

In the cross-case analysis between SEB and Handelsbanken it can be seen that both banks consider the relation with their customers as most important. The banks are quite similar in their PR regarding importance of relations. Great differences can be found in how PR activities are set up and evaluated. Handelsbanken has no framework for set-up and evaluation, while SEB have frameworks developed. At SEB, there are specific frameworks developed for each PR tool instead of a general framework. It is clear that both banks utilize most of the available PR tools, but difference can be found in how the banks rank them in importance. The freedom of utilizing PR activities at local level also differs between the banks, as result of centralization versus decentralization in the bank strategy. Handelsbanken only evaluates the publicity in media. No other measurements are done, except from economical results and outcomes on branch level. On other hand, SEB measure what is measurable and evaluate almost all PR activities. Both Handelsbanken and SEB use external agents to measure publicity in media.

Trust and Reputation

- PR develops trust with the customers.
- Trust can increase customer satisfaction and customer loyalty.
- Personal relationships are the most important part when developing trust.
- Professional advice and information to the customer is utilized to develop trust.
- The bank perceives that they succeed in keeping customer loyalty and satisfaction high as a result of developed trust.

The bank realizes the importance of being trustworthy.

- Corporate reputation
- Corporate reputation is believed to be a result of the PR and communication efforts.
- Corporate reputation can give competitive advantages to the bank.
- Corporate reputation can be seen as a signal of future performance.
- Corporate reputation, if actively managed with PR, can be changed in a short period of time.
- Preserving of corporate reputation is of great importance when considering the industry.

- Importance of corporate reputation is emphasized in the entire organization.
- Reputation management is proactive.
- Reputation management is an emerging business function.

When analyzing the data concerning trust, it can be seen that the banks are highly similar in the way that trust is understood in the organization. The matter of trust is emphasized and managed fairly similar by the banks.

Also when analyzing corporate reputation, the banks are to a high degree similar. Both organizations understand the importance, value, and impact of corporate reputation management. SEB though differs in two matters from Handelsbanken. SEB sees reputation management as an emerging business function, and also believes that corporate reputation, if managed correctly can be changed in a short period of time. Handelsbanken believes that corporate reputation is developed in a long-term perspective, and is not that easily repaired or changed with PR. Handelsbanken also believes that the management of corporate reputation has been important for long time, and is not an emerging business function. In this chapter the research questions stated in chapter one are going to be answered, based on the data and analysis conducted in chapter four and five. Further, implications of this study for management, theory, and future research will be provided.

CONCLUSIONS

How can roles and objectives of PR in banks' promotion mix be described? It can be concluded from the two cases that roles and objectives of the banks are quite similar. It is understood by both banks that setting up general corporate communication strategies at top management level is of great importance. PR and corporate communications are also understood as important to utilize in the entire organization by both banks.

When reviewing the definitions of PR activities it can be concluded, that the two banks differ. SEB defines PR internally as a very narrow media activity. Theory explains that publicity is often called PR on a regular basis at companies, and this is also the case at SEB. On other hand Handelsbanken does not define PR as anything specific; in fact they do not use the terminology PR. Conclusions drawn from the cases are that there is an obvious problem in defining PR and the work that falls under it When concluding the overall objectives with PR there are similarities, as well as differences between the banks. Handelsbanken's main objective is to build strong relationships with the various publics with priority given to existing customers. A second objective is to market the bank in best possible way toward the publics. With this marketing objective, PR seems to gain further importance for Handelsbanken since they do not utilize marketing in traditional ways.

The objectives of SEB are to build relationships with existing customers, to reach new customers, and to strengthen the bank image. The relationship focus is similar between the banks, but the other objectives differ.

When observing the results from Hutton's framework for defining PR, it can be concluded that both banks position themselves quite close to each other in the role of relationship management. It is no surprise, since the market of financial services is characterized as strict with little room for failure, and organizations involved need to adapt and adjust to the specific conditions. Since the customers, both private individuals and companies often trust the bank with all their assets; the customer relationship is getting into focus. It is also important to establish relationships with other publics, to be able to build a trustworthy impression in the society as a whole.

When looking at Hutton's hierarchy of PR, the overall PR characteristics of the banks can be identified. When analyzing the outcomes from the model, the similarities of PR's role in banks get even more obvious.

From the two cases of SEB and Handelsbanken it may be concluded that the banking industry has a specific way when handling PR matters. It appears that the reputation management role, with personal relations as priority, is the most important issue for Swedish banks. With such a small sample selection it is hard to generalize, nevertheless the banking industry's tendencies seen in this study are obvious.

It can be concluded that:

- There is a relationship objective at both banks that is quite similar. Other objectives differ between the banks.
- Banks aim at reputation management as their role in PR.
- Banks are highly similar in the overall PR and communication aspect with a few exceptions.

In addition:

- The overall corporate philosophy influence to a high degree in what way PR activities are conducted. But organizational differences in structuring PR do not conflict with the results of the activities.
- Banks set up general guidelines for PR at top level, and understand the importance of active communication with the publics.
- PR is very actively utilized in banks, but it may not necessarily be called and defined PR, as it is referred to in theory. There is an obvious problem when defining PR and what falls into the area.

How can PR's functions and tools utilized by banks' be described?

Based on the two cases of SEB and Handelsbanken it can be concluded that relationships are utilized quite similarly by the banks. Both banks define their target groups broadly, and to a large degree see members of the community in hole as their target group. It can be concluded that the most important relation is the customer relations, which include media-, financial-, and corporate relations.

Another conclusion that can be drawn is that there are differences in how banks set up and evaluate their PR activities. Findings show that the nature of the organizational structure, if it is centralized or decentralized, can affect the implementation of guidelines and frameworks for PR activities. It can be concluded that it is easier for a centralized organisation to implement such guidelines and frameworks, compared to a decentralized organization. In a decentralized organization, extensive effort is needed to be able to implement guidelines and frameworks.

Both SEB and Handelsbanken utilize most of the PR tools described in theory, even though there are differences in the importance of the tools. The importance of local activities at branch level is high at both banks, even though it is of higher priority at Handelsbanken, where PR activities primarily are utilized at local level. Another conclusion that can be drawn is that both banks utilize local PR activities, to be able to encounter the demand of local markets. It can also be seen that a decentralized strategy makes it easier for the bank when adapting to local markets.

At SEB, PR mainly falls under the corporate information department, marketing department and it is to some extent performed at local branch level. At Handelsbanken the central PR falls under the corporate communication department, but much focus is laid on the local branches, where the main PR activities are conducted. When evaluating the effectiveness of PR activities initiated by the banks, there are some differences. Based on this research it can be concluded that no evaluation except measuring publicity is done at Handelsbanken. Instead the bank relies on evaluation of economical results and outputs from the business itself. In opposite, SEB heavily rely on evaluation, and therefore practice various types of measurements for their PR. Finally, we can conclude that there is no general PR evaluation theory or framework that directly fits into the banking industry. Frameworks and guidelines have to be developed for specific organizational settings and purposes. By the fact that both organizations are successful and profitable, but only one utilize thorough evaluation; we can conclude that evaluation of PR activities is not necessarily needed for success.

Further, it can be concluded that Handelsbanken's highly decentralized organization pushes the PR responsibility out to branch level where branch managers have great responsibility and large freedom when planning and conducting PR activities. This make the bank's PR highly flexible. In contrast, SEB has a more centralized organization which is built to control PR activities in a different way from central level. The branch managers have not the same freedom to decide how to utilize PR at the local market. This way of working makes PR fairly flexible, but SEB is not as flexible as Handelsbanken. Even though the organizational overall strategies differ in such a high degree, it can be observed that it does not conflict with the quality of the PR activities considerably. The two banks structure their PR work in different ways, but both achieve desired results. The major difference in the management of PR between the two banks comes from their overall corporate strategies.

After discussing the second research question, the following are concluded:

- Local PR activities at branch level are important for banks.
- Personal relations as a PR tool is emphasized quite similarly in the banking industry.
- Most important PR relation is the customer relations.
- The banks have no PR department. Instead PR work is divided under different departments and sections of the organization.

Evaluation of PR activities is not necessary for success, and there is no general evaluation theory or framework suited for the banking industry In addition:

- The nature of the organizational structure is affecting implementation of guidelines and frameworks. It can be seen that implementation of frameworks and guidelines is easier in centralized organizations.
- A decentralized organizational structure leads to increased importance of local PR activities.

How can corporate reputation and trust as viewed by banks be described?

When looking at the importance of trust and reputation at the two banks, similar priorities can be found. Trust and reputation seems to be the most important characteristics in the financial service industry. It can be concluded that a bank, managing private individuals and companies' entire assets, is highly dependent in the ability to develop trust with various publics, and needs to maintain the corporate reputation. Even though banks realize the importance of managing trustworthiness and reputation, there are differences in how it actually is done. The variation is mainly a result of the organizations overall strategy.

Handelsbanken can be seen as a very local bank and is to high degree emphasizing personal relations with their publics, as a result of the organizations decentralized philosophy. Since Handelsbanken has no marketing in traditional meaning, it can be concluded that their PR and personal relations gets of vital importance when developing trust and reputation. Since reputation is seen as something that is easily ruined, the reputation management is highly proactive, and emphasized throughout the entire organization. At Handelsbanken reputation management is not seen as an emerging business function.

SEB also relies in personal relations, however not with same priority as Handelsbanken. Instead more focus is put in professional advice and information services at the bank. It is believed at SEB, that corporate reputation can be managed fairly quickly with active use of PR. Therefore the bank puts more importance in the reactive management of the reputation.

At SEB reputation management is seen as an emerging business function that already is emphasized in large parts of the organization.

Therefore it can be concluded that:

- Trust and reputation has very high priority at banks.
- There are differences in how banks manage corporate reputation in the aspect of pro-activity versus reactivity, and also to what level PR is utilized in the entire organization when developing trust and reputation.

- Reputation management is not seen as an emerging business function by both banks.

Implications and Recommendations

Conclusions that have been drawn in the previous section finally bring this thesis to an end. In this section implications for various fields where this study can be useful will be presented. These are implications for practitioners and management, as well as ideas for theory and future research.

Implications for Practitioners and Management

This thesis has investigated how commercial banks utilize PR. There are several issues' that can be given as implications for management. Our implications for management are listed below:

When setting up communication and PR objectives, large organizations have to realize the importance of setting the strategies at top management level.

Whatever the organization is calling their PR activities, it is important that some kind of structure is describing and navigating the communication strategy. The effects of conducted PR should in some way be measured and evaluated so that the organization can get an understanding of the impact of the utilized activity. Otherwise the company can continue using PR tools that are not fully effective. Flexibility in PR strategies and activities is highly desirable since the public opinion is constantly changing. In this way the corporate communications can be constantly up to date, meeting the requirements of the publics. Therefore PR activities should be planned to be highly flexible. Organizations in the banking industry should define their publics broadly, and utilize image building PR campaigns in the community as hole. The PR strategies should mainly be planned as proactive so that the organization can build a positive consciousness in the mind of the publics. With consideration of the evolvement of Internet the past decade, PR tools such as the company website should be seen as very important when communicating with the publics.

The corporate reputation and trustworthiness of the organization in front of the publics should be one of the main priorities. If utilizing PR in the right way, a positive outcome can be observed also in these areas.

Implications for Theory

The purpose of this study was to gain a better understanding of how banks' utilize PR in communicating with their publics. This study has to some extent been exploratory since we have gained a better understanding of the area of research through gathering information. This thesis has contributed to theory in terms of a broader understanding of PR activities within the Swedish bank sector. When looking at existing theories and compare these to the collected empirical data, some deviations can be found. This has contributed to theory and strengthens the fact that the term PR is vast, and hard to define due to its various definitions and roles. The general understanding of PR is "publicity in media", instead of the broader definitions stated by theories. Therefore it could be better to define PR in general as corporate communication; this could reduce the problem with defining PR. This thesis also contributes to theory, and confirms that there is no general method of evaluating effectiveness in PR activities in the banking industry; instead it is obvious that different ways can be successful.

Implications for Further Research

The empirical findings from two case studies can be a basis for further research within the area of PR. During the work with this thesis, issues and questions related to the research questions have arisen. Time limitation prevented us to answer all the questions and issues. Therefore we recommend further research within the area of PR in the following lines.

CONCLUSIONS AND IMPLICATIONS

Due to time limitations, only two cases could be conducted, it would be interesting to perform the same study with a larger sample. In this way it could be possible to generalize the outcomes in a different way.

It would also be interesting to conduct the same study in other industries. The specific characteristics of different industries would give varying data in the same research area. It would be interesting to observe how Hutton's framework for defining PR, would describe the roles of PR in other industries.

Specific parts of this study could be looked into with further depth with a wider sample selection. For example explanatory research could be conducted to examine cause and effect of the different PR activities.

It would also be interesting to conduct the same research internationally; in other countries internally, or in comparing across borders, to be able to identify differences that are brought up by cultural diversity. Research on how specific publics perceive the banks PR efforts would also be interesting to do. The study could be conducted from the publics' point of view.

10

Classification and Functions of Banks

Banking institutions are specialized dealers in and guarantors of credits. The evolution of our system of credit has been characterized by the same division of labor which dominates our social and economic structure. Not only have credit institutions separated from the merchant and industrial institutions, but the credit institutions have themselves specialized on the basis of function. This differentiation of functions affords the most useful classification of banks. Banks may be viewed, of course, from an economic or social point of view as well as from that of business.

The economist and sociologist consider the services of the bank with reference to the furtherance of human welfare. The banker, however, thinks of his bank as a profit-making institution; he may philosophize on its economic and social influences, but unless moved by a high sense of public duty he is prone to think most of dividends. His customers, moreover, are likely to think of the bank from the purely business point of view - as an institution from which to secure loans, in which to deposit money, and by the aid of which securities may be floated and estates managed.

CLASSIFICATION BY FUNCTIONS

The most common classification of American banks based on bank functions makes three divisions, namely:

1. Commercial banks.
2. Investment institutions, including savings banks and bond houses or investment banks.
3. Trust Companies.

But further division on the same basis is possible. The New York State banking law has special sections for the following classes: state and national (commercial) banks, federal reserve banks, credit unions, foreign banking corporations, investment bankers, investment companies, Land Bank of the State of New York, personal loan brokers, personal loan companies, private bankers, state deposit companies, savings and loan associations, savings banks, trust companies, discount companies, acceptance houses, note-brokers, and others. Indeed the subclasses that are possible are limited in number only by the number of functions and combinations of functions open to such institutions.

Classified as to source of authority to do business, banks are commonly grouped as federal or national, state, private, and foreign. Another classification is into parent or mother bank, branch, agency, and correspondent. Still another is into joint-stock, mutual, private, and individual. And in any system the banks may be specified as central, member, or non-member; as bank of issue or non-issue; as reserve city bank, central reserve city bank, or country bank; as land bank, agricultural bank, mercantile bank, industrial bank, and so forth.

FUNCTIONS OF COMMERCIAL BANKS

The major functions of commercial banks have already been described as the testing and guaranty of credit, and the extension of credit by means of notes, deposits, and acceptances. Commercial banks extend short-time loans, handle short-time mercantile paper, receive deposits subject to check, issue bank notes, issue letters of credit, and accept bills drawn upon themselves. In carrying on these main activities many incidental services are performed for customers. In a circular published recently a metropolitan bank advertised "forty-three separate service divisions - all working for a single object, namely, to render a powerful and well-balanced banking service." In their competition for business, banks adapt their services to their actual and prospective customers' needs, adding feature after feature. In this point of service, by the way, there is probably opportunity for both the large and small banks. The smaller banks can render their fewer customers services that are probably more intimate and personal than the great metropolitan banks, whereas the latter can offer facilities more powerful, varied, complete, and expert.

The accessory and minor functions of commercial banks will be discussed in detail in the body of this text. The nature of these functions appears in the statement that from his bank the business man receives the ready accommodation of a loan or the prompt cash conversion of commercial papers; he finds it convenient to keep his money and make his payments at the bank; he is adviced in the purchase and sale of securities and their handling; the bank assembles vast credit files which are open to him; his funds are transmitted over distances, his foreign trade is facilitated, his business operations planned and guided for him.

From the point of view of economics, bank credit obviates the use of metallic money and conserves the metals for use in the arts; it facilitates the production, movement, and exchange of goods more effectually even than money does; it stabilizes credit, resting it upon long-established, widely extended, conservatively managed institutions. The banker determines the personnel of the business world, by extending credit to persons of character and capacity and by choosing as debtors those who have either proved abilities or give reasonable promise. Capital is thus diverted into channels and hands where it is most productive and most useful to society. The bank assembles the stray and hoarded funds of the country into its vaults and puts them to productive use. Capital is thereby conserved. The benefits of thrift are taught and the importance and equity of keeping contracts to the letter are brought home to the commercial world.

SPECIALIZATION OF COMMERCIAL BANKS

Commercial banks specialize in loans, adapting their services to their locality or to a special clientele. Some carry specialization to such degree as to relinquish many of their banking functions. For instance, to facilitate the production and marketing of cattle, "cattle loan companies" conduct a banking business in the primary livestock markets and production centers. Certain banks in close touch with speculative exchanges cater to brokers and commission men. Others in our great seaports cater to foreign trade and international finance. Devotion to a limited field of operations results in expertness and ability to perform a particular sort of loan or service better and at lower rates than is possible for competitors who are less specialized.

But side by side with this tendency of certain banks to limit themselves to narrower fields, there has been a movement in the opposite direction. Banking institutions find it advisable to be able to perform for their customers all the financial services for which they have need rather than to let them depend in part on outsiders. In view of the expense of organization and overhead which the bank must carry in any event, to undertake these additional services may be economically very desirable. State and national banking laws have hedged the banks with restrictions on their field of operations, but commercial banks are gradually developing such side lines as long-term and agricultural loans, acceptances, trust business, insurance agency, loan brokerage, safe deposit and storage, investment buying and selling, and so forth. The trust companies in the several states are pushing their commercial banking departments, and national banks are being permitted by federal and state law to handle trusts. An identity of function will probably not be developed soon but the evolution is toward a close approximation.

Savings Banks

Mutual or Trustee Savings Banks. The savings bank started as a mutual savings association and is commonly regarded as a benevolent institution. A mutual savings bank is a financial establishment which receives deposits up to a fixed maximum amount from individuals, provides safe-keeping for the funds and, having aggregated them, invests them in securities declared by the state legislature legitimate for trust funds; the interest from these investments, after the bank's expenses are deducted, accrues to the depositors in proportion to their deposits. The relation between depositor and bank is one of trust; the funds of the bank are held by its officers as trustees; the assets, profits, and losses are distributed ratably among depositors, and the officers get no profits, but receive trustee fees.

The rate of interest on the investments is generally very low, for the reason that safety rather than earning capacity guides the legislature in defining eligible investments. The deposits received are not subject to check, nor are they subject to withdrawal except by pass-book and due notice of 30, 60, or 90 days, varying with the bank and the amount to be withdrawn. The pass-book constitutes the contract of deposit; the terms are described therein; entries and signatures in it become very important from a legal point of view. The depositor is moved to make the deposits by the motive of thrift and the interest inducement offered by the bank; he does not expect to withdraw them soon inasmuch as they represent his savings. He does not have the privilege of paying by check which the commercial bank accords nor does he get short-term accommodation. The savings bank invests in long-term securities and not (though recently to a limited degree in some states) in short-term commercial paper; its deposits turn slowly and it relies on its ability, within the period of notice of intended withdrawal of deposits, to sell its securities at other than sacrifice prices. Mortgages and bonds form the bulk of such a bank's investments.

Joint-Stock Savings Banks. In the West and South the dominant type of savings bank is the joint-stock bank, an institution which, like a commercial bank, is conducted for the profit of the shareholders. Deposits are received as in other savings banks, but instead of the depositors being paid a net return from the investments above expenses, they receive a definite rate of interest as arranged at the time of making their deposits. The margin between the earnings of the investments and the interest paid on deposits constitutes the sum that covers expenses and profits to the stockholders. These net profits the shareholders divide on the basis of shares owned.

While joint-stock savings banks may contribute as much to the economic and social welfare as trustee savings banks, they are purely private business enterprises and not eleemosynary institutions. In the trustee savings bank the risk of high or low earnings and of loss of principal is borne by the depositor; in the joint-stock bank the shareholders assume these risks and guarantee the interest and principal to the depositor. In the former the depositors, being creators of a trust, have the control; in the joint-stock bank they are simply creditors and have no voice in its management.

The mutual type prevails in New England and the eastern states where the historical and social conditions are favorable to it, where the communities are old, sentiment strong, and a philanthropic and public-spirited attitude is prevalent; it is not adapted to the West, which is dominantly commercial, nor to the South still impoverished from the Rebellion and lacking on the whole a thrifty population.

The trustee who starts a mutual bank gains no financial advantage from it; in fact, he assumes a large risk and responsibility to the community. He must be a man of highest type, holding the unswerving confidence of the depositors, not only as to personal character but also as to business capacity; he acts primarily from philanthropic motives, although some lawyers and other business men may promote mutual banks for the purpose of gaining clients.

Guaranty and Other Types of Savings Banks. New Hampshire is unique in having a hybrid type of savings bank, combining the chief features of the two previously mentioned types. Instead of capital stock and shareholders, this type of savings bank has "special deposits" and "special depositors." It pays a certain stipulated rate of interest to its general depositors, and any surplus earnings go to the special depositors. The special deposits constitute a guaranty fund for the general depositors and are limited to 10 per cent of the total deposits. Except for their name and the method of determining their amount, these special deposits have all the characteristics of the capital stock of joint-stock banks.

There are many other kinds of savings banks which are too numerous to describe here; for instance, the municipal savings banks, school savings banks, postal savings banks, and various groups of co-operative credit institutions, such as building and loan associations, farmers' co-operative credit societies, and the new farm loan bank system. The co-operative credit institutions, while formed primarily to provide on their joint credit long-term credits on realty at lower rates than the co-operators could obtain on their individual credit, tend to fulfil much the same social and economic ends as other savings banks.

FUNCTIONS OF SAVINGS BANKS

The essential economic and social functions of savings banks are three in number, as follows:

1. They assemble the capital of the community, conserve the idle wealth, and having aggregated it into sizable funds, loan it to business enterprisers.
2. They add to the peace and comfort and available consumption of society by providing a safe outlet for the funds of those who have the will and capacity to save but do not have the ability either to use the funds industrially themselves or to invest them with safety and profit.
3. They Promote Thrift More Than Any Other Financial Institution.

The prudent investment of interest and accumulated principal, which together constitute savings, lessens profligacy, provides against the adversities of old age and sickness, helps the thrifty to buy a home and to enjoy better living conditions, builds up independence and stability of character, and improves the social and political life of the community.

FUNCTIONS OF THE BOND HOUSE AND INVESTMENT BANK

Whereas savings banks aim to assemble funds for the purchase of investments, and whereas the bond houses or investment banks are concerned with the sale and distribution of securities, both promote investment from the opposite end.

In marketing securities, three groups of institutions are successively engaged: The securities are purchased by one group, are underwritten by another, and are distributed among ultimate buyers by a third. These functions overlap, it is true, and in some instances one house may perform all three of them, and the bond house may operate in any or all of these ways.

1. Purchasing Securities

The houses which buy first hand the largest blocks of securities are relatively few in number and strong financially, with central offices in New York, Philadelphia, Boston, or Chicago. There are, of course, in these and other cities many houses which are competent to handle somewhat smaller blocks of securities. Institutions which buy securities on a large scale must command large resources, occupy a position of financial influence, and have a record of successes which will assure the company issuing the securities of the success of the flotation. Such houses determine the direction of industrial and commercial development and the selection of the personnel of business enterprises worthy of financial support. They may act either independently or in conjunction with others.

The promoter brings his proposition to one of the financial houses at a time; if his negotiations fail he approaches another; but he will not find the financial houses actively competing with one another, nor do they actively bid for his proposition. Active competition by bond houses might result in reckless extensions of credit and overfinancing; the bankers prefer to act in a more professional capacity and to select their clients with an eye to an intimate, confident, and permanent relationship.

A few years ago the cry arose that the financial houses constituted a "money trust," denying financial assistance to warrantable business undertakings mainly because the latter interfered or competed with the vested interests. The extensive investigations of the Pujo Committee failed to make out a conclusive case for these allegations.

In purchasing a block of municipal securities a preliminary investigation, unless it is the issue of a well-known municipality, is made by an agent who inquires into the physical and financial condition of the city to determine its ability and willingness to meet its present and prospective obligations.

The securities issued by business corporations are usually submitted to the bond houses by a representative of the company or by a promoter. The bond houses, except under very favorable conditions, refuse to handle securities of a business with which they are unfamiliar. They reject issues in excess of the physical value of the mortgaged property and they likewise refuse securities of corporations with narrow margins of net earnings above fixed charges, and of corporations owned or operated by men of low business morality.

If a favorable price can be agreed upon, accountants, engineers, and investigators are sent to make a thorough examination of the conditions, and after the proposition is finally accepted the bond house may insist upon having representation upon the board of directors until the securities are disposed of. Some houses finally handle only securities of well-established earning power. This insistence upon high quality reacts favorably upon corporate finance in general.

2. Underwriting

A bond house which has bought a big block of securities endangers itself by the high concentration of risk; this risk is usually distributed by having the issue underwritten by a group of banks through what is known as a "syndicate agreement." There are four basic types of syndicate agreements, with several variations. It will suffice to illustrate but one type: Suppose that a bond house takes over the bond issue of a corpora-.tion at 97.5 and that a syndicate is formed, the members of which are offered and agree to take parts of the issue at 98.29 in case the public does not take them at 99.04. The bond house might be successful in closing out the issue directly to purchasers at 99.04, but rather than run the risks attendant on underwriting so large a block, it is content to make a smaller margin of profit through offering the securities to the underwriting syndicate. If the public absorbs the securities at 99.04, the underwriters make 3/4 per cent for having assumed the risk; but if the market offers only 96 the underwriters take them over at 98.29, and thus tie up their funds indefinitely or until the market rises. The members of the underwriting syndicate co-operate to establish and maintain the market for the issue. Bond houses like to participate in syndicates so as to diversify their security offerings and be able to offer such a variety of investments as will be sure to attract and retain customers.

3. Distributing Securities

Bond and brokerage houses prefer to sell large issues at small commissions rather than small issues at larger commissions. The expense of investigating a small issue is nearly as heavy as a large issue; the selling expense per share is likely to be smaller in the case of the large issue as it can be sold in larger blocks; and the large issue probably comes from a larger, better known institution and will therefore sell more easily. The commission rates vary widely, the general range being 1 1/2 to 10 per cent; the chief factors determining the rate are the size of the issue, the condition of the market, the borrowing corporation, and the publicity that will be required. In addition to the commission, the borrowing corporation must pay legal expenses and fees to accountants, intermediary brokers, and others, which expenses may run to a high figure.

Some bond houses have developed a clientele to whom they sell by mail; some sell through local independent bankers on a commission basis; some have developed a great sales organization and reach old and new customers by advertisements, circulars, and traveling salesmen. A selling campaign may be very extensive and highly organized; the more underwriters the more widely dispersed will the sales be. The buyers are insurance companies, banks in smaller cities, secondary syndicates, individual trustees and estates, trust companies, savings banks, and individuals.

The bond house or syndicate manager undertaking to market an issue of securities may, particularly if the issue is a large one, have the securities listed on the stock exchange and try to sell part of the issue through that avenue. Thus a ready market is at once established and many people whose names do not appear in the lists of prospects of the various bond houses, or who prefer to buy or sell through the exchange rather than "over the counter," may be attracted and buy the securities. The sellers then proceed "to make a market," by creating a volume of transactions sufficiently large to draw the interest of brokers and speculators. The syndicate buys and sells the securities and otherwise manipulates the market, in this way controlling the price and gradually unloading the securities on the investing and speculative public. Meanwhile a campaign of publicity is being conducted in the financial press and daily newspapers.

Having investigated carefully the history, physical property, earning capacity, present and prospective business policy, and organization of the corporation before undertaking to market its securities, the bond house is in a position to recommend them to its customers. The good-will of a representative bond house achieved by conservative practice, good counsel, and painstaking service, would, of course, be endangered by recommending securities which prove to be of poor quality, and therefore customers come to put implicit confidence in its advertisements, circulars, and daily news sheets. Bond houses thus function as advisors and directors of investment.

Though the policy of the bond houses in protecting their customers varies greatly, it is not unusual for them to contract explicitly to make good their counsels and recommendations as to purchases, and if the price of securities recommended declines below the selling price, the house stands ready to repurchase and thus protect the buyer. The buyer is often protected, however, quite as much by the moral responsibility which the house feels towards its client as by an explicit contract.

BANKING AND OTHER OPERATIONS OF BOND HOUSES

The intimate relations between a bond house and its customers are furthered by certain of its banking operations. A special department is established for the safe deposit of funds which, together with accruals of interest and additions from time to time, the depositor purposes to invest in securities offered by the bond house. The banking department also makes loans to customers who wish to purchase securities but who have not sufficient funds to pay in full at the time of purchase. In conjunction with the deposits destined for purchase of securities, the banking department may accept other deposits subject to check; this service is, however, mainly incidental. It would seem best for the investment market and the commercial bank market to be kept relatively distinct. Some investment banks by adding service to service have become general banking institutions, handling securities, savings, trusts, and deposits.

A further activity of bond houses is to act as fiscal agents for business corporations and bodies politic. The payment of dividends, interest, and principal on stocks and bonds, the flotation of their securities and their financial advertising are all matters entrusted to well-known bond houses in the central markets. Undoubtedly this arrangement improves the financial stability of the country, for in performing these operations of corporate finance the bond houses seek to build and maintain a good-will which less permanent promoters would fail to consider.

General Functions Of Trust Companies

A trust is something committed to another person's care for use or management and for which an account must be rendered. The original and essential function of a trust company was to accept and handle trusts of a business nature. To execute trusts efficiently, however, the trust company found it expedient to undertake many lines of collateral business, thus adding function after function to its province until today it represents the most inclusive and complete financial institution.

A representative trust company performs the following general functions:

1. Banking functions: savings and commercial banking operations.
2. Trust and agency functions:
   (a) For individuals: private agreements, probate, investment, real estate, and insolvency operations.
   (b) For corporations: trustee of mortgages and funds, transfer agent, registrar, corporate reorganization and financing operations.
3. Insurance and Safe-Deposit Functions.

Advantages of Corporate Over Individual Trustee

A trust company can perform the various functions of trustee better than an individual. As a corporation its existence is not limited, so that it can carry through to the end any trusts committed to it, whereas the individual trustee may die or become incompetent, making it necessary to instal another trustee, with incident delay and expense. The convenience of the creator of the trust and the public is enhanced when a trust company acts as trustee rather than an individual, since it has a regular place of business, well known and open every business day. It has all the facilities for executing trusts efficiently - an organization, expert officers, a clerical staff, a legal department, a good bookkeeping and auditing system, safe-deposit vaults, a wide clientele, and so forth. To this work it gives its almost exclusive attention, whereas an individual trustee is prone to make his trust secondary to his own business. Furthermore, the trust company is expert in the law of trusteeships and has had long experience in handling them; its customers who have created trusts with it get the benefit of its legal advice and investment ability, and thus the income from the trust is likely to be higher and the expenses lower; and the trust company is able to make temporary loans to the advantage and preservation of the estate. Finally, the trust is much safer in the hands of a company, which executes the estate in an impersonal way, free from the personal prejudices and biases common to individual trustees; which also provides a capital and surplus to protect its customers; and which desires to perpetuate the good-will of the institution. Such influences as these make for additional security.

Trust Functions For Individuals

Trusts undertaken for individuals are of various kinds and arise for numerous reasons. Persons who feel themselves incompetent to care for their estates, travelers, absentee property-owners, endowed charities or bequests, and others, commit their properties to the care and management of trust companies. Trust companies act as custodians of life insurance policies, collect the proceeds of the policies, and pay them as annuities to beneficiaries. In all such trusts the trustee's fees are stated in the trust contract, and the funds are kept distinct from the trustee's own assets and are held in the name of the trust company as trustee.

In many states the trust company is empowered by law to act as executor, administrator, trustee, guardian, and conservator. An executor is a person appointed by the terms of a will to take and execute an estate according to the terms of that document. An administrator is a person appointed by the probate court to take and execute according to the inheritance laws of the state an estate of one who has died intestate.

An "administrator with the will annexed" is a person appointed by the court to take and execute an estate when the deceased did not name an executor in the will, or when the executor named dies, refuses to act, or is incapacitated from acting. The trust company may serve in any of these capacities and in doing so take charge of the estate, subject to the supervision of the court, to which, after the final distribution of the estate according to the will or the state inheritance laws, the company makes an itemized report of all receipts and expenditures under the trust. The trust company may be appointed a guardian to care for the estates of minors, or a conservator to care for the estates of insane, idiots, habitual drunkards, spendthrifts, or others incapable of looking after their own affairs. All such duties are carried out under the surveillance of the court, to which also reports are made. The fees may be fixed by law or by the court. State statutes generally permit trust companies to act as depositories for court funds and for others acting as executors and the like.

The conduct of the trust functions of a trust company gives occasion for the investment and reinvestment of trust funds; and the trust company has funds of its own to invest. To carry out these investment operations a special department is developed which deals in high-grade securities for itself, its clients who have established trusts with it, and other customers, and functions as a bond house. One favorite line of investments is mortgages or debentures issued by mortgage bond houses, or the trust companies may issue such bonds themselves and sell them to their customers. Under investment-deposit agreements, deposits received from customers are invested in securities which are held in trust for the depositors.

Another type of service is the care of real estate committed to a trust company by private agreement, by will, or by appointment of court. This line of activity may develop into a real estate business engaged in the purchase, sale, and renting of real estate on commission. Trust companies are permitted in some states to act as assignees, receivers, and trustees in bankruptcy. An assignee or trustee in bankruptcy cares for the just distribution of the assets of insolvent persons, firms, or corporations among their creditors. The assets are taken over, some or all of them are converted into cash, the preferred claims are paid, and the rest of the assets are distributed among the creditors on the basis of their claims. Assignees and trustees are accountable to the court having jurisdiction.

A receiver is a person or a corporation appointed by the court to take charge of a property in dispute. If the shareholders of a company or the partners of a firm are dissatisfied with its management the court may be asked to handle the property until the dispute is settled. Sometimes, although a company is insolvent, the prospect for early rehabilitation may be good and the court may appoint a receiver to handle the property during the period of recovery. On the other hand, the company may be so insolvent as to be hopeless, and the receiver may be appointed to cut down fixed charges, assess the present holders, borrow funds, and put the reorganized company on its feet again. The trust company, by reason of its experience, good credit, and financial responsibility, is well fitted to act in any of these cases.

Trust Functions for Corporations

A trust company commonly acts as trustee under the trust deed or mortgage securing an issue of bonds. It certifies to the regularity of the issue and to the genuineness of the document, but does not guarantee the value or payment of the bond. In this capacity the company acts for the interest of the bondholders, and in case of default of the issuing company it could foreclose on the property covered by the deed or mortgage.

Another trust activity is to act as fiscal agent for states, municipalities, railroads, and industrials, handling the payments relating to the bonds, coupons, interest, dividends, taxes, acting as depository for the above corporations, receiving subscriptions to their securities, and delivering the issues.

Trust companies act as transfer agents for stocks and registrars for stocks and bonds, their duty being, in that connection, to prevent the fraudulent overissue of securities. The transfer agent cancels old certificates of stock and issues new ones in the names of the new owners. Bonds are registered as to principal or interest, or both, and usually the trustee of the mortgage underlying the bonds acts also as registrar of the bonds.

Other important operations of trust companies are connected with corporate reorganization and financing. This is a risky line of service and if the trust company is to maintain its good-will it must handle only conservative propositions. When charged with such work the trust company determines upon a plan of reorganization, recalls the outstanding certificates, distributes the new ones, makes assessments, and manages the reorganized company until it is an assured success. When a new enterprise is to be financed, the trust company investigates the concern and the value of its physical and other assets, undertakes the sale of its securities, and acts as a regular investment banker.

Insurance and Safe-Deposit Functions

Some few states permit trust companies to do a fidelity insurance and title insurance business similar to that done by regular bond or surety companies. Fidelity insurance is devoted chiefly to acting as surety for the honesty and fidelity of officers and employees holding positions of trust and responsibility. Such an arrangement is better for all concerned than to have friends go surety for the person bonded, for the person signing the bond, and for the security afforded the beneficiary named in the bond. The fidelity company receives compensation for its service, assumes the risk as an actuarial business matter, and protects the beneficiary with its known financial responsibility. Title insurance is an agreement of the trust compay to defend, at its own expense, all litigation directed against the title insured by it, and in case of unsuccessful defense to bear losses up to the full sum insured for.

Trust companies also do a safe-deposit business, maintaining vaults so constructed as to be proof alike against burglars and mobs, fire, and water. Boxes are rented for the keeping of money, jewels, and valuable papers and access thereto is given only when the vault guard is in attendance.

While there are other minor functions performed by trust companies, those just described are the most important and indicate the wide variety and complexity of the trust banking business.

The banking system of the United States is dual in the sense that some institutions are authorized by federal statute and charters and other institutions by state statute and charters, and the two classes have developed in competition with each other.

The financial institutions to which federal charters are granted or which operate under federal law include:

1. Federal Reserve Banks.
2. National Banks, Some Of Which Have Local Or Foreign Branches.
3. Federal Land Banks.
4. Federal Joint-Stock Land Banks.
5. National Farm Loan Associations.
6. Postal Savings Depositories, Including Branch Post-Offices And Stations.
7. "Edge" Corporations.
8. The War Finance Corporation.

The state institutions are more varied in their nature, purpose, and operations. They embrace:

1. Commercial Chartered Banks.
2. Private Individual Banks.
3. Trust Companies.
4. Mutual Or Trustee Savings Banks.
5. Joint-Stock And "Special Deposits" Savings Banks.
6. Bond Houses And Investment Companies.
7. Co-Operative Savings Associations And Building And Loan Associations.
8. Morris-Plan Banks.
9. Personal Loan Companies.
10. Personal Loan Brokers.
11. Land Banks.
12. Mortgage Loan Companies.
13. Credit Unions.
14. Discount Houses.
15. Acceptance Houses.
16. Note Brokerage Houses.

17. Finance Companies.
18. Cattle Loan Companies.

THE FIRST BANK OF THE UNITED STATES

As part of a general scheme to support public credit in 1791, Alexander Hamilton prevailed upon Congress to institute the first Bank of the United States. His main arguments in support of the institution were:

1. The demonstrated success and usefulness of national banks in the chief European countries.
2. The more effective utilization of capital by concentrating the savings of the community for business uses.
3. The possible services of such a bank to the government in advancing loans and facilitating the payment of taxes.
4. The Desirability of A Bank Note Currency.

The opposition to the scheme was led by Madison and came from the southern states.

The law provided for a Bank of the United States, located at Philadelphia, capitalized at $10,000,000, with shares at $400 each, subscriptions payable one-fourth in specie and three-fourths in United States securities bearing 6 per cent interest and payable within two years. The United States government subscribed $2,000,000, which sum was loaned by the bank to the government, the loan to be repaid in ten annual instalments. Thus the payment of the government subscription was effected by what were virtually stock notes - a very faulty banking operation. The subscriptions in government securities were thought to give the bank a wider basis for note issue than would otherwise have been possible, as it would have been difficult to assemble $10,000,000 in gold.

The bank was privately controlled by a board of directors of 25 members, one-fourth of whom at the end of each year became ineligible for re-election. Stockholders in foreign countries could not vote by proxy. The votes allowed per share decreased with the increase in the number of shares held by any one stockholder, thus providing for decentralized control, and no subscription, save that of the government, was to exceed 1,000 shares.

The bank was authorized to issue notes which were a legal tender in payment of all debts to the United States. The bank's debts were limited to the amount of the capital. This limitation could be exceeded only by authorization of Congress, and the directors were personally liable for the excess. The bank was forbidden to trade in merchandise, it was permitted to sell - but not to buy - United States securities, and its real estate investments were limited to its bank buildings and site. The bank was to make no loan to the United States in excess of $100,000, nor to any state in excess of $50,000, nor to any foreign country without the authorization of Congress. The maximum rate for loans and discounts was fixed at 6 per cent. The directors were empowered to establish branches within the United States. The bank was required to report its condition to the Secretary of the Treasury at his demand, but not oftener than once a week. The Secretary of the Treasury had the right to inspect the books of the bank. The charter ran for twenty years and meanwhile the government was to establish no other bank.

In 1792 the bank established in the chief cities of the country eight branches, among which the $10,000,000 capital was apportioned.

Bank notes were issued by the parent bank and its branches in denominations of $5 and more, the total amount in circulation at any one time never exceeding $6,000,000. As the parent bank refused to redeem the notes of its branches, this forced each branch to be self-reliant and tended to prevent overextension; this policy also relieved the parent bank from a sudden demand for large payment at any one of its branches. The bank used "half-notes" and "post-notes" to make payments at a distance. As these notes circulated widely, they had a salutary effect in restraining the overissue of notes by state banks.

SERVICES OF FIRST BANK TO GOVERNMENT

The government enjoyed many advantages from the bank, such as the $2,000,000 loan for its stock subscription, which bore only

6 per cent interest, whereas the dividend rate on the stock was 8 per cent, the 2 per cent difference representing a net profit to the government. The Treasury also borrowed on short-term notes from the bank. When by 1795 long-term loans to the government amounted to $6,200,000, or nearly two-thirds of its entire capital, this concentration of loans crippled its services to commerce and industry and also made it difficult for the institution to help the government with short-term accommodation. To liquidate its debt to the bank the government, between 1797 and 1802, sold its shares of the bank's stock - at premiums aggregating $671,860. Meanwhile the government had received dividends amounting to $1,101,720.

The relations between the Treasury and the bank were intimate. The bank granted loans to the Treasury, helped it to perform its foreign exchange business - for the bank did most of the foreign and domestic exchange business of the country - acted as government depository, paying no interest on the public deposits, and in compensation for the use of the deposits transmitted public moneys from place to place free of charge. In addition the bank was of service to importers in the payment of custom duties, which were commonly paid in post-notes. After 1800 the Collector of the Internal Revenue used the bank as well as its branches to collect the maturing revenue bonds, promoting thereby greater punctuality and economy in the service.

DISSOLUTION OF FIRST BANK

Because the bank was regarded as a Federalist institution, Jefferson and the Democrats were opposed to it, yet the institution was managed capably and with a view to profits and kept aloof from political controversies. Gallatin, who pleaded the bank's cause with Jefferson, was willing to waive political objections in consideration of the fiscal and business advantages of its operation, and in 1808 when the original charter was soon to expire he advocated its renewal. The objection which weighed most heavily against the bank was the large holdings of the bank's stock abroad and the consequent payment of dividends to foreigners. The trade organizations of the country in general favored the renewal of the charter but state jealousy of the national institution and the repressive effect of the bank and its branches on the smaller new state banks, served to fan political opposition. As a result Congress refused to renew the charter, and in 1811 the bank closed. Its officials attempted to procure a state charter for it in Pennsylvania, but failed. They obtained one, however, in New York under the name, Bank of America, and the concern continued to do business as a state institution.

The first Bank of the United States failed of success because of political opposition, despite the fact that it had served well both the government and the financial and commercial world.

THE SECOND BANK OF THE UNITED STATES

After the dissolution of the first Bank of the United States and during the war against Great Britain, the money market became badly disorganized, specie payments were suspended except in New England, and the public credit sank to a low ebb. A demand for the re-establishment of the bank arose spontaneously, the main reason being to restore to the country an orderly currency through the resumption of specie payments. Accordingly a bill was passed in 1816 creating a new bank, with a charter to run for twenty years.

The new bank was capitalized at $35,000,000, in $100 shares, one-fifth to be subscribed by the government and four-fifths by private subscribers. No one subscription was to exceed $390,000. Subscriptions were payable within a year, one-fourth in specie, and the remainder in either specie or government bonds. The board of directors consisted of 25 members, 5 of whom were appointed annually by the President of the United States from several states, and the other 20 by the stockholders under a system of restricted voting. Not all the directors were eligible for re-election and no director could be a director of any other bank.

The bank was authorized to deal in bills of exchange and bullion and to sell goods pledged for loans, but was not to deal in any public stock. Loans to the United States were limited to $500,000, and to any state to $50,000. Debts, excluding deposits, were not to exceed the capital. The smallest denomination of bank note issued was $5. All bank notes below $100 denomination were payable upon demand, and were legal tender in payments to the government. The larger notes could run for terms up to 60 days. The organization of branches of the bank was required under certain conditions, and control of the branch was lodged with the parent institution by the appointment of the branch directors.

The bank was required to transmit public moneys at par and free of charge. The Treasurer was directed to deposit the government funds in the bank or its branches; and if for any reason he did not do so, he was to report the reasons to Congress. In case of the suspension of specie payments, the obligations of the bank were subject to 12 per cent interest until resumption of such payments. The bank was to make periodical statements, not more often than once a week, to the Secretary of the Treasury, and he was empowered to inspect its books. A bonus of $1,500,000 was levied upon the bank for its franchise.

HISTORY OF SECOND BANK

Professor Dewey summarizes the history of the bank somewhat as follows. The bank was chartered on April 10, 1816, and on April 30 Congress ordered the resumption of specie payments to go into effect on February 20, 1817. The bank was quickly organized under the presidency of one Jones, and began operations in January, 1817. Owing to mismanagement, Jones was forced to resign in 1818, and Langdon Cheves became president. He held office until 1823, when he was succeeded by Nicholas Biddle. In June, 1829, Senator Woodbury of New Hampshire brought complaints against Jeremiah Mason, manager of the Portsmouth branch; in the following December President Jackson in his annual message questioned the constitutionality of the bank and accused it of failing to establish a sound currency.

On April 30, 1830, a committee of the House of Representatives reported at length on the questions raised by Jackson, its conclusions being entirely favorable to the bank. A Senate report was likewise friendly. In 1831 Senator Benton supported a resolution against rechartering the bank. In January, 1832, the bank petitioned for recharter. This petition was favorably acted upon by committees of the Senate and the House and a bill for recharter was passed. The bill, however, was vetoed by Jackson, July 10, 1832. In the autumn of the same year Jackson was re-elected President, and he interpreted the vote as an indorsement of his opposition to the bank. In December, 1832, he raised the question as to whether the funds of the government were safe in the custody of the bank. An investigation was ordered by the House, and a majority report of the Committee on Ways and Means upheld the policy of the bank and was adopted March 2, 1833, by a vote of 109 to 46. Notwithstanding this recommendation the President determined to remove the deposits, and in order to accomplish his purpose, on September 23 he dismissed Duane, Secretary of the Treasury, who objected to the removal, and appointed Taney in his place. The latter, on September 26, ordered that deposits henceforth be made in certain state banks, and on December 3, 1833, he reported to the Senate his reasons for their removal. In 1836 the charter of the bank expired.

Weaknesses in Operation of Second Bank

A number of weaknesses developed in the operations of the second bank during its earlier years. The subscription to its stock by means of stock notes was a mistake in that the method of payment amounted to a margin purchase of the stock and was therefore speculative in character; besides, the payments on the notes were very dilatory and renewals were freely made.

Friction also developed with the state banks over the transfer of public deposits and over the credit to be given to state bank notes. The state banks, with the exception of those in New York, Philadelphia, and Baltimore, refused to help the national bank effect the resumption of specie payments, and when this resumption was accomplished without their help they became embittered. When the national bank charged the delinquent banks interest on overdue balances, they regarded this as "an unprecedented grievance." The withdrawal of government deposits from a state bank usually led to a collision, not with the Treasury but with the national bank with which the funds were placed.

A controversy which centered in the West, where inflation had been carried further than elsewhere, arose over the acceptance of state bank notes tendered in payment of public revenues. The Treasury and the bank instead of co-operating in the matter worked at cross-purposes. The Treasury permitted the collectors of internal revenue to receive state bank notes, the collection of which was thrown upon the national bank. This responsibility brought the latter into collision with the state banks, which were unable or unwilling to redeem promptly. The national bank held that whatever loss was incurred in the collection of the notes should devolve upon the Treasury, but the Treasury threatened to remove all public deposits rather than deprive the people of the means of paying for public lands and for their taxes. Naturally this dispute also contributed to the unpopularity of the national bank.

Political expediency as well as the terms of the charter demanded that many branches be established, and 27 in all were founded. Almost every state had at least one, and this was too many for the best business efficiency. Losses were greater in the branches than in the parent bank, for the reason that they were run more loosely and their management tended to yield to local pressure for favors in operation and policy. The branches were established with an eye to equalizing banking facilities over the country and consequently excessive amounts of cash were transferred to the South and West. Despite the number of branches, however, it was impracticable to open one in every collection district, and this was a further cause of complaint.

The volume of deposits fluctuated widely from month to month and this fluctuation was a very disturbing factor in the bank's loan operations. The original theory was that the bank and its branches were a unit and, since the bank was required to transmit government funds free of charge, the Treasury drew upon the bank at any place where public money was deposited, whether public funds happened to be there at that time or not, it being understood that the Treasury would give the bank reasonable notice of withdrawal so that provision might be made for meeting the draft. Trouble soon arose between the bank and the Treasury because of lack of sufficient notice, but later a schedule of lengths of notice was arranged. The transfer of public moneys by the bank was a convenient arrangement for the government, and better than any that could have been provided by the state banks.

Defects of Note Redemption System

Though the original system of bank note redemption aided in effecting resumption by forcing the state banks to improve the standing of their notes and created a good national currency accepted everywhere, it was nevertheless defective. The parent bank agreed to redeem its own notes and those of the branches north of Charleston, without distinction, at any branch. One result was that the parent bank did not know where or when notes were likely to be presented. Loans were also created freely by certain branches, for the loaning branch knew that its notes would be presented elsewhere for redemption. In consequence, sudden and great demands were made, varying with the balance of trade, and it became useless for any one branch to be conservative.

For these reasons the system broke down in 1818, and the bank resolved that no branch should take the notes of other branches except in payments due to the United States. It further resolved that no branch should reissue notes of the parent bank or other branches except when it was a creditor of the other bank, and then only when the exchanges indicated that such reissue was for the interest of the parent bank. By making notes of $5 denomination issued by any branch or by the parent bank acceptable at the others, however, a good currency was provided. But the burden of signing these notes of small denomination was so great that the bank officers sought relief from Congress; failing to secure this relief the bank in 1827 invented "branch drafts," in $5 and $10 denominations. These drafts were signed by the branch president and cashier, and drawn upon the parent bank; they resembled bank notes in form, were indorsed payable to bearer, and circulated freely, supplanting the notes in certain areas. Their issue, however, was a leading cause of complaint against the parent bank, because such drafts were held to be contrary to the provisions of the bank's charter and harmful because they contracted the circulation of the state banks.

Services of Second Bank to Commerce

The second Bank of the United States operated in domestic exchange, the sale of drafts to the public constituting no small part of its business. The public and the Treasury argued that the bank ought to sell these drafts at par; but the bank charged varying rates of exchange, averaging 1/2 per cent. These varying rates gave rise to the complaint that the bank showed favoritism and that it charged excessive and usurious rates. After 1820, however, the bank bought bills heavily and increasingly, and this helped to facilitate commerce and to equalize exchange. In this business it competed with the state banks. The exchange operations gave the bank a considerable control over the local currency by purchasing, or refusing to purchase, bills from the different areas.

During the first few years of the second bank's existence its services to commerce were restricted through the tying up of an undue proportion of its capital in stock notes received for subscriptions. With the change of management, however, its service improved and commercial loans of short-term usance were readily granted, mostly on pledge of personalty. Not only by aiding commerce in this and other ways, but also by its influence upon the state institutions, the bank proved its value to the community as a national institution.

Causes of Dissolution of Second Bank

The opposition which brought the bank to an untimely end was largely inspired by political intrigue and by selfish jealousy on the part of the state banks. The charges of Jackson and other critics were that some of its officers who were incompetent were retained in office by political influence, that it tried to influence political elections and state legislation, and that some of the branches were established for political effect. It was further alleged that the bank was monopolistic and undemocratic in character and therefore dangerous to our institutions. On other grounds it was argued that the bank was unconstitutional. Some of its banking operations were held to be objectionable and violations of its charter, such, for instance, as the use of branch drafts, the practice of usury in exchange dealings, the sale of coin, trading in public securities, speculation in real estate, and the like. The aggressive and peculiar character of the Democratic President, with his large political following from the West and South, really explains why the inconsequential charges brought against so serviceable and successful an institution led to its dissolution.

State Banks Before the Civil War

Banking in the United States really dates from 1781, when Robert Morris, Superintendent of Finance of the Revolution, founded the Bank of North America at Philadelphia to promote the financing of Washington's army. The institution was chartered by the Continental Congress and was organized as a means of creating credits based upon the small amount of specie that existed and of making advances to the government. It was a complete success as a war measure and had a benign commercial influence as well. In 1782 it was chartered as a state bank in Pennsylvania, and under this charter, renewed from time to time, it enjoyed a very successful career until 1864, when it became a national bank, and is still a leading bank of Philadelphia.

In 1784 Massachusetts chartered the Bank of Massachusetts, and in New York, under Hamilton's influence, the Bank of New York was founded and put into operation but the state refused to grant it a charter until 1791. The tendency in both these states, as time passed, was to lay heavier restrictions upon their banks. The restrictions included the imposition of personal liability upon directors for any violation of the law that debts should not exceed some specified multiple of the paid-in capital, the limitation of notes to large denominations, the prohibition of dealing in merchandise or stocks, and the requirement of reports of condition.

By the year 1800 the number of state banks had increased to 28, and by 1811, to 88. This rapid increase, though it indicated the need of credit institutions, was also a leading cause of the opposition to the rechartering of the first Bank of the United States. In the period from 1812 to 1816 the Treasury of the United States employed the state banks as depositories of the public funds. The poor conduct of the national finances, particularly the failure to levy taxes, the heavy issue of Treasury circulating notes, and the drain of specie abroad precipitated suspension of specie payments by all state banks, except those in New England, and tied up the government deposits.

The failure to recharter the first Bank of the United States left the field free to the state banks, which increased from 88 in 1811 to 246 in 1816, and expanded their bank note issues to $100,000,000. These banks were organized on very defective credit principles, the loans being based heavily upon lands and government securities. The export of specie due to the adverse balance of trade made the situation still worse. The Treasury operations were thrown into confusion by the disordered currency. At this juncture, in the year 1816, the demand for a second Bank of the United States became strong enough to force Congress to grant a charter.

From its organization in 1816 down to 1834, the year in which the second Bank of the United States was refused an extension of its charter, the state banks grew in number. Good statistics are not available as to their number, for no general reporting system existed and, moreover, through a peculiar policy of secrecy, several states concealed the operations of their banks. The available records, however, indicate that in 1829 there were 329 banks, the character of which varied greatly, depending upon state law, local conditions, and individual management.

After Jackson's re-election in 1832 he became more determined in his opposition to the second Bank of the United States and decided to sever relations between the government and the institution, removing the public deposits and putting them in state banks. These state banks, although selected with reasonable care and subjected to fairly strict conditions, were called Jackson's "pets," and political motives were alleged to have entered into their selection.

The entire period from 1816 to 1837 was one of rapid development and speculative prosperity. Land speculation, internal improvements, and the development of cotton farming were particularly active features of finance, and banks in consequence sprang into existence in great numbers. The hope of procuring some of the redistributed public surplus during Jackson's administration was a further stimulus. By 1836 the number of state depository banks increased To 89 And By 1837 the state banks increased to 788, with a circulation of $149,000,000.

Causes of Panic of 1837

In 1836 the Treasury issued the "specie circular," an order to its public land agents to receive for the sale of public lands only specie, and to refuse the notes issued by the banks. The order aimed to repress land frauds, to discourage the extension of bank notes and bank credits, and to protect the Treasury.

The circular restricted particularly the activities of western banks and their eastern agents. This restriction, in conjunction with the failure of a number of foreign banks and the failure of the crops between 1835 and 1837, precipitated a panic which had been brewing for some time.

When the transfer of public deposits was suddenly halted, banks and projects founded on the expectation of receiving these funds failed straightway and the government lost heavily. During the long period of depression that followed, the number of banks, after increasing to 901 in 1840, declined to 691 in 1843, and their circulation contracted from $149,000,000 in 1837 to $59,000,000 in 1843.

The Independent Treasury System

After the crisis of 1837 many projects were advanced to substitute for the banks some other form of financial institution as public depositories. Two national banks had failed for political reasons, and losses had been sustained by the Treasury during the intervening periods, 1812-1816 and 1832-1836, when it had used the state banks. After a long legislative struggle an independent treasury was created in 1840, the law having a "specie clause" to the effect that the government would accept only specie in payments to itself. The Whigs in 1842 repealed the Independent Treasury Act and attempted in vain to establish a national bank.

The Democrats in 1846 re-established the Independent Treasury by legislation which permitted only specie and treasury notes to be received by the government, and public funds to be kept only in the Treasury, sub-treasuries, the mints, and the custom-houses. The Independent Treasury system worked fairly well during the period before the Civil War.

The inauguration of the system was plainly forced by the abuses and failure of the banking system of the day, and was a protest both against the central national bank and the state bank systems. Before the Civil War the state banks had increased in number from 691 in 1843, to 1,601 in 1861; in circulation from $59,000,-000, to $202,000,000; and in deposits from $56,000,000, to $ 257,000,000. Some states had developed a body of sound banking laws and methods of supervising their banks, thereby increasing their utility as commercial and public institutions.

Bases of Note Issue Before the Civil War

The period between 1790 and 1861 was one of experimental banking in a new country rich in natural resources and settled with an energetic, inventive, and independent people who worked things out for themselves locally. But the country was poor in specie, in loanable capital, in financial institutions, and in experience. Such a combination led to a wide variety of experiments which always sought a maximum of benefit from a minimum of specie. Banks of many kinds were developed, and four types of note, issue stand out, based upon or protected by:

1. General Assets.
2. A General Safety Fund.
3. Bond Security.
4. The Credit of The Several States.

General Assets. Of the banks whose issues rested upon general assets, the best examples were those of New England. The original Bank of Massachusetts was of this type and was singularly free from legal limitations. Later laws restricted the amount of issue to a multiple of the capital and specified the minimum denomination of the notes, but no provision was made for the special protection of the notes. The banks were required to report their condition from time to time to the state. They grew up in a conservative area and were sounder than those in other parts of the country. As a result, in 1814 they alone of all banks did not suspend specie payments. In 1837 Massachusetts adopted a system of examinations by state bank commissioners. Though repealed in 1842, the system was readopted in 1851.

The banks of New England were modeled upon those of Massachusetts, and they maintained intimate relations with the banks of Boston. The Boston banks in 1818 instituted the Suffolk system of note redemption, in order to prevent the note issues of interior banks from driving out of circulation the issues of the sound Boston banks. This system required the country banks to keep, in addition to a sum sufficient for the current redemption of its notes, a permanent deposit with the Suffolk Bank. The notes of any bank which refused to make this deposit were sent home for redemption. A large majority of the New England banks came into the system, some quite reluctantly, and the circulating notes of the area were thus brought to par in Boston. The bank notes were redeemed through this agency on an average ten times a year, and this redemption constantly tested the solvency of the issuing bank and kept the volume of issue elastic.

Safety Fund. The safety fund system was illustrated in New York. It was inaugurated at the instance of Governor Van Buren, in 1829, as a protection for notes only, but by accident the fund was made to cover deposits also. Each bank was to pay annually to the State Treasurer a sum equal to 1/2 per cent of its capital until the payments aggregated 3 per cent. Any deficit, after the assets of a failed bank had been liquidated and the proceeds applied to its notes and deposits, was paid from this fund. In 1837 the law was changed to provide for the immediate payment of the notes of an insolvent bank whose debts in excess of assets were less than two-thirds of the bank fund. In 1842 the fund was specifically set aside for the redemption of bank notes alone, and the other liabilities of the bank were charges against the assets. Had the fund not been made to cover both notes and deposits, it would have succeeded, for calculation shows that the annual assessment required to pay the losses from 1829 to 1865 would have been less than 1/4 Per cent of the capital and 3/8 per cent of the average circulation of the banks. The fund should have been proportioned to the volume of the note issue rather than to the capitalization.

Bond Security. The panic of 1837 proved the defects of the safety fund system of protecting bank notes as employed in New York State, and the next year the Free Banking Act was passed. Banking was "free" in the sense that any individuals or associations were free to open a bank and to issue notes upon deposit with the State Comptroller of securities of the United States, or of New York, or of any other state approved by the Comptroller. After 1840 the securities of other states were not accepted. Provision was also made, though little used, for the issue of notes against deposit of approved mortgages. Though this method of note issue lacked elasticity, it was relatively sound, and in 1863 it became the model of the national bank note system. Many other states also adopted the method of protection by deposit of securities, but usually without due safeguards, so that in some states an endless chain of debt creation and note issue developed until the securities fell below par.

State Credit. The fourth system of note issue was based on state credit, that is, on the credit of banks owned and managed by the state. Though the Constitution forbade the states to issue bills of credit, in 1837 the Supreme Court decided that an issue by a bank owned in whole or part by the state was not thereby prohibited. Such banks had been in operation even before this date, but the experiences of Kentucky, Alabama, Mississippi, Florida, Illinois, Louisiana, and other states, with their note issues, were most unfortunate. On the other hand, the state bank of Indiana was very successful. It based its note on commercial assets and required the payment of its capital in actual cash, whether the subscriptions were by the state government or by private citizens. The state made good profits on its investment and its natural resources were developed very well indeed through the help of the bank.

EVILS OF EARLY BANK NOTE ISSUES

Prior to the year 1860 the state bank notes consisted of a heterogeneous currency, lacking all uniformity, under diverse systems of issue, with varying degrees of protection and of limitations on issues. The bank notes of the New York banks, where the banking law was rigidly enforced, attained wide circulation; the mutual redemption system in New England also gave currency to the notes of the stronger banks. With these and a few other exceptions, state bank notes enjoyed only a local credit.

As bank notes constituted practically the whole circulating media, the difficulties confronting travelers in procuring acceptable media for their expenses can readily be realized. The currency of the western states was so motley and contained so many doubtful notes that their recipient had to have almost the expert knowledge of a note-detector. The notes issued in one state were accepted at varying rates of discount in others, and the consequent losses were large. Exchange on eastern cities was quoted in the Mid-west at high premiums, ranging from 1 to 10 per cent. After its unfortunate experiences in the panic of 1837, the national government refused to accept bank notes and insisted upon specie in payments to itself.

Noteholders, particularly the poorer and more ignorant classes into whose hands the worst notes drifted, lost heavily from failures of the issuing banks. In 1861 a writer in the Chicago Tribune said the "bank nuisance had become unbearable." According to that writer many banks made it their chief business to manufacture and put out as large an amount as they could by any contrivance keep in circulation, regardless of the dearth of reserves. Some were "merely banks of circulation without capital and doing no business at their nominal locations," the notes being issued at goodly distances from the place of redemption so as to delay presentation.

Since the notes circulated some time before redemption, they became dirty, greasy, mutilated, and worn - facts which made them not only unfit for circulation but also facilitated counterfeiting. It was necessary to inspect all bills carefully and the receiving tellers of banks had to be very expert and acute to recognize and reject the spurious notes. Publications, known as "Counterfeit Detectors," with weekly supplements, found a useful place in every counting-room. A writer in 1863, examining these "Detectors," claimed that there were in existence nearly 1,600 banks issuing daily 10,000 different kinds of notes, a large portion having been copied and issued by counterfeiters.

Considering the number of issues, the different forms and pictorial designs, the various denominations, the numerous counterfeits and raised notes, and the notes of fraudulent and failed banks, that formed the currency of the day, it is not surprising that reform was advocated. The poorer and more ignorant classes, who were least able to refuse tendered notes and to detect and reject worthless ones, suffered most and yet could not make their protests heard.

During periods of depression the quantity of note circulation was considerably decreased by failures of issuing banks, but prosperous years gave birth to new issues. The volume in circulation was also summarily increased or decreased by fits of legislative enactments permitting or suppressing note issues.

Another evil of the day inherent in the bank note system was the speculation and traffic in bank notes. Speculators would buy up certain issues at discounts and carry them to redemption points or put them out in regions where they circulated at higher values; they would also speculate in the changes in note values effected by time. In 1861 the risks and difficulties of note circulation were increased by the suspension of the banks, a suspension which relieved them from the test of redeeming in specie their issues on presentation, but allowed them to redeem with the fluctuating greenbacks, if redeemed at all. A sound, sufficient, and uniform currency was also rendered necessary by the government's suspension of specie payments and by the passage of the Internal Revenue Bill, for the collection of revenues would have been farcical or unequal if the revenues could have been paid in the existing legal tenders or bank notes.

PROPOSED ADVANTAGES OF NATIONAL BANK NOTE ISSUE

In his finance report of 1861, Secretary Chase first stated the advantages to be derived from "the preparation and delivery to institutions and associations of notes prepared for circulation under national direction and secured as to prompt convertibility into coin by the pledge of United States bonds." The advantages claimed were:

1. Uniformity In Currency.
2. Uniformity In Security.
3. Effectual safeguard, if effectual safeguard is possible, against depreciation.
4. Protection From Losses On Discounts And Exchanges.
5. A Large Demand For Government Securities.
6. Increased Facilities For Obtaining War Loans.
7. Some alleviation of the burdens on industry, through a diminution of the rate of interest or a participation in the profit of circulation without risking the peril of a great money monopoly.

8. Increased security to the Union, springing from the common interest in its preservation, created by the distribution of its stocks to associations throughout the country as the basis of circulation.
9. Easy and desirable method of accomplishment through voluntary action of existing institutions.

In 1862 Chase drew attention to the further advantage that the note-issuing banks would provide the government with safe and convenient agencies for the deposit of government moneys. His two fundamental motives were: to create a safe uniform currency, and to secure a market for government bonds. He opposed making the greenbacks legal tender and objected to their issue, suggesting as an alternative the issue of bond-secured bank notes. The plan necessitated the nationalization of the banks, a step which the banks strongly opposed in Congress on the grounds that: (1) nationalization would force the state bonds already deposited against circulation on the market in competition with United States bonds; (2) the total note circulation was but $200,000,000, and the market created for bonds would therefore be negligible; (3) nationalization would take place slowly and the government would secure no considerable relief for two or three years.

The National Banking Act

The National Banking Act became a law on February 25, 1863. On October 1 the Secretary reported the organization of but 66 national banks, and these were small institutions with the foundation of which the leading financiers had nothing to do. During the early part of 1864 Chase urged a prohibitive tax on state bank notes as a means of forcing the state banks to nationalize, the argument being based on:

1. The Desirability Of An Exclusive National Currency.
2. The support which the bond sales would afford to the credit of the government.
3. The convenience and utility of the national banks to the government. On June 3, 1864, the act was amended, the new

act constituting what is commonly called the National Banking Act. On March 3, 1865, an act was passed imposing a tax of 10 per cent on the amount of notes issued by state banks after July 1, 1866. Up to November 15, 1864, only 584 national banks had been organized, with $81,961,450 capital. The effect of the tax by October 1, 1865, was to raise the number of banks to 1,566, with $276,-219,450 capital. Though during the Civil War the national bank system failed to provide either a uniform currency (which seems to have been Chase's main motive), or a market for government bonds, after the amendment of March 3, 1865, the plan quickly established a safe and uniform note circulation and a permanent market for government bonds.

THE GROWTH OF THE NATIONAL BANKING SYSTEM

The nationalization of those state banks which desired to continue to issue bank notes was rapidly consummated during the years 1865 and 1866. Since that time the number of banks has increased eightfold, with periods of growth between 1871 and 1875, 1880 and 1892, and 1900 and 1919, and periods of contraction between 1867 and 1869, 1876 and 1879, 1894 and 1898, and in 1916. The most rapid expansion occurred after 1900, at which date the minimum required capitalization, as well as the tax on circulation, was reduced. The volume of national bank notes is not an adequate index to the growth of the banks. The rapid growth between the dates 1877 and 1882 was due to the expansion of the country; their growth between 1895 and 1914 was also due to the expansion of the country, but more particularly, after 1900, to the lower capital requirements for national banks. The two periods of their decline were between the years 1883 and 1891, when the government debt was being paid off, and between 1915 and 1917 when the Aldrich-Vreeland currency was being contracted. The two best indexes of banking activity are the deposits and aggregate resources. Except during the panic periods of 1873-1878, 1883-1887, and 1903, our banks have grown in number and in the extent of their operations, and the panic of 1907 and the depression of 1913-1914 retarded but did not reverse this tendency.

MOVEMENT TO REFORM NATIONAL BANKING SYSTEM

Certain defects in the national banking system appeared early, particularly in the geographical distribution of the banks and in the reduction of national bank note circulation as the national bonds were paid off. The inability of the system to meet and stem panics had been demonstrated in 1884, 1890, and 1893. During 1893 an acute scarcity of currency started the reform movement which has culminated in the federal reserve. At the meeting of the American Bankers' Association at Baltimore in 1893 a plan for a currency protected by a joint guaranty fund contributed by all the banks was advocated; this "Baltimore plan" of "currency reform" was based on the Canadian system. In 1896 the reform of the banking currency became involved with the question of bimetallism versus the gold standard. The Indianapolis Currency Commission, a body composed of representatives of boards of trade and commercial organizations, recommended the establishment of the gold standard, the segregation of the reserve gold fund against greenbacks and its automatic repletion by issue of bonds, and the issue of bank notes based upon commercial paper and protected in several ways.

The Gold Standard Act of 1900 accomplished the first two of these recommendations, and further provided for the refunding of the government bonds into 2 per cent consols and the establishment of national banks with a smaller capitalization than had been allowed theretofore, and permitted the issue of notes up to 100 per cent instead of 90 per cent of the par value of the bonds. This legislation temporarily satisfied the demand for currency, but it did not remedy any of the inherent defects of the national bank plan.

The aim of reform henceforth was to reorganize the system completely. In 1901 and succeeding years the Banking and Currency

Committee of the House of Representatives presented bills to establish an elastic currency and a centralized banking system. Several banking students advocated in private circulars, in the press, and in Congressional bills, various schemes of centralization.

The movement thus well under way was precipitated by the panic of 1907. In the spring of 1908 the Banking and Currency Committee of the House reported the Fowler Bill advocating the issue of currency based on commercial paper, and the Senate Committee on Finance reported the Aldrich Bill advocating the issue of notes against other kinds of bonds than United States bonds. As a compromise, the Aldrich-Vreeland Act of May 30, 1908, was passed, providing for the issue of currency based on commercial paper by associations of banks known as "national currency associations," and for the issue of national bank notes based on deposits of special kinds of municipal and other bonds. This act, which was regarded as a makeshift on the eve of a presidential election, provided for a National Monetary Commission with wide powers to make an investigation of the currency and banking situation and report to Congress.

The commission made an extensive investigation and published an excellent series of books with the object of helping to educate the business and financial world in the banking problem. In 1910 Senator Aldrich presented in a bill the outlines of the Aldrich or Monetary Commission plan. A Republican Congress meanwhile had become Democratic in character and the Aldrich Bill in consequence died in committee. The Democratic Banking and Currency Committee of the House, out of the vast amount of information assembled, and with the help of the Aldrich, Fowler, Muehlman, and other bills, prepared, during 1912 and 1913, a preliminary draft of what later became the Federal Reserve Act. After three months of consideration and amendment the measure passed Congress and was signed by the President on December 23, 1913. It is known as the Currency Act, or more commonly and properly the Federal Reserve Act, and is the most important piece of financial legislation since the National Bank Act of 1863

11

Credit Confidence and Time Element

The discussion of money has so far dealt only with the metallic forms. Transactions in which immediate payment of standard metallic money is made are primarily barter transactions - as when one hat is exchanged for one ounce of gold; they are transactions, however, which differ from the original barter transactions, inasmuch as the receiver of the gold does not take it for his present industrial or personal use but as a representative of those things for which he is confident he can exchange it.

This purposed exchange may be direct or indirect. One man, Brown, accepts gold because he is confident that another, Jones, will take it from him for shoes which Brown wishes and which Jones has. This confidence is born of custom and rests upon the inertia of custom to change, and is seldom if ever consciously acted upon. Brown, however, may accept silver or paper which he knows Jones will not accept for the shoes, but which he knows Smith will accept in exchange for gold. That is, Brown knows that by indirection he can get the shoes from Jones. This confidence that Smith stands ready to exchange gold for silver or paper rests upon custom, upon Smith's promise, or upon law or public opinion compelling Smith to make such exchanges. Smith's function is to convert or redeem silver or paper with gold. Thus the very foundation of the money concept is faith in another. This faith is "credit." "He believes." Brown believes that Jones will accept and Smith will redeem. It is a confidence which extends over a period of time, that is, Brown accepts now, believing that Jones or Smith will accept later. The coin or paper is the tangible evidence of that faith and the measure of its amount. A gold eagle or a $20 bill accepted by Brown is evidence that he trusts custom, promise, or law to that amount.

THE CONTRACT ELEMENT

Indeed, Brown may desire the shoes but he may not have gold or another commodity acceptable to Jones, but Jones, having confidence in Brown's future ability and willingness to provide acceptable commodities, may therefore be willing to transfer the shoes to Brown at once and trust him to transfer acceptable commodities later. The payment, in other words, is deferred. Since either man or both is likely to forget the exact nature and terms of this deferred payment, some written evidence is usually prepared to describe it. This written evidence may be simply a book entry, or it may be a special instrument drawn up to which Brown subscribes. In any case the credit precedes and exists independently of the instrument; contracts, written or parol (oral), characterize a credit economy and may well be regarded an essential attribute of credits, but emphasis on this feature is likely to becloud the more fundamental element - confidence.

Reduction of the credit contract to writing serves several purposes, but parol credit is just as thoroughly credit as is that evidenced by written instruments. Writing gives the contract legal definiteness; what was possibly vague, easily forgotten, and therefore subject to dispute, becomes definite and lasting. If left in the form of an entry in an open book account, it is still subject to dispute by the debtor, and the burden of proof of its validity and correctness rests upon the creditor. But if reduced to writing and signed by the debtor, the law presumes that it was then and is now valid and correct, hence the burden of proof to the contrary is upon the debtor. Writing also makes the contract more easily transferable. Writing, however, does not change its credit basis; the credit instrument cannot be better than the credit which it embodies; its safety and security do not lie in the form, but in the credit conditions underlying its creation; the promissory note by which a book account is closed has no greater security than the book account itself; it simply renders the account in a more convenient form for the creditor.

Jones, however, at the time he grants credit to Brown, may not know what specific commodities he may want at the maturity of the credit; it serves his convenience, therefore, to have Brown promise to pay in terms of the most commonly acceptable commodity in the community, which Jones believes he can exchange for things then wanted. It is, therefore, drawn in terms of money. Money is the standard of deferred payment. Credit is the deferred payment. The credit instrument is the certificate of such deferred payment. The four attributes of credit are, therefore, standard money, confidence, time, and contract.

CREDIT A SUBSTITUTE FOR MONEY

Credit serves the convenience of Brown and Jones in another way. So long as metallic money was passed at the time of exchange, every exchange necessitated the handling and testing of two commodities - the article bought and the gold given. The gold had to be carried to market, and as exchange grew in frequency, volume, and distance, to carry and count metallic money became bothersome, dangerous, and expensive. The receipt of actual metallic money was no advantage except that it might be more widely acceptable than the private credit of the buyer.

If, however, Jones accepts Brown's credit and Brown accepts Jones's credit, the burden of actual money transactions can be greatly reduced. Promises may be balanced against each other and only the net balances actually paid in metallic money. Credit operations, therefore, while making use of standard money as a unit of account and as a standard of deferred payment, obviate to a large degree the use of money as a means of payment; hence credit comes to play an even more important role than standard money as a circulating medium. As standard money facilitates exchange over the barter economy, so credit facilitates exchange over the money economy. A credit transaction is a form of exchange in which credit is given by one of the parties; it may be a deferred payment either of goods or of money, but it is usually stated, for reasons shown, in terms of the standard money; it is a present transfer of money or economic goods or services in consideration of a promise of a future return of probably greater value. But it may also be an exchange of credit against credit, of credit against a title to goods. To illustrate: Jones may have a promissory note from Brown which arose from a deferred payment for shoes, and Smith may have a similar note against White; Jones and Smith may exchange these credits so that Smith becomes Brown's creditor and Jones becomes White's. Such operations occur every time a commercial instrument is sold for government or bank credit money and constitute the prime business of the banks and of the discount market. In fact, credit transactions constitute practically the whole business of finance as now conducted.

The Personal Element in Credit

It is important to conceive the exact nature of a credit. If Brown promises to pay to Jones at some later date, he creates a property right; Jones thereafter has a claim on Brown and Brown's wealth; the state has found it politically and economically expedient to guarantee, under certain conditions, this right; it is a " chose in action," recoverable by law. Fundamentally it is a jus in personam - a, right against the person of the promissor, and once in the history of jurisprudence was collectible by forced service from him. Slavery and imprisonment for debt have, however, been abandoned by the civil state, and such rights, in the absence of wealth of the debtor, are rather moral claims against him than anything else. The importance of the consideration of the moral qualities of the debtor by the creditor is, therefore, apparent; his ability to pay is best indicated by his present capital and his earning capacity, but his willingness to pay depends upon his character.

Credit is deferred payment; the creditor has confidence in the debtor's willingness and ability to pay; both willingness and ability to pay rest upon personal as well as impersonal elements. Willingness to pay is more a personal than an impersonal matter; and ability to pay is rather a matter of capital than of character, although the debtor's character - his business abilities - determine in no small degree his ownership or control of capital. The law supports the creditor as against the debtor who is able to pay but will not; but the law cannot make him willing to pay. Because his willingness is subject to caprice, it is difficult to estimate and so limits his credit to small compass. As business operations and discounting become more extensive and complex, the necessity of eliminating or reducing the personal element of credit or of reinforcing it increases, for intimate knowledge of the personal character of the debtors is more difficult to ascertain.

Secured Credit

The personal element can be reduced by attaching to the credit a concrete article of wealth or property right which, having assured and easily determined value, can be readily sold and converted into money. This insures ability to pay and the law will avail to collect payment. Such is the method of collateral security. The promise in the collateral note is backed by the pledged wealth or property. Ability to pay can also be practically assured by basing the credit upon a strictly commercial transaction the completion of which will put the debtor in funds within the period of the debt. Such credits are said to be "self-liquidating," since they assure the debtor of ability to pay, provided the business is sound. These two methods may be combined in one, the collateral being commercial documents by which the commercial transaction is effected, for example, bills of lading attached to a commercial bill of exchange.

Credit Indorsement and Substitution

The personal element can be reinforced by getting, in the words of the customary expression, "someone to go your security," that is, getting more "names" on the paper to evidence the credit; the purpose of these indorsements is to divide the risks. Synchronous complete failures of all the indorsers are, by the law of chance, very unlikely. Hence the security of the credit becomes as strong as the ability, joint and several, of the indorsers to pay, but no stronger.

The personal element can also be reinforced by getting some party who is better known, stronger in wealth and connection, and with good financial record, to substitute as debtor. The practice of issuing and using letters of credit is based upon this idea. A New York bank makes arrangements with an English bank whereby the latter agrees to accept bills drawn on it by a Brazilian exporter; otherwise the New York importer would have to be drawn on and the Brazilian could get from the Rio de Janeiro bank but a very low price for the bill as compared with one drawn on the English bank. This substitution of debtor constitutes the fundamental difference between the bank acceptance and the trade acceptance.

Commercial and Financial Credits

Credit is deferred payment; there is a period of trust, and it may be long or short. The longer the period the more the contingencies against which the creditor must provide. "Commercial credits" have come to differentiate themselves from "financial credits" on the basis of the term; the former are for 10, 20, 30, 60, 90, and 120 days, and are evidenced by promissory notes, checks, drafts, bills of exchange, acceptances, and so forth; the latter are for periods of 1, 2, 3, 5, 10, 20, and 40 years, and are evidenced by various forms of notes, bonds, and certificates. Commercial or mercantile credits are used to conduct the daily operations of business life. It is always assumed that the money or goods are to be used in such ways that the debtor will be in a position to realize upon his transaction within the period of the credit and so will be able to pay upon maturity.

Financial credits, on the other hand, being for long terms of years, are issued with the idea that the money or wealth which the creditor contributes to the debtor is for quite permanent use. If the creditor wishes to regain his funds before maturity he does so by selling the credit instrument to another who may wish to become creditor to the debtor; and it is commonly understood that the debtor will never make repayment in his own money or goods, but that the present credit will be met at maturity by refunding, that is, borrowing further funds either from the same creditor or others. There are, however, various practices by which commercial credits function in real fact as long-term credits.

Definition of Commercial Credit

Exact agreement does not exist among financial men and writers as to the definition of commercial credits. In the United States the term "commercial paper" is widely used in a very technical sense, and refers only to such paper as is marketed through note-brokers. Such paper is short term, but is in large part continually renewed at maturity and sold to present holders or others, and therefore represents long-term advances. Another restrictive definition makes commercial credit relate only to credit extensions which facilitate the marketing of products. This definition is too restrictive; industrial loans for the purpose of buying raw materials and paying wages to workers may be as self - liquidating, may be for as short terms, and as safe for temporary investment as mercantile loans. This definition would exclude also loans to speculators and brokers, a considerable part of which are characterized by the two essentials of commercial credit, namely, short term, and self-liquidation. Important differences of opinion as to banking policy often arise from the inability to agree on a strict definition of commercial credit.

EFFECT OF TIME ELEMENT ON CREDIT VALUES

The time element in a credit ordinarily gives rise to discount when the credit is exchanged against money. If a promissory note does not mature till 30 days hence, the holder cannot hope to find in the business world a purchaser who will pay down at once its face value for it, since such a purchaser would be deprived of the use of the purchase price for 30 days; for this reason a purchaser would deduct the interest in advance and pay the proceeds. In practice this is calculated either as true or as bank discount, depending upon the purchaser. Long-term instruments, such as bonds, are invariably valued by true discount. The time element, however, is ordinarily ignored in case of credit instruments payable upon demand and about which there is no doubt as to the willingness and ability of the debtor to pay.

Promises of the government to pay on demand, and similar promises of reputable banks, are accepted without discount because these promises will themselves function as a medium of exchange, and the person who accepts them in exchange for a credit instrument, goods, or services will not lose the use of the funds during the time until the promissory notes can be redeemed. These promises can be used immediately and without discrimination or discount. They circulate as money themselves. To give such demand instruments is one method of paying, whereas to give a time instrument that is subject to discount is not, in common parlance, "paying"; one does not pay by giving his note. The commonest forms of demand instruments that circulate as money, and are money, are government notes and bank notes, and also bank deposits but for their limited acceptability attain to the r61e of money.

Other Kinds of Credit

Another form of credit is commonly called "personal," or "consumptive," credit, on the theory that such credits "spend themselves in the consumption or annihilation of necessities and articles of luxury as opposed to those utilities of credit which assume a productive or distributive character." This kind of credit was the earliest historically, and gave birth to our credit system by educating men in the honest keeping of contracts; but personal credit constitutes a relatively small fraction of present-day credits and is discouraged by credit-givers.

Still another form of credit may be specified in this classification on the basis of uses to which the funds are devoted. It is "public" credit. The debtor is the body politic, and the funds raised are diverted to the uses of the state. Such credits are usually long term and, being strictly financial credits, partake of the qualities of the bonded debt of corporations.

Relation of Credits to Wealth

The credit instruments are many and, to facilitate their various uses, are highly specialized. Book credits, promissory notes, bills of exchange, drafts, acceptances, certificates of indebtedness, checks, bank notes, bonds, and the like all arise from credit transactions, however much the instruments themselves may differ in their details of form and terms, in their power to circulate, and in their creation by debtor or creditor. They purport to be claims for money, are evidences of debt of the debtor and of credit by the creditor, and are used to facilitate the exchange of goods and the investment of funds.

The issue of credit does not, however, by itself directly increase the wealth of the community. If Brown gives Jones a promissory note the volume of credit in the community has been increased by that amount, but the volume of wealth has not been affected one iota by that act. The deferment of the payment may, however, leave the capital in Brown's hands, and Brown may be a more efficient producer of wealth than Jones; the net result of the credit transaction for the community will thus indirectly be an increase of wealth.

The presumption is that the borrower is a more efficient producer than the lender, else the lender would use the capital in his own productive activities. One of the greatest functions of credit is just this - it throws control of productive capital into the hands of the most efficient producers, and this control results in additional consumable commodities for the community. One of the commonest of errors is to fail to keep in mind the fundamental fact that credits are not wealth, but at best claims to wealth, and that their issue does not add directly to the wealth of the community. The issue, for instance, of multiplied millions of dollars of credits by the government does not increase our national wealth directly, however prone the owner of a dollar bill is to regard it as part of his wealth.

Fundamental Basis of Credit

A credit rests upon the person or wealth of the debtor; even when apparently based upon credits the ultimate basis is concrete wealth. For instance, a mortgage company may pledge mortgages and mortgage notes as security for debenture bonds issued by them and sold to the public; the holder of such a debenture bond may pledge it with his bank to secure an advance to his account; then the holder of a check drawn by this bank customer has a credit instrument which, in its ultimate analysis, is a property right in the mortgaged land.

This illustration shows how very useful credit is in making fixed wealth rapidly transferable and marketable so that it may be diverted to that operator who can make best use of it. The land remains intact and the operator is able, by the issue of credit based upon it, to procure seed, machinery, fertilizer, and the like, with which to work the land. Persons in other parts of the country who have funds - titles of purchasing power - are willing to exchange these funds for credits based upon land.

RELATION OF CREDITS TO INTEREST

It is human nature to prefer present economic goods or services to future economic goods or services, the degree of preference varying with the person - with his personal characteristics and the nature of his income. If Brown is less impatient for income than Jones, he will lend to the latter, but if more impatient, he will borrow; borrowing tends to lower the impatience of the borrower and raise it for the lender. Given a market of borrowers and lenders there will result a market rate about which borrowing and lending will crystallize. This rate measures the general notion as to how much, in a certain community at a certain time, present goods are preferred to future goods; it denotes, in other words, that lenders are willing to lend \$100 today for \$105 repaid one year later; the premium, 5 per cent, is our market rate of interest. Whenever a credit is drawn, this element of time preference enters, and the value of the goods or the money returned at maturity must exceed the value of the goods or money originally paid. A borrower is willing to pay this premium for the use of goods, or for money which represents goods, for various reasons, but in any case the borrower must be satisfied that the goods are worth more to him (at the market rate of interest) than to the lender. One of these reasons would be that he feels himself by the amount of the interest a more efficient producer than the lender.

Credits as Circulating Media

In its function of facilitating exchange, credit may become the actual medium. An earnest of this was seen in the treatment of subsidiary, fiduciary, or token, coins. A credit medium is more economical than a metallic medium. The expenditure of labor and capital in producing metals for monetary use is a big item of expense for society. Moreover, these metals have industrial uses and the erection of a superstructure of credit on a reserve of metallic money conserves the metal for use in the arts. Since the creation of a credit currency is done with less effort than that of a metallic currency, there is an economic advantage in substituting credit for metallic media wherever possible. Such substitution, though not without danger, is within limits highly beneficial.

Any medium circulates for one or more fundamental reasons. Certain counters may circulate by express or implicit agreement among a limited group, as gamblers' poker chips. It has been shown that commodity money attains and maintains this function because of a belief in the stability and the persistence of social custom. Credit rests upon confidence in the issuer. The issuer may be a government, a corporation, a firm, or an individual; in any case the credit issued will have a more or less extensive circulation, dependent upon the public's opinion of the ability and willingness of the issuer to meet his promises. Credit may be classified, therefore, on the basis of whether or not it has general acceptability. Those forms of credit which do possess general acceptability perform all the functions of money, and usually more efficiently than money.

Media which have only a restricted circulation are: i. Securities (stocks and bonds). These are usually too highly specialized, too technical, too dependent upon market conditions, and too large in denomination to acquire a general circulation. They are, however, quite commonly used in making large payments at great distances, as overseas. Where the expense of shipping gold runs high, securities of international reputation may be used to settle credit balances.

Credit instruments, like checks, drafts, promissory notes, acceptances, and the like, which have only a local circulation among a limited circle who know the issuer, drawee, drawer, or acceptor.

Credit media which have a general circulation are:

1. Government issues:

(A) Convertible Metallic Money, As Nickels And Coppers.

(B) Certificates Of Deposit Of Metallic Money.

(C) Convertible Paper Money.

(D) Inconvertible Paper Money.

2. Bank issues:1

(A) Deposits, Represented By Checks.

(B) Bank Notes.

GOVERNMENT PAPER OR CREDIT MONEY

From the creditor's point of view, credit represents the trust he has in the debtor; from the debtor's point of view, credit is borrowing power, the power he has to induce the creditor to put economic goods at his disposal for a period of time, on the promise of repayment at maturity. The power of the borrower coincides in all respects with the trust of the creditor, the one being but an opposite aspect of the other.

A government enjoys higher borrowing power than other borrowers. The war loans of 1914-1919, towering into scores of billions, exceeded all previous credit operations. Such credits indeed were quite beyond the estimates of the most sanguine financier before 1914; the way the people of the belligerent countries have loaned to their governments is amazing. Nevertheless there are limits to a government's credit, however elastic they may seem under the spur of patriotism, efficient publicity, and appeal, and practically every existing government has at some time experienced a want of unhesitating financial support.

The emphasis here is on the breadth of government credit. People visualize the state only dimly and consequently are prone to feel it is quite omnipotent. Since it draws its powers from the people and is held to be as just as their ideals, it is believed to be not only able but also willing to keep its promises. It takes a catastrophe to shake this confidence. Credit instruments of the state, in small round denominations and payable on demand, are, because of this high confidence in the government, most likely to be freely accepted by any citizen of the country and to pass readily from person to person at par, rousing scarcely a thought of having them redeemed in metallic money. One man buys goods from another, but instead of paying standard money, or giving his note, or having the debt charged on a book account, may pay with a note issued by the government, which note has come into his hands by some previous business transaction. That is to say, the first man was for a time the creditor of his government and now the second man becomes creditor. This ready shift in the ownership of a government note and in the personnel of the creditor constitutes its circulation. So long as the government note circulates freely it performs all the functions of money and is popularly and rightly understood to be money.

CLASSIFICATION OF GOVERNMENT CREDIT MONEY

Government paper money is of three sorts, the classification being based on the proportionate reserve of standard money which the Treasury keeps on hand to redeem credit money, and to instil into the people's mind the government's intent and ability to redeem on demand. The longer the credit money stays in circulation, that is, the fewer the presentations for redemptions, the smaller may this reserve be; but the very size of this reserve may be a deciding factor in delaying such presentations.

Certificates. The first class of government paper has full face value in standard money in reserve. The silver dollar by reason of its size and weight is awkward and burdensome for commercial uses; except in limited areas of the country which have become thoroughly habituated to its use, it will not circulate, but drifts at once to bank reserves and the government Treasury. Nor is its circulation desirable, for the losses from erosion are heavy. A simple device used by the government to obviate these difficulties is to give to any depositor of silver dollars or silver bullion certificates of deposit certifying that the government holds on hand face value of silver which is payable upon demand.

As only a few of the certificates will be presented for redemption, it is not necessary that much of the silver be coined.

Certificates are really warehouse receipts and, like any receipt of this kind, their value takes into consideration the character of the warehouseman and his warehouse. Because the government and the Treasury stand in such high esteem, currency certificates are accepted generally and without equivocation, but that this form of paper money does not add to the total of existing currency is nevertheless evident.

Convertible Paper. The second class of paper money has a fraction of its face value held in reserve in standard money, to meet demands for redemption. It is spoken of as "convertible," that is, the Treasury stands ready to redeem it at any time. As long as this convertible money is faithfully and freely redeemed, the promises are worth their face value; any distrust, however, results in a run on the Treasury, which, if great and long continued, may exhaust the reserve fund. The government may also suffer reverses in revenue receipts, or expenditures may be extraordinary, and its ability to carry on conversion may be impaired. While a reserve of 100 per cent is at no time necessary, since there is no probability of a simultaneous demand on the part of all holders, it is nevertheless expedient to keep a considerable reserve; one of the best evidences of the intention and ability of the government to fulfil its promises to redeem is the creation and maintenance of a special fund for this purpose. The fund should be separate from the general funds of the Treasury and be used exclusively for redemption purposes; the size of the fund must vary with the probability of the demand for conversion, which must be determined from experience and from the contingencies of the government credit.

It is also important to note that ultimate redeemability is not equivalent to immediate convertibility. If the paper is immediately convertible it stays at par, but if redeemable only after a period of indefinite length it will be regarded as an investment or as a deferred payment, and its present value will differ from its face value by discount for interest and risk. In this case it does not matter whether the issuing government is rich in natural resources; it is the present means of payment that maintains the parity.

The reserve held may be determined in several ways, such as the following: It may be a minimum percentage required, the issue and the reserve bearing a predetermined minimum ratio; or it may be a certain fixed minimum quantity of specie whose ratio to the issue would vary inversely with the amount of issue; or the reserve may consist of securities and gold, the law fixing the maximum amount of the "uncovered" issue (the notes backed by the pledged securities) and requiring the excess above that amount to be "covered" by 100 per cent of gold.

Inconvertible Paper. The third class of government paper money is variously called "fiat" money, "political" money, and "inconvertible" paper money. This kind usually results from excessive issues of convertible paper money so large that the citizens doubt the government's ability or intention to redeem on demand, a doubt which is later justified by an actual suspension of specie payments. These inconvertible bills are promises of the government to pay on demand, though at the time of issue the government may have no intention of keeping its promise.

Sometimes they are issued as orders on the Treasury to pay upon demand, the government well knowing the Treasury's inability to meet such demands; and sometimes they are simply printed statements proclaiming the bills to be the equivalent of such and such amounts of metallic money.

Value of Inconvertible Money

To give acceptability to inconvertible paper, the government usually makes special provisions. One is to declare it legal tender in payment of private and public dues. Unless the people unite to boycott the use of inconvertible money, the government's legal sanction can force its receipt at par for debts, with the result that its acceptability for other purposes will follow. Of course, the existence of inconvertible money does not prevent a creditor from contracting in terms of gold, nor does it prevent his asking a higher sum in payment, if the contract be drawn in terms of general money. Its depreciation may, therefore, persist despite legal - tender laws.

The extent to which the paper declared is legal tender may, however, be limited to the payment of taxes and debts to the government. If issued in anticipation of taxes soon to be levied and in amounts equal to those taxes, it will likely keep at par, for the people accepting it will really be paying their taxes in advance, and when the taxes come due they will not care whether they pay in standard or in inconvertible money. Such issues will not be excessive; the tax levy will act as governor of the issue, and loss of faith in the issue is, therefore, unlikely. If, however, issues exceed taxes, laid or to be laid, the volume of circulation will be inflated by the excess.

The above methods of promoting acceptability and maintaining parity are unavailing if the issues become excessive. The volume issued may be so large as to discredit the government's ability or intention to redeem, and far exceed its capacity to absorb by way of taxes. Depreciation then becomes inevitable. After the public has become used to convertible paper a certain volume that is inconvertible will by force of habit circulate without question. If the issue thereafter is limited to the growing needs of business at the existing price level, there will be no depreciation; greater issues, however, will result in depreciated values in terms of gold inversely proportional to the volume. The most effectual method of maintaining the value of inconvertible money is, therefore, to limit its issue. There is no way of determining in advance the amount which a country may issue and keep at par; the risk is psychological, varying with the people, time, and conditions. In times of peace, normal order, and ready collection of taxes, a much larger sum of credit can be supported than in times of panic, war, or falling tax receipts.

Danger of Overissue of Government Paper Money

The danger or likelihood of overissue is the greatest objection to government paper money. Overissue brings about inflation, rising prices, bigger profits, business boom, and a demand for more and more issues; the cycle once begun is intoxicating and in democracies the legislatures are likely to yield to the popular clamor for new issues. Every issue, however, means an inflation of prices, a scaling of debts and contracts. The train of attendant evils is dire, and ultimate catastrophe is inevitable. Credit thus defeats itself. Moreover, a paper money party invariably arises which preaches the doctrine that paper money, being cheap and easily created and performing the functions of money satisfactorily, is the best kind of money, and a better means of finance indeed than taxes - which directly affect pocketbooks - or than bond sales - which must later be repaid with interest. Paper issues work out their results so insidiously and indirectly through inflation that for a time only their virtues are perceived, while their evils work unhindered.

The issuing government is not without guides to determine when an issue is excessive. One indication is a premium on gold; paper will be accepted only at a discount, the premium varying with the issues and with the government credit. Since foreign payments must be settled in gold, foreign exchange rates in a paper money country will rise and fall as the price of gold in terms of paper fluctuates. Metallic money, first the standard money and then subsidiary forms, will be withdrawn from circulation and go into hiding, into the melting pot, or abroad. Prices payable in paper will rise largely and rapidly, but a holder of specie can really buy on approximately the old basis by exchanging his gold for paper and buying at the paper prices. The premium on gold is thus a rough index to the appreciation of prices of goods.

ADVANTAGES AND DISADVANTAGES OF PAPER MONEY

The advantages of the issue of government paper money are:

1. It is economical, since it substitutes a less expensive material than metal for money and conserves the metal for the arts.
2. It is easily and quickly increased; the printing press is more expeditious than the mine, smelter, and mint.
3. It has fiscal advantages; in emergencies, before taxes can be laid or bonds sold, paper money may be run off in anticipation of taxes or receipts from sales of bonds; it can be used to pay the obligations of the state, and amounts to a forced loan without interest.
4. It is more convenient than metallic money; it is light in weight and the weight does not increase with the amount; it is easy to conceal and to ship by mail or express.
5. If Properly Issued, It Provides A Certain Elasticity To The Currency.

Paper money has also many disadvantages and attendant evils:

1. The greatest has been pointed out - the high probability of overissue, with consequent disturbance of contracts, business morale and relationships, and foreign exchanges.
2. The government may also suffer; it is a heavy purchaser, especially at such times as free resort is likely to be made to inconvertible issues, and it pays, like individuals, the higher prices due to inflation; the government expenditures are increased and the purchasing power of its receipts decreased, and as a net result the public debt is expanded.
3. The area of circulation of paper money is very limited; gold will be accepted internationally but paper only in the country issuing it; it cannot be used in international settlements. Its value, therefore, depends on the accidents of a limited area, and is more subject to fluctuation than that of gold, which is steadied by the equalizing tendencies of parts of a broad area.

4. Paper money has less stability of value, also, for the reason that it has only one use, namely, its monetary use. The metals, on the other hand have an equal or greater use in the arts, for which the demand is relatively constant, inasmuch as social usages change slowly and the demand for silver or gold utensils shifts but little. The total demand for the metal is, therefore, on a wider basis than the demand for paper money, and its value is thereby stabilized.

Government Paper Money Issued by the United States

The issues of paper money of the United States government now current for which the government is direct debtor embrace the United States notes, the treasury notes of 1890, the gold and silver certificates, the gold order certificates, and the federal reserve notes. Our history is replete with experiments in government money. The colonies issued such money to finance wars or the ordinary expenses of government, and to make loans to individuals. The various colonial issues differed in the degrees to which they were made legal tender and bore interest; but overissue characterized practically every lot. During the Revolution the "continentals" were used to finance the war, and excessive issues so depreciated their value that they became worthless. In the period 1812-1815 successive issues of legal tenders were made, with the result that specie payments were suspended and gold commanded a premium. Later issues were made during the distress following the panic of 1837, which extended over the years 1837-1842, and in connection with the financing of the Mexican War, and again after the panic of 1857. These issues were in moderate amounts and were not objectionable. During the Civil War, however, the real disaster came with the issue of United States notes, popularly called "legal tenders," or "greenbacks." The Confederacy also, as well as many of the Confederate States, issued overwhelming quantities of notes.

Greenbacks

The greenback issues were started in 1861 and continued throughout the war. The government suspended specie payments in 1862 and the greenbacks depreciated until, in 1864, they brought less than 40 cents on the dollar in gold. The fluctuations in value were wide and frequent, varying with the fortunes of war and the markets.

Contraction was undertaken at the conclusion of the war, but abandoned in 1868. In 1879 specie payments, according to the pledge of the Specie Resumption Act of 1875, were resumed, the Secretary of the Treasury having accumulated a specie reserve of about $100,000,000 for this purpose. The sum of greenbacks left in circulation was $346,681,016, and it became the accepted idea that the government would retain a reserve of $100,000,000 in gold for their redemption. This reserve proved sufficient until the redemptions during the depression that followed the panic of 1893, when an endless chain of redemptions and reissues threatened to extinguish the reserve; the balance of trade was adverse and holders of greenbacks presented them for gold to ship abroad, but because of deficits the Treasury was forced to reissue the redeemed notes to meet its ordinary expenses. To replenish the reserve, the Treasury sold bonds for gold.

In 1900 a separate reserve fund of $150,000,000 was authorized and adequate powers were extended to the Secretary of the Treasury for maintaining it; the fund was to be separated from the general Treasury funds; the greenbacks when redeemed were not to be reissued until the fund was again replete; the Treasury was to pay any gold in its possession into this fund to refill it, and was also empowered to sell bonds to fill the reserve when it should drop below $100,000,000. By the Federal Reserve Act in 1913 the government's share of the net earnings of the federal reserve banks may, at the discretion of the Secretary of the Treasury, be used to supplement the $150,000,000 reserve.

These greenbacks are promises of the United States to pay on demand. Between 1862 and 1879 this promise was not kept and the notes possessed all the features of inconvertible paper; but since 1879 they have been convertible and at par. They are now legal tender for payment of all debts, public and private, except for payment of interest on government debt and for payment of revenue duties. The denominations issued are 1,000's, 500's, 100's, 50's, 20's, 10's, 5's, 2's, and i's. As a constituent of our money system they are a menace, are an inelastic form of currency, and should be redeemed and discarded. Their menace becomes less as they come to constitute a smaller fraction of our total circulating media, as they become bills of smaller denominations, and as the reserve becomes larger - all of which tendencies are now at work.

Treasury Notes Of 1890

The treasury notes of 1890 are similar to the greenbacks in quality. They were issued under the Sherman Silver Law of that year to pay for the silver bought by the government. They created an additional demand upon the gold reserve against the greenbacks, which was already too small. The issues are:

Issue And Retirement Of Treasury Notes (In Millions)

Fiscal Year	Treasury Notes Issued	Silver Dollars Coined from Bullion of Act of 1890	Amount of Treasury Notes Redeemed in Silver and Canceled	Amount of Treasury Notes Outstanding
1891	$ 50.5	$27.3		$ 50.2
1892	51.1	34	....	101.7
1893	45.5	5.3	....	147.2
1894	8.7	.0	$ 3.3	152.6
1895		3.9	6.5	146.0
1896		7.5	16.4	129.7
1897		21.2	14.8	114.9
1898*		3.8	8.5	106.3
Total...	$155.9	$72.6	$49.6	

* First 6 months only.

The Act of 1900 provided for the retirement of an amount equal to the amount of silver coined from that bought with the notes; this has now all been coined and as the notes are turned in for redemption, silver certificates are substituted for them. Of the $155.9 millions originally issued, only $1.7 millions were outstanding

September 1, 1919; there are probably very few in existence, and most of these will be held as souvenirs and in numismatic collections. They are redeemable on demand in either gold or silver, at the discretion of the Secretary of the Treasury.

Gold and Silver Certificates

The United States has two forms of representative paper money, the gold certificate (or note) and the silver certificate. In 1863 Congress authorized the issue of gold notes against deposits of gold coin and bullion. They are receipts for the gold coin and redeemable in gold. They were not legal tender until 1920, but have been receivable for customs, taxes, and all public dues, and previous to July 15, 1916, might be used as reserves in national banks. The denominations issued are 10,000's, 5,000's, 1,000's, 500's, 100's, 50's, 20's, and 10's. The gold held to redeem these notes may be coined or uncoined; by an Act of 1916 two-thirds may be kept in bullion form.

The silver certificates were authorized by Congress in 1878, to facilitate the circulation of the standard silver dollar. They are redeemable in silver only and are not legal tender, but are receivable for all public debts, customs, and taxes. By the Act of 1878 the denominations issued were 1,000's, 500's, 100's, 50's, 20's, 10's, 2's, and i's. In 1891 an act was passed limiting the denominations to $10 and under, except that one-tenth of the total issue might, in the discretion of the United States Treasurer, be issued in denominations of 20's, 50's, and 100's. The large notes, when redeemed by the Treasurer, are retired and canceled, and certificates of the denominations of 10's or less substituted. The

Pittman Act of 1918 made provision for the reduction of silver dollars to bullion for shipment to India. This forced the retirement of silver certificates representing the silver dollars. The federal reserve banks issued a request to the member banks to forward at their expense all silver certificates above $5 denomination and to receive in their place federal reserve bank notes; a little later smaller denomination certificates were called in and federal reserve bank notes given in exchange. This process ended in 1919, as the emergency of the war passed. These federal reserve bank notes are being replaced by silver certificates as silver is purchased by the government to replenish its stock.

Gold Order Certificates

One other form of government certificate is the gold order certificate, issued at the discretion of the Treasurer of the United States, against deposits of gold coin or gold bearer notes, of ten-thousand denomination only. Prior to July 1, 1914, the sub-treasury in New York issued this form of certificate to the order of the New York Clearing House in settlement of its debit balances. Such certificates were formerly carried by the national banks as part of their reserve.

Federal Reserve Notes

The federal reserve notes are obligations of the United States government and are, strictly speaking, a form of government paper money, but their qualities and the method of issue can be more easily treated.

Method of Issuance

The United States Treasury has Divisions of Issue and Redemption, to which are assigned respectively the accounts relating to the issue and redemption of United States notes, gold certificates, silver certificates, and currency certificates. The federal reserve notes, the federal reserve bank notes, and the national bank notes, against which redemption funds are specifically kept, are issued and redeemed through the Comptroller of the Currency. The reserve fund for redemption of United States notes and treasury notes, the gold coin and bullion held against outstanding gold certificates, and the silver dollars and bullion held against outstanding silver certificates, are held as separate trust funds for the redemption of the notes or certificates for which they are respectively pledged, and can be used for no other purpose.

New United States notes are issued upon request in return for United States notes unfit for circulation, also for federal reserve notes, federal reserve bank notes, national bank notes, subsidiary silver coin, or minor coin, received for redemption or exchange. Gold certificates are issued by the Treasurer upon deposit of gold coin and silver certificates upon deposit of standard silver dollars.

Method of Redemption

United States notes and gold certificates are redeemable by the Treasurer in gold coin, treasury notes of 1890 in gold coin or silver dollars, and silver certificates in silver dollars. National bank notes and federal reserve bank notes are redeemable in lawful money by the Treasurer, and also over the counter of the issuing bank. Federal reserve notes are redeemable in gold by the Treasurer.

Since the abolition of the subtreasuries in 1920-1921, the federal reserve banks have redeemed United States currency, national bank notes, federal reserve bank notes, and coin for non-member banks, business concerns, and individuals. It is not necessary to effect such redemptions for the member banks inasmuch as they may forward paper money or coin, whether fit or unfit for circulation, to the federal reserve bank for credit to their reserve account, and they may order paper money or coin fit for circulation from this bank as needed.

All United States notes, treasury notes, and gold and silver certificates unfit for circulation, when not mutilated to a greater extent than two-fifths of the whole, are redeemed by the government at their full face value. All notes mutilated so that less than three-fifths, but clearly more than two-fifths, remain, are redeemed by the Treasurer at Washington at one-half the face value of the whole note. Fragments less than three-fifths may be redeemed at full face value if accompanied by an affidavit of the owner that the missing portions have been totally destroyed; this affidavit must state the cause and manner of the mutilation and must be sworn to by a notary.

When remittances are received for redemption by the Treasury from a place in which there is no federal reserve bank or branch bank, returns are made in new United States notes, subsidiary silver, or minor coin, by mail (postage and insurance deducted) unless requested otherwise, in which case the charges for transportation are paid by the consignee. If the remittances are received from a place in which there is a federal reserve bank or branch bank, the Treasurer may make returns by check payable at the federal reserve bank or branch bank, if it suits his convenience.

Paper currency for redemption must be assorted by kinds and denominations, and each 100 notes or less enclosed in a paper strap marked with the amount.

The Treasury gives other instructions in case of large packages. With each package should be enclosed a memorandum giving an inventory of the contents, the sender's name and address, and the disposition to be made of the proceeds. United States notes, treasury notes of 1890, gold certificates, and silver certificates may be sent in the same package and should be marked "Unfit United States currency for redemption." National bank notes, federal reserve notes, and federal reserve bank notes may be sent in the same package, marked "National and federal reserve currency for redemption." Charges are paid by the government on unfit national bank notes, federal reserve notes, and federal reserve bank notes, when sent to the department at Washington "charges collect," but not on any other kind of currency.

The total redemptions during the fiscal year 1919 were:

United States currency............ $731.4 millions

Federal Reserve Notes............... 877.3

Federal Reserve Bank Notes.......... 31.8

National Bank Notes............... 294.2

MONEY CIRCULATING IN THE UNITED STATES

The total money in circulation in the United States on June 30 in recent years is shown in the following table:

Money In Circulation In The United States, June 30 (In Millions)

	1914	1915	1916	1917	1918	1919	1920
Gold coin	$ 611	$ 590	$ 637	$1,036	$1,114	$1,172	$ 834
Gold certificates	1,026	1,072	1,413	1,392	818	542	390
Standard silver dollars.........	70	64	66	71	77	81	134
Silver certificates	478	481	489	477	379	169	118
Subsidiary silever	159	159	171	193	216	232	251
United States notes	337	332	341	335	340	332	337
Notes of 1890	2	2	2	I	I	1	1
Total......................	$2,683	$2,700	$3,119	$3,505	$2,945	$2,529	$2,066
Federal reserve notes		$ 80	$ 173	$ 544	$1,713	$2,493	$3,122
Federal reserve bank notes.....				12	15	163	199
National bank notes	$ 715	785	728	698	703	649	696
Total	$ 715	$ 865	$ 901	$1,254	$2,531	$3,305	$4,018
Grand Total Circulation	$3,398	$3,565	$4,020	$4,759	$5,476	$5,841	$6,084
Per Capita Circulation	$34.35	$35.44	$39.28	$45.74	$50.81	$54.28	$56.79

12

Nature of Bank Credit-specialization in Credit Issue

The credits issued by the government are incidental to its major functions of making, executing, and interpreting the law. The credits issued by the business man are incidental to the conduct of his commercial operations. The personal credits issued are occasional and for personal consumptive uses. None of these parties specializes in the issue of credits or devotes time primarily to that function. The commercial banks have undertaken this specialized function. Their business is the issue and guaranty of credits for business uses; they are dealers in credits, and are sometimes, although too narrowly, called "manufacturies" of credit. As will appear in the later chapters on banking practices, commercial banks function in many ways which do not bear strictly upon credits, and which concern financial as well as commercial credits. The fundamentals of banking, however, are most easily grasped from the point of view of purely commercial credit operations.

FORMS OF BANK CREDIT

The liabilities of a bank to creditors take four chief forms:

1. Deposits
2. Bank Notes
3. Acceptances And Letters Of Credit
4. Bills Payable

Deposits are rights to draw on the bank for money. A depositor commonly gets such rights in one or more of the following possible ways:

1. By The Deposit Of Cash Or Cash Items.
2. By Depositing Time Items For Collection And Credit.
3. By remitting securities or other property to the bank for sale and credit.
4. By The Process Of Loan And Discount.
5. By the sale of securities, real estate, personalty, or services to the bank for credit.

Bank notes are promises of the bank to pay money on demand; issued in round denominations and transferable without indorsement, they are designed to circulate in lieu of metallic money. The transferee becomes the noteholder and creditor of the bank; the bank note may come into his hands in the ordinary transactions of his business, or through any one of the five methods described above by which a depositor gets deposits.

Acceptances are bills of exchange drawn on the bank, which, for a commission, it obligates itself to pay, but to provide funds for which payment the person for whom the letter of credit is procured is obligated to the bank. Letters of credit are agreements by the bank to accept, and to pay at maturity or demand, bills of exchange drawn under certain specified conditions.

Bills payable are promissory notes, secured or unsecured, interest-bearing, and running for a period of time, by which a bank borrows in large, irregular sums, at various times.

Sometimes the borrowing is done by selling some of the bills receivable, acceptances, or other commercial paper which the bank has in its portfolio, a process which incurs the contingent liability of indorsement or agreement to repurchase.

Bank credit extensions more commonly take the forms of deposits and bank notes, and therefore the theory of these two forms will be fully developed.

NATURE OF CASH DEPOSITS

Suppose a person, Mr. White, from motives of hire, public interest, or business efficiency, undertakes to accept moneys from a certain number of persons, Messrs. Black, Brown, Green, and Blue, who have mutual business transactions, to act as trustee and common custodian of the funds, to keep a record of receipts and withdrawals, and to permit and care for the transfer of title to these funds on his books. The transfer of title to these funds would become the common method of payment in their business transactions. Such transfers would be accomplished most easily by Black ordering White to debit his account a certain number of dollars and to credit Brown's account the same number of dollars; other orders might be written by Green on White in favor of Black, and by Blue on White in favor of Brown, and so forth. If a number of such orders were presented to White, all the payments could be handled by the simple cancellation of debits and credits on his books. Trade would be much convenienced.

Instead of White acting in the capacity of trustee, the traders, Black, Brown, Green, and Blue, might be content to loan White the funds on his promise to repay the loaner, or the person presenting the loaner's written order, on demand; title to the funds would then pass to White, while the traders would become demand creditors of White with rights to draw on that credit at their pleasure. These rights to draw are deposits, and in this case they arise through the deposit of cash. White is essentially a bank of deposit. The orders for withdrawals are checks or drafts. White's balance sheet (supposing he had no other funds or wealth) would then stand as follows:

Assets Cash................. $100,000

Liabilities Deposits..............$100,000

Items for deposit may consist of cash or cash items, "cash items" being the term applied to items payable on demand. Immediate credit would be given by White (the receiving bank) for cash, and might also be given for cash items received for collection. The receiving bank (White in this case) has usually a definitepolicy to which it adheres in this matter; it usually gives credit only after collection or after the average time consumed in making such collections. If interest were being paid on the deposits or if the depositor expected to draw at once against his credit, the bank would be likely to delay credit until collection had been made. Collections on institutions in the city or the vicinity would thus receive credit sooner than items on more distant institutions; clearing house items would be given immediate credit.

MOTIVES IN DEPOSITING CASH FUNDS

Customers have various motives in making deposits of cash funds. One motive is the desire for safety. The depositor gives up his right to any particular cash when he makes a deposit; he cannot properly say he has "money in the bank"; he has simply the right to draw money from the bank, and it is very unlikely that he would get back the identical cash which he actually deposited. If the depositor thinks in terms of the extraordinary facilities which the bank has for the safe-keeping of its moneys and valuables, he is quite likely to err as to the exact nature of deposits. He may make a "special deposit," having the banker "earmark" it and keep it out of the general fund of the bank's cash, so that the identical money deposited can be repaid; but this would be rather a warehouse business than commercial banking, and deposits are not of this nature. The safe-keeping, therefore, when rightly understood, refers, not to the depositor's funds, but to the bank's funds. The depositor's funds are safe only in the sense that a claim against the bank is good and the facilities for safe-keeping (vaults, guards, burglar alarms, etc.) of the bank's funds add to the value of a depositor's claims.

Another motive for depositing cash funds with a bank is convenience. Payment by check is more convenient than payment by money. The use of checks saves the bother and expense of counting and of shipment; checks are relatively safe against theft and loss in transit; they are payable only to the payee or indorsee; the voucher becomes a receipt; and large sums may be paid with the same ease as small ones.

A third motive may be the receipt of interest on the deposits. In communities where the competition for accounts is intense, banks offer interest on the average balance carried by the depositor; this is especially likely in the case of large accounts, as of the governmental units, corporations, or other banks. The interest paid ranges from 2 to 4 per cent, varying with the account and the bank. The policy of the bank may be open, explicit, and the same to all, or arrangements with the depositor may be secret. Paying interest on deposits is discouraged by bankers, for it adds to the expenses, forces the bank to negotiate loans which have high earning capacity but inadequate security, and at times, when deposits are increasing faster than loans or when the market money rates are low, eats up the bank's profits. If interest is paid, it should be done sparingly and on a sliding scale of rates which varies with the market rate, and the burden should be on time deposits.

The bank performs many services for the depositor which, because of its large clientele and organization, it is better equipped to perform than the depositor himself. It collects his cash items and other papers through its clearing house, messengers, or transit and collection departments; it keeps and cares for his securities, and upon order will buy or sell these for him; it offers free advisory service about credits, market conditions, signatures, and so forth. The exact nature of these and other services which are tendered to the depositor who maintains with the bank a fair dependable balance, will appear in the following chapters.

A more important motive than any of these is bank "accommodation," as it is called. The depositor wishes to be assured that he will have someone from whom he can get loans in case of need, and a bank which has enjoyed the use of a good balance from a worthy customer assumes an implicit responsibility to accommodate that depositor with loans when appeal is made. In this sense the relations between customer and bank are mutual. In the depositor's daily business transactions, occasions frequently arise when he wishes to procure loans on his own note or by the discount of paper in his portfolio, and the bank stands ready to provide customers with its own credit in exchange for their credit or that of other persons. The bank offers a market for procuring and selling credits and so facilitates business in this incomparable way.

NATURE OF LOANS

The last paragraph introduces the subject of loans and discounts. The person or bank, here termed "White," soon observes that, although payments of checks are being continually made, cash is as continually being redeposited by the payee or others; that, although payments and receipts are not synchronous or equal in amount, there is a continuous balance left in his hands, which varies but little in amount. As there is slight probability that all depositors will at one time demand the full amount of their deposits, White is therefore safe in loaning to any would-be borrowers, on their promissory notes, a sum, say, of $45,000. White's balance sheet would then stand as follows:

(1) If cash is paid out to the borrowers:

Assets

Cash.................. $55,000

Loans (Promissory Notes Of Borrowers)........ 45,000

Liabilities Deposits............. $100,000 or (2) if the borrowers preferred to leave the funds on deposit with White, subject to later withdrawal:

Assets

Cash................ $100,000

Loans (Promissory Notes Of Borrowers)....... 45,000

Liabilities Deposits.............. $145,000

In this process deposits have been created; the borrower has come to possess rights to draw money from White, although the cash which he nominally borrowed and redeposited at no time left the possession and ownership of White. From the borrower, White has accepted an interest-bearing promissory note payable at a specified date, and in exchange for this note has given the borrower the right to draw on him to the amount of the note, with the implied agreement that he will pay such requisitions on demand. The ratio of his cash to his demand liabilities has been changed from 100: 100 to 55:100, or 100:145. White does not normally allow interest to Black for such credits, however long it may be until Black demands payment of them; rather than allow interest on deposits created by loans, the rate of interest on the loan would be lowered. Receiving interest-bearing promissory notes in exchange for the right of the depositor to draw later is, in effect, lending with interest and borrowing without interest, by means of which White is able to make a profit, which is the motive of his business.

NATURE OF DISCOUNTS

It may be supposed that the loans placed by White in this way do not exhaust the sum that may be loaned by him without endangering his ability to meet all demands made upon him, and that some of his customers have promissory notes, bills of exchange, or acceptances, which have come into their hands in the daily transactions of their businesses and which they are willing to sell. White may buy these to the face amount, say, of $35,000, but he will pay less than their face value by the amount of the interest on their face value till due. This interest is taken in advance, and the proceeds are either paid in cash or credited as deposits to the parties selling the paper. The interest taken in advance and calculated, not on the sum actually paid in cash or credited as deposits (that is, the sum actually loaned) but on the face of the paper, is called "discount," and the act of selling a note when discount is taken is called "discounting" the paper. At the time when White buys the paper the discount is not yet earned, but it is nevertheless credited at once. His balance sheet, based on the last above, will then stand: (1) If cash is paid:

Assets

Cash................. $66,000

Loans (Promissory Notes Of Borrowers)........ 45,000

Discounts (Promissory Notes And Other Paper Discounted).......... 35,000

Liabilities

Deposits.............. $145,000

Discount............. 1,000 or (2) if paid by creating deposits:

Assets

Cash................. $100,000

Loans................ 45,000

Discounts............ 35,000

Liabilities

Deposits.............. $179,000

Discount............. 1,000

The process of discount results in the creation of deposits, in much the same manner as did loans. White has now in his portfolio commercial papers bearing the names of makers, drawers, and indorsers - claims against these parties, these claims being earning assets, with the earnings taken in advance. In exchange for these White has given either cash or deposits. If cash is paid, the payee may possibly redeposit it. The discount is profit, since no interest is allowed on the credits which White gives the seller of the paper.

NATURE OF DISCOUNTS

It may be supposed that the loans placed by White in this way do not exhaust the sum that may be loaned by him without endangering his ability to meet all demands made upon him, and that some of his customers have promissory notes, bills of exchange, or acceptances, which have come into their hands in the daily transactions of their businesses and which they are willing to sell.

White may buy these to the face amount, say, of $35,000, but he will pay less than their face value by the amount of the interest on their face value till due. This interest is taken in advance, and the proceeds are either paid in cash or credited as deposits to the parties selling the paper. The interest taken in advance and calculated, not on the sum actually paid in cash or credited as deposits (that is, the sum actually loaned) but on the face of the paper, is called "discount," and the act of selling a note when discount is taken is called "discounting" the paper. At the time when White buys the paper the discount is not yet earned, but it is nevertheless credited at once. His balance sheet, based on the last above, will then stand: (1) If cash is paid:

Assets

Cash................. $66,000

Loans (Promissory Notes Of Borrowers)........ 45,000

Discounts (Promissory Notes And Other Paper Discounted).......... 35,000

Liabilities

Deposits.............. $145,000

Discount............. 1,000 or (2) if paid by creating deposits:

Assets

Cash................. $100,000

Loans................ 45,000

Discounts............ 35,000

Liabilities

Deposits.............. $179,000

Discount............. 1,000

The process of discount results in the creation of deposits, in much the same manner as did loans. White has now in his portfolio commercial papers bearing the names of makers, drawers, and indorsers - claims against these parties, these claims being earning assets, with the earnings taken in advance.

In exchange for these White has given either cash or deposits. If cash is paid, the payee may possibly redeposit it. The discount is profit, since no interest is allowed on the credits which White gives the seller of the paper.

RATIONALE OF EXCHANGE OF CREDITS

The rationale of this exchange of credits is that the seller (or borrower) gives less widely known credit for the more widely known credit of the bank. The bank essentially guarantees the private credits, the bank credit being more widely accepted and therefore more useful to the customer in his business operations.

The exact nature of this substitution or guaranty of credits should be fully perceived, for it constitutes the fundamental principle of commercial banking.

There is an exchange of less known credit for better known credit; of less useful credit for more useful credit; of credit in which the time element is considerable for credit in which the time element is inconsiderable, the check or draft on a bank being payable upon demand; of credit subject to interest and discount for credit freed from such depreciation.

To illustrate, suppose a retailer buys goods from a jobber on 30 days' time. The common methods of financing the transaction are three.

The first method is for the jobber to carry the retailer on open account for 30 days. In this case the jobber will probably have to borrow at his bank funds to meet his own debts maturing meanwhile. He gives his own note, payable to the bank, and gets in exchange deposit rights which he transfers by check to his creditors. The bank in this way becomes the direct presumptive debtor to these creditors, and remains so until the checks are presented and paid. Such an operation is a substitution of credits.

But the jobber was able to get this substitution only by showing to, or pledging with, the bank his account receivable, that is, the retailer's credit, the retailer's implied promise to pay in 30 days. The bank accepted the jobber's credit, supported by a contingent right to the retailer's credit, giving in return its own credit. The bank accepted credit items in which the time element was considerable and gave demand credit items.

The second method is for the retailer to give to the jobber a promissory note for 30 days, or to accept (that is, sign) a draft drawn on him by the jobber by which the retailer agrees to pay in 30 days. The jobber can indorse (and thereby guarantee) this explicit promise of the retailer to pay, and can sell or pledge it with the bank for credit to his own account.

The jobber can then draw checks and remit to his creditors, and the bank becomes debtor to his creditors until the checks are presented for payment. The bank looks primarily to the retailer and secondarily to the jobber for payment; for the credit of these two men it substitutes its own.

The third method is for the retailer to borrow at his bank, giving his note for 30 days, and either receive credit to his account against which he can check and pay the jobber, thereby substituting the bank as debtor to the jobber till the checks are presented; or to have the bank authorize the jobber to draw against it and agree to accept the draft drawn payable in 30 days and to pay at maturity, thereby substituting time credit of the bank for the retailer's time credit.

LIMITATION ON CREATION OF DEPOSITS OF BANK IN SYSTEM

In an earlier paragraph it is stated that the creation of deposits by White was limited by the declining ratio of White's cash to his deposits. So far the hypothesis has been that White was the only bank in existence, or was an isolated bank, and that when customers drew checks against White and gave them to their creditors, cash to the amount of those checks was withdrawn by the latter and stayed out in circulation.

If, however, these creditors are also customers of the bank, they will probably deposit the checks for credit to their own account, in which case the process of payment amounts to a transfer of deposits on the books of the bank, and, inasmuch as no cash is demanded in such cases, a smaller reserve need be held by White as the proportion of his customers to the whole population becomes larger. If all the people are White's customers and all the payments in the community are made by checks on the bank, it will need to keep no reserve whatever, and the creation of deposits through loans will be unlimited so long as the deposits remain acceptable circulating media.

Profits, too, will be limited only by the demands of borrowers for loans. But the supposition of a sole or isolated bank is far removed from business facts. In the United States there are thousands of banks; many communities have more than one between which customers divide their patronage. A customer of bank A may hand a check to a customer of bank B, who will deposit it with B, and B will collect the cash from A.

The loss of cash by A in meeting such collections over the counter, through the mails, and at the clearing house, would seriously affect the ratio of cash to deposits and endanger the ability of the bank to meet its demand liabilities. Now if one bank, by the method of loans and discounts, creates an unduly large sum of deposits, it is sure to suffer adverse clearing house balances, for, although many of the checks drawn against these accounts will be redeposited in the drawee bank by holders into whose hands they fall, many others will be deposited in other banks which will collect cash from that bank.

Of course, if all other banks of the system are creating deposits at the same pace, it is possible that the checks drawn against A and deposited in banks B, C, D, and E, will just equal those drawn against B, C, or D, respectively, and deposited in A. But if any one bank creates deposits out of proportion to the others, it faces the impossibility of maintaining its cash. For the banking system as a whole the deposits may reach a high multiple of the cash reserve, but the multiple for any one bank of the system must approximate that prevailing in other banks.

If a customer of A applies to A for a loan, one of the factors determining whether it will be granted is the average daily balance of his account with A. Furthermore it is quite common for banks to insist that their borrowing customers maintain balances at or above some minimum percentage of their borrowings.

Probably 20 per cent is the commonest requirement; that is, if a loan of $100,000 is extended, the average daily balance of the borrower for the period of the loan must not be less than $20,000. From the date of the loan, the credit is checked against until it reaches some minimum amount; then a few days before maturity the borrower will probably build up his balance so that he may pay the loan.

His checks drawn during the loan reach other near and distant banks, which present them to A for payment. The attendant loss of cash by A forces it to reduce or limit loans, but this acquisition of cash by bank B makes it possible for B to extend loans. Part of this cash will stay with B, but the larger part will be drawn out by bank C when C collects checks against B; in turn, C will extend loans and B will retract.

By a continuation of this process the cash will be widely dispersed and become the basis for successive expansions of loans and deposits, but in smaller and smaller amounts.

The sum of these deposits created by the loans process and based upon an increment of cash reserve deposited in some bank of the system may increase until the ratio of the cash to the new deposits approximates the ratio for the system as a whole. The total expansion of the system's deposits derived by the loans method is therefore determined by the cash reserve and the prevailing ratio of reserve to deposits.

The deposits, however, arising out of loans by one bank in a system of otherwise homogeneous banks cannot exceed the increment of cash reserve probably by more than 25 per cent, because when such deposits are created the borrower proceeds to check out all but a minimum balance during the life of the loan and the checks may be largely presented through the clearing house or otherwise for payment. Nor can such deposits be much out of proportion to deposits derived by other banks from loans.

ILLUSTRATION OF NEED OF COMMON RATIO

The necessity of this common ratio as among the banks of a system may be illustrated numerically. Assume the following data: Bank A has $100,000 cash reserve, and likewise all the other banks, B, C, D, and E, have together, $100,000 cash reserve; bank A keeps 10 per cent reserve, the other banks, B, C, D, and E, keep 20 per cent; one-fifth of the deposits of each bank is not checked out, three-fourths of the checks are redeposited in the drawee bank, and the rest are deposited in the other banks and presented through the clearing house. Then the situation will be as follows:

		All Other Banks, B, C, D, and E		
	Bank A	Each Smaller Than A	Each Equal to A	Each Larger Than A
Cash Reserve........	$ 100,000	$100,000	$ 400,000	$ 800,000
Per cent Reserve......	10%	20%	20%	20%
Deposits	1,000,000	500,000	2,000,000	4,000,000
Checks Drawn........	800,000	400,000	1,600,000	3,200,000
Checks Redeposited in Drawee Bank......	600,000	300,000	1,200,000	2,400,000
Checks on it Presented Through Clearing House	200,000	100,000	400,000	800,000

It is seen that bank A suffers an adverse clearing house balance of $200,000 less $100,000, or $100,000, which wipes out its reserve. Had it kept the same per cent reserve as the other banks its clearing house balance would have been zero. On the other hand, a more slender reserve would have resulted in suspension and failure. In fact, the above adverse balance of $100,000 is a minimum, for in all probability some of the checks on B would have been deposited in C, D, or E, and presented by them and not by A at the clearing house. If the cash reserve of B, C, D, and E combined had been assumed to be less than $100,000, the adverse balance of A would have been greater.

If, instead of supposing that bank A's cash reserve is equal to the total reserve of banks B, C, D, and E, combined, we suppose that the reserve of each bank is $100,000, then the total reserve for B, C, D, and E will be $400,000, deposits $2,000,000, and clearing house items $400,000.

One-fourth of $400,000, or $100,-000, of these clearing house items will be presented against, let us say, B. The banks presenting checks on B are A, C, D, and E, and, as it has been assumed that they are all the same size, one-fourth of $100,000, or $25,000, will be presented by A. By the same reasoning A will present $25,000 against each of the other banks, C, D, and E, in the group, thus presenting a total of only $100,000 to be deducted from the $200,000 which B, C, D, and E present against it. Under these assumptions it is evident that A would suffer an adverse clearing house balance of $100,000.

If instead of supposing A equal to B, C, D, and E, combined, or equal to B, C, D, and E, severally, A is assumed to be smaller than B, C, D, and E, severally, adverse balances will likewise exist. For if it is assumed that each of the banks B, C, D, and E, has, say, twice the cash reserve that A has, then the checks on B presented by A, C, D, and E, will be divided somewhat in the proportions of 1, 2, 2, and 2; and one-seventh of $800,000, or $114,285, will be less than the checks presented against A.

Therefore, whether bank A is considered as smaller, equal to, or greater than the other banks, it may expect adverse clearing house balances if its ratio of reserve to deposits is more slender than that which the other banks of the system maintain. This limitation does not apply to deposit rights arising from the deposit of cash; it applies only to those additional deposits built upon cash holdings by the method of loan and discount.

For if $100,000 in cash is deposited, checks drawn later to that amount can be fully met. Any one bank can build up any amount of deposit liabilities by the cash method, and proceed to loan them all out except such a proportion as business expediency proves proper as a reserve.

The adverse clearing house balances which follow the loans will be met by the cash that has been received over the window. Accordingly bankers solicit accounts and offer various inducements to get cash deposits and build up their demand liabilities in that way, whereas they guard very carefully against overextension of demand liabilities by the loans process.

RATIO OF LOANS TO DEPOSITS

Because a very large proportion of deposit liabilities are created by the method of loans and discounts, and because receipts of cash deposits ease the bank's position and incline it to extend loans to an amount about equal to the cash received, deposit liabilities tend to increase and decrease pari passu with loans and discounts over a period of time.

Temporary conditions may obtain in which deposits of any one bank or group of banks may expand faster than loans, or loans may even be decreasing. Instance the New York Clearing House banks the first week of April, 1917, when loans contracted nearly $40 million while deposits expanded over $86 million; the contraction largely reflected the withdrawal of funds from the time market in anticipation of the Victory Loan, and the expansion of deposits represented the flow of funds from interior banks to New York for investment in the call market.

During 1915-1916-1917, before the United States entered the war, the heavy importations of gold from abroad created such an easy money market that bankers found real difficulty in loaning funds as fast as they came from depositors. On the other hand, loans may increase faster than deposits, and then the money market will tighten.

Bank Notes

White's last two statements (see page 73 above) of assets and liabilities showed the alternative effects of his paying for discounts with cash or deposits; the two previous statements showed the similar alternative effects of his making loans in cash or deposits; and the first statement showed deposits arising by the deposit of cash or cash items. Another alternative was open to White in each case. Instead of paying cash or crediting deposits to be drawn later by order, White might have paid by simple promissory demand notes payable to bearer.

These notes would be in small denominations, round amounts, and convenient size, and, if White was well-reputed, would be readily accepted by others and would tend to circulate as money. If the proceeds of the $35,000 of discounts had been paid in bank notes, the financial statement in this case, starting with the figures given in the last statement on page 73, would have been as follows:

Assets

Cash................. $100,000

Loans And Discounts... 80,000

Liabilities

Deposits.............. $145,000

Bank Notes Outstanding 34,000

Discount............. 1,000

Obviously many variations may be introduced here to indicate part payments of loans, discounts, collections, and so forth, in cash, deposits, and bank notes. For instance, items to the amount of $27,000 may be discounted and the proceeds, $25,000, be paid, one-fifth in cash, two-fifths in bank notes, and the rest credited as deposits, with the following results on the last statement:

Assets

Cash................ $ 95,000

Loans And Discounts... 107,000

Liabilities

Deposits.............. $155,000

Bank Notes Outstanding 44,000

Discount.............. 3,000

Summary. The Three Functions Of Commercial Banking

The three fundamental functions of commercial banking are, then, discount, deposits, and note issue; discount (and loan) is, in practice, but one method of creating deposits and note issue; and the three functions readily reduce themselves to one, namely, the guaranty of the credit of individuals. The guaranty is effected by a highly developed, specialized, and well-known institution, holding a liquid cash reserve, as well as quickly convertible assets, and standing ready to exchange its own credits for those of customers.

Capital

In the discussion in the previous sections, White has been doing business entirely on his customers' money and his own credit. No mention has been made of any direct contribution of funds by himself; he started with a deposit transfer business, and later developed a loan and discount business and a bank note issue business.

Undoubtedly any person who deposited money directly with White or who borrowed from or sold discounts to White and left the proceeds on deposit with him, or took his notes in payment, that is, any person who became his creditor, would more readily become creditor if White himself were willing to put up a guaranty fund and thus increase the assets out of which the creditor could recover. Such contributions by A are generally made from the very start; they give confidence to would-be creditors that he will be willing and able to repay and make good his promises, and, of course, the greater such contributions the greater the security to the creditors, for they can collect, not only against the assets procured by White through their own cash deposits, but also against the assets procured by White through his own contributions.

Such original contributions are called "capital." White usually associates with himself other persons who likewise contribute capital. Ownership of the assets of the association is then in proportion to the contributions; profits, losses, and responsibilities are proportioned upon the same basis.

The association may be incorporated under the laws of the state and capitalized at, say, $100,000, the capital contributions and ownership being evidenced by $100 shares of capital stock. Subscriptions (contributions) to the capital stock may be in cash, real estate, securities, promissory notes, or other assets. If the subscription is paid in cash, some of it would be immediately invested in a bank building, furniture, and fixtures, and the rest of it, along with funds deposited by depositors, gradually absorbed in investments, loans, and discounts, real estate, cash reserve, and so forth.

As a result of all this White has now become a full-fledged banking company.

SURPLUS AND UNDIVIDED PROFITS

The company may, voluntarily or by force of law, over a period of years add to the original capital contributions by withholding part of its earnings, not declaring them in dividends and converting them into a "surplus" fund. The state law, as a protection to the bank's creditors and as a means of adding to the stability of financial institutions, may require that the bank accumulate a surplus equal to, say, 40 per cent of its capital and that a certain fraction of the yearly earnings be diverted to that fund until it is filled. To make their bank's statement somewhat more comparable to those of other institutions, and also to reduce the extra liability that may attach to stock ownership, the founders of the bank may start with a capital of $100,000 and a surplus of $100,000 rather than with a capital of $200,000. The surplus accumulated in an old bank may be many times its capital.

Public policy requires that capitalization bear a rough proportion to the size of the business done; and, since size of business is roughly proportional to the population of the domiciling city, the state and federal laws have fixed the minimum capitalization of banks in various sized cities.

The existence of a fair-sized surplus also promotes stability in corporate control.

If in bad years net operating deficits had to be met by assessing the stockholders rather than by using up the surplus, the wealthy stockholders would be at an advantage over the poorer, who would find it difficult to meet the assessments.

In fact the corporation might fall into the control of unscrupulous men who would purposely operate it at a deficit in order to "freeze out" the weak stockholders. This operation, however, is less likely to succeed if a large surplus must be exhausted before assessments can be put on stockholders.

To maintain a working balance, the bank does not declare all its earnings as dividends nor convert them into surplus, but retains a relatively small amount as "undivided profits."

The capital, surplus, and undivided profits represent the original and accumulated contributions of the owners of the bank, and serve as a buffer to reinforce the claims of the bank's creditors. These contributions, along with the funds contributed by creditors, are invested in various assets, only a small part of which is held as cash reserve.

It is wholly wrong to think that surplus and undivided profits constitute a fund of cash in the bank, or any other particular form of assets. The surplus together with the undivided profits is a property right (in proportion to the shares owned) of the stockholders in the general assets, and as such is a valuation item in the financial statement. The accumulated aggregate assets have a book valuation more or less equal to the market valuation.

This book valuation, less the creditor liabilities and the capitalization, is the surplus. If the book valuation exceeds the market valuation, the surplus is not substantial; on the other hand, if the assets are undervalued, the bank creditors have more protection than is shown. Capital and surplus protect depositors and noteholders, for in case of liquidation the greater the actual value of the assets belonging to stockholders the more are the funds that can be realized for the bank's creditors.

Bibliography

Auerbach, Alan J.: *Fiscal Policy, Lessons from Economic Research*, The MIT Press, Cambridge Massachusetts, London, 1997.

Besley, T.: *How do Merket Failures Justify Interventions in Rural Credit Markets?*, Washington, D. C., World Bank, 1994

Bhagwati, J.: *Trade, Balance of Payments and Growth: Essays in Honor of C. P. Kindleberger*, Amsterdam, North-Holland Publishing Company, 1971.

Bookman, Zarkovic: *The Political Economy of Commercial Banking*, New York, Praeger, 1991.

Cooper, S. Kerry and Donald, R. Fraser: *Banking Deregulation and the New Competition in Financial Services*, Ballinger Publishing Company, Cambridge 1984.

Ferraro, Gary P.: *The Cultural Dimension of International Banking*, Englewood Cliffs, Prentice Hall, 1997.

Goldsmith, W.: *The Financial Development of India, 1860-1977*, New Haven, Yale University Press, 1983.

Goodhart, Charles: *The Evolution of Commercial Banks*, The MIT Press, Cambridge, 1988.

Homoud, S.H., 1985. *Islamic Banking*, Arabian Information, London.

Irshad, S.A., 1964. *Interest-Free Banking*, Orient Press of Pakistan, Karachi.

Le Prestre, Philippe: *The World Bank and the Environmental Challenge*, London, Associated University Presses, 1989.

Mowlana, H.: *Global Information and World Communication: New Frontiers in International Relations*, London, Sage Publications, 1997.

Ranade, Sudhanshu: *Rural Banking Adrift*, Bombay, Jaico Publishing House, 1984.

Victor, David A.: *International Business Communication*, New York, Harper Collins Publishers, 1992.

Index

M

N

O

P

R

S

T

□□□